A FAMILY AFFAIR

Before 1993, few people could say how the McCains ran their successful company from the tiny village nestled on the banks of the Saint John River. Theirs was a privately held company in the K. C. Irving mould: make all the money you can and keep your business affairs to yourself. Why tell the world what you earned—or how—when you had no legal obligation to disclose anything?

All that the world knew about McCain Foods Ltd. was that Wallace and Harrison McCain had turned their father's respectable potato business into one of Canada's most profitable food companies. Their success was a modern-day fairy story set in a fairy tale village.

Harrison and Wallace accomplished what they did, they liked to say, because they worked together as a team. They had adjoining offices, connected by an unlocked door. They talked nonstop by intercom or by shouting through the wall.

By the end of the 1980s, they no longer worked as a team, and they were no longer best friends.

FAMILY TIES:
The Real
Story of the
McCain Feud

MICHAEL WOLOSCHUK

SEAL BOOKS
McClelland-Bantam, Inc.
Toronto

*This edition contains the complete text
of the original hardcover edition.*
NOT ONE WORD HAS BEEN OMITTED.

FAMILY TIES

A Seal Book / published by arrangement with Key Porter Books Limited

PUBLISHING HISTORY
*Key Porter Books edition published 1995
Seal edition / November 1996*
CIP: 95-931721-X
*All rights reserved.
Copyright © 1995 by Michael Woloschuk.
Author photo by Gary Dimmock.
Cover design by Peter Maher.*
No part of this book may be reproduced or transmitted in any form or
by any means, electronic or mechanical, including photocopying,
recording, or by any information storage and retrieval system, without
permission in writing from the publisher.
*For information address:
Key Porter Books Limited
70 The Esplanade
Toronto, Ontario
Canada M5E 1R2*

ISBN 0-770-42730-8

Seal Books are published by McClelland-Bantam, Inc. Its trademark,
consisting of the words "Seal Books" and the portrayal of a seal, is
the property of McClelland-Bantam, Inc., 105 Bond Street, Toronto,
Ontario M5B 1Y3, Canada. This trademark has been duly registered in
the Trademark Office of Canada. The trademark consisting of the
words "Bantam Books" and the portrayal of a rooster is the property
of and is used with the consent of Bantam Books, 1540 Broadway,
New York, New York 10036. This trademark has been duly registered
in the Trademark Office of Canada and elsewhere.

PRINTED IN CANADA

UNI   0 9 8 7 6 5 4 3 2 1

Contents

Acknowledgements

It will become quickly apparent that this book is not about number crunching; it is about people. And it could not have been written without the help of friendly people—lots of them. I would have floundered in New Brunswick without the support of such loyal friends as Roger Nason, a treasure trove of historical facts and inside information who *always* came through with a document or a contact at the drop of a hat. And the indefatigable Oxymoron Club—John Baxter, Dalton Camp, Gordon Gregory, Dan Skaling, Barry Toole and a half dozen other political desperadoes—who accepted me into their ranks, and kindly offered guidance and advice.

Some, such as Peter Walsh and Jennifer Gibson, even threw open the doors of their homes for me. During a two-week stay in Saint John, Peter and Jennifer provided me a comfortable bed to sleep in and a basement office to work in. They brought me fresh coffee in the morning, made sure I ate a hot meal every night, and allowed me to run up a massive telephone bill. I will never forget the kindness and hospitality they showed me.

I am especially thankful to Neil Reynolds, who nurtured my hungry inquisitiveness, first at *The Kingston Whig-Standard*, and later, at the *Telegraph Journal* in Saint John. Every time I write a sentence, I owe a debt of gratitude to him.

I am also grateful to some of my former colleagues at the *Telegraph Journal*, most notably Gary Dimmock in

Fredericton, Charles Enman in Saint John, Jacques Poitras in Moncton, and Jonathan Stone, now in Quebec City. They all provided valuable research and encouragement.

A last-minute find was Janet Maclellan Toole of the New Brunswick archives department, who faxed me a wealth of information on Hugh John Flemming's involvement in the start-up of McCain Foods. I am also grateful to the staff at the legislative library in Fredericton, who dug up many old magazine clippings and obscure references during my early research. And to Joan Weinman, NDP leader Elizabeth Weir's executive assistant, who freely moonlighted for me and telephoned often to make sure I was still alive.

Initially, I was told that getting people in Florenceville to talk about the McCains would be impossible. I am thankful to those who proved this assumption wrong. Bev O'Keefe, even while laid up in a Woodstock hospital, spent hours with me and my tape recorder. I hope he doesn't punch me in the nose for calling him a courageous man. I am also thankful to Alan and Stephen Morris, who gave their time and offered an insider's perspective of Florenceville. Equally important in my Florenceville research were Barb Carter, Don Marmen, Fred McCain, Ernie Stickney, David Watson—and Mary Walters, who fed me the world's best peanut-butter cookies.

Much interviewing was done during the winter months, when those who can, fly south. To the following, who took time from the beach to gab with me on the telephone, a big thank you: Elbert Day, Mrs. Helen Depow, Joe Palmer, Senator Louis Robichaud, Cy Sherwood and George Urquhart.

There would be no book, however, without Anna Porter and Charis Wahl. Anna gambled on my ability to produce a final manuscript on time. I am forever grateful for her encouraging me when I faced a blank computer screen as my deadline zoomed towards me, and for personally overseeing the project from start to finish. Charis took my pile of rambling prose and whipped it into shape. I don't know how she did it, but again, I am thankful.

A big thank you goes to those McCains—Wallace, Margaret, Michael, Scott, Harrison and Andrew—who took time from their hectic schedules to talk with me. They breathed life into the book.

I would also like to thank my wife, Julie Green, for putting up with a single-minded zombie for six months, and for giving me a corner of sanity to crawl into when the day was over.

Last, there is Jackie Webster, the godmother of New Brunswick journalism. Jackie has lived a long time and knows everyone worth knowing in the province. She is a reporter's ideal source and a helluva good storyteller. More important, however, she is a rock-solid friend. From developing story ideas to turning me on to ginseng, Jackie has been there every step of the way—and I owe her big time.

CHAPTER ONE

In the Beginning

STAND ALMOST ANYWHERE IN CARLETON COUNTY, NEW Brunswick, and you'll see potato fields stretching in every direction. The fertile soil along the snakelike St. John River is unlike that anywhere else in the province, and the people here are grateful to the Lord for it. There are more churches here than Irving gas stations. This is the New Brunswick where parents name their children Chastity and Faith, and Saturday night "singspirations" are popular community events. Politicians who talk about gay rights, gun control and multiculturalism get nowhere in Carleton County. Just ask the provincial NDP candidate who tried—and finished dead last, with only 85 votes.

In Hartland, home of the world's longest covered bridge and the final resting place of freewheeling Premier Richard Hatfield, sits the New Brunswick Bible Institute. The poet Alden Nowlan, who lived in Hartland for 11 years, wrote that the town needed more atheists. But the chance of most Hartlanders ever reading Nowlan is remote, because the only bookshop in the county is The Valley Light Bible Bookstore in Woodstock. It doesn't stock modern Canadian literature.

The earliest settlers in Carleton County were Loyalists, refugees from the American Revolution, who fled to New Brunswick from Maine and New England. Armed with axes,

1

saws and scythes, the settlers, mostly hardworking and God-fearing Presbyterians, moved into the forest, chopped immense white pines down to half-metre butt ends and set fire to the stumps. Winter and summer the immigrants hacked and cut until, exhausted, Nature gave up and red earth lay exposed like an open sore. By the 1820s, log cabins had sprung up along the banks of the St. John River, on 40-hectare swatches carved from the woods. About 160 kilometres from Fredericton, in the middle of nowhere, the village was called Buttermilk Creek, in honour of the white effluent the local creamery spewed into the river.

During that half-century of building, missionary preachers such as Henry Alline came up from Maine, spouting fire-and-brimstone Baptism. Carleton County settlers took to it like fish to water: one frigid winter day in 1800, 500 of the faithful got together to watch a preacher break the St. John River ice and baptize a newly converted woman by total immersion.

God is in just about every nook and cranny of Carleton County, but even if you are blind to His presence, there is no missing the McCains. They may be bigger here than God. Harrison and Wallace McCain, the french-fry kings, have homes in what once was Buttermilk Creek. Renamed in the late 1800s after Florence Nightingale, Florenceville and the heart of the $3-billion McCain empire sit smack dab in the middle of the Bible belt, for which the locals are grateful. For while most New Brunswick villages have to struggle to maintain such basic services as snow removal for their communities, Florenceville is a boomtown.

With a population of only 694, Florenceville has a tax base of $60 million. Factoring in the McCains and their army of corporate vice-presidents and managers, the average per capita income here is higher than in most New Brunswick towns. BMWs, Jeep Cherokees and Jaguars tool around Florenceville's streets. Thanks to the McCains Florenceville has a $700,000 public library, a million-dollar arena, a curling club, a fitness centre with indoor tennis courts, and a decent hospital, an anomaly in rural New Brunswick. The McCains even fund roadside flower beds so the village will look pretty in the summer.

It is only fitting that the best view in the village is owned by Harrison and Wallace. Up a hillside that the locals call "McCain Hill," their houses are separated by a lawn some three or four football-fields wide. When either Harrison or Wallace gazes out the picture windows of his enormous white plantation-style home, he is truly the lord of all he surveys. The McCains have owned so much of Florenceville for so long that even the oldest folk here can't remember when a McCain wasn't the most prosperous gent in town.

• • •

The first record of the McCain family in New Brunswick dates back to 1826, when Andrew McCain petitioned Lieutenant-Governor Sir Howard Douglas for a grant of land in Greenfield, on the outskirts of Buttermilk Creek. Andrew was 21 years old, and had been a New Brunswick resident for three and a half years. In the spring of 1823, Andrew, his two older brothers and younger sister had disembarked from an immigrant ship in Rivière-du-Loup. The young family travelled south, following what would later become the "Great Road" between Edmundston and Fredericton, along the east bank of the St. John River into New Brunswick.

Young William, James, Andrew and Jane McCain had been born on a farm near Castlefinn, County Donegal. Bordering Northern Ireland on the west, hilly, bog-filled Donegal was one of the few Protestant counties in Ireland. It was also one of the poorest.

The McCains were part of a wave of emigrants from the British Isles that began in the 1820s. During the first two decades of the nineteenth century, emigration to North America had been almost impossible, because of Napoleon's naval blockade of British shipping. After Wellington defeated the French at Waterloo in 1815, the British poured into the New World, their hopes pegged on reports of fertile, unoccupied land for the having.

The Maritime provinces were natural destination points, being both the closest ports and familiar to British sea captains. When Napoleon's blockade cut England off from her traditional timber suppliers in Scandinavia and the Balkans, Britain was forced to import lumber from the North American colonies. Shipowners who hauled timber transported emigrants for a relatively cheap price, rather than return empty to North America.

The McCain brothers were strict Presbyterians who worked hard six days a week and kept the seventh day for God, forbidding even newspaper reading on Sundays. They hired out as farm hands and lumbermen, saving their money for land. Thus, in 1832, Andrew received the 40-hectare provincial land grant he had petitioned, and brothers William and James together bought 300 hectares of land between 1834 and 1836. The 340 hectares of McCain land were contiguous and the three brothers, of necessity, worked them together.

De-foresting major tracts of land was back-breaking work. Apart from the dangers of felling trees, burning the stumps sometimes had tragic results. In dry weather, the smouldering fields of stubbed pines might spark to the forest, destroying farms and farm houses. So difficult and risky was the work that uncleared land could be purchased for half the price of cleared land.

McCain family raising began as soon as the family became land owners. Jane married John Elkins of Fredericton in 1834 and settled on a farm in Greenfield, near her brothers' land. She bore 11 children, with one named after each of her brothers. William married a local woman, Jane Kilpatrick of Greenfield; Andrew and James sent for brides from the Old Country. In 1834, Andrew married Margaret Ferguson; James married her sister, Isabella, a year later. The McCain brothers produced 26 children.

Around 1850, a feud erupted between the three McCain brothers and their sister Jane. No early record of the family survives, but the McCain family version has it that John Elkins was not the McCains' social equal. The Elkins family's claim to have run a food supply business back in Ireland put them in better society than the McCains. Whatever the problem, sometime around 1850 the brothers shut their sister and her husband out of their lives forever. The McCains could also feed a grudge: although they live scant kilometres apart, the sides have not spoken to each other since.

The younger McCain brothers almost started married life as rich men. The Ferguson sisters' inheritances totalled $60,000, a fortune at the time, but the money disappeared. Another Ferguson sister, Mary, married a U.S. lawyer named Henning, who convinced the family to invest with him. That was the last they saw of their money. Henning may have been a poor investor, but McCain family lore paints him as a swindler who snookered the ancestors out of their rightful wealth.

Even without the kick-start of a handsome inheritance, by mid-century the three families were running successful farms. According to the Canadian census of 1861, the McCains owned 256 hectares of farmland, with a cash value of more than $5,000. They owned cattle, sheep and hogs, and that year produced 2,132 kilograms of slaughtered pork, 635 kilograms of butter, 136 kilograms of wool, 102,000 litres of oats, 62,000 litres of buckwheat and 31,000 litres of potatoes.

The McCains' success exacted a heavy price. In 1860, Andrew's son and namesake died of pneumonia at the age of 19, after driving a herd of cattle to Woodstock in the middle of winter. And family solidarity was developing deep rifts.

The youngest brother, Andrew, produced two sons who would lay the foundation of the McCain empire. Before Andrew died in 1867, at age 62, he divided his assets among his children, perhaps to avoid a squabble over the inheritance. He deeded his 97 hectares among his four sons, the bulk of the land going to the eldest, John, and youngest, Hugh Henderson, known as H.H. to avoid confusion with other Hugh McCains.

John and H.H. McCain were the first McCains to market their crop beyond Carleton County, selling as far away as Saint John. By 1890, however, John's creditors were pressing. He sold his produce business to H.H., who agreed to pay off his debts in exchange for John's farm in Greenfield. H.H. now controlled more than 80 hectares of good farmland and, in 1890, was able to print letterhead for his business that read: "H.H. McCain. Dealer in hay, oats, beef, pork, etc. Florenceville, N.B."

H.H. was born in 1853, just four years before his mother died. After his father's death, when H.H. was 12 years old, he was raised by his sister Margaret. In 1877 H.H. married Frances Kilpatrick, whose father had emigrated from County Donegal with the McCains in the 1820s. He bought another farm, which added substantial acreage, and built a large house for his new bride on the west side of the river.

H.H. was an innovator, a man who looked opportunity in the eye and then grabbed it by the tail. He grew experimental strains of apples on his farm. In addition to his produce business, H.H. owned a general store, and was the first merchant in the area to pay farmers for their produce in cash rather than goods. His was also one of the first farms to have running water in the home, after he laid an 800-metre-long wooden pipe-line from a nearby spring to the farmhouse and barn. Raised in the Presbyterian church, H.H. caught the Baptist fever and became a staunch churchman, hauling the lumber for the Florenceville Baptist Church, where he later became a deacon and choir member. He also saw the benefits of political ties, running for and winning a seat in the provincial legislature for the Liberal Party in the 1895 and 1899 elections.

As the county grew, and with it the population of cattle and work horses, so did the demand for hay. H.H. purchased moveable hay presses: when he wasn't baling his own hay, he was hiring out work crews to county farmers to press theirs. He also bought a threshing machine, which he rented out for harvesting. At the turn of the century came the Boer War, the last war in which cavalry horses would rule the battlefield. Demand for hay skyrocketed. H.H. won a large hay contract with the federal Liberal government of Wilfrid Laurier. (As he was still an MLA, H.H. sent his son Andrew to Ottawa to sign the contract.) H.H. then bought up all the Carleton County hay he could.

He also bought a high-pressure, steam-powered press and installed it in a large warehouse near the railroad station in Florenceville. The baler could squeeze hay into the 50-centimetre bales needed for shipping the crop to South Africa. H.H. expanded the warehouse, installing sleeping quarters and a makeshift kitchen for the work crews, which operated the baling machines around the clock.

Even the local newspaper started taking notice of H.H. McCain. On February 26, 1902, *The Hartland Advertiser* reported that "H.H. McCain has replaced the engine that drove his steam hay press with one of 25 or 30 horsepower. Mr. McCain's press was the first steam press to be made in Canada and he is keeping the first bundle it pressed as a souvenir."

In a few months, however, H.H. would have hundreds of thousands of souvenirs. By the summer of 1902, he was on the verge of bankruptcy. There are two versions of what happened. The first is that when the Boer War suddenly ended May 31, 1902, H.H. was left with tons of hay and nowhere to sell it. The more likely story is found in Hugh Gordon's *The McCain Family of Florenceville, New Brunswick*, written with the help of Muriel McCain, H.H.'s daughter. Gordon tells us that Frank Carvell, a Woodstock newspaper owner, lawyer and Liberal politician, found a number of errors in the McCain contract and had it cancelled. Carvell then took over the supply arrangements himself, and had the hay supplied by Bohan's, a produce competitor of McCain's in nearby Bath. Needless to say, Carvell bought no hay from McCain. H.H. was forced to buy the thousands of tons of hay he had contracted from local farmers, and to sell it at fire-sale prices. He went into debt, and it was only McCain family solidarity that kept the company afloat.

H.H.'s wife, Frances, bore three daughters and one son, Andrew Davis, who would sacrifice his medical career to bail his father out of the financial crisis. Born September 19, 1878, at his parents' White Marsh farm, A.D., as he was later called, was given responsibilities beyond his years. When he was 13 years old H.H. sent him alone to Boston, 800 kilometres from Florenceville, to collect debt. And at 20, he was sent to England, during Queen Victoria's Diamond Jubilee, to look into possible new markets for the company.

A.D. was in his second year at the Horton Academy, a residential high school run by the Baptist Educational Society at Wolfville, Nova Scotia, when he was called back to Florenceville to help his father through the hay crisis. He joined his father in a stand against the creditors and helped sell the hay; but there was no money for A.D. to fulfil his ambition of becoming a doctor. All they had gleaned and more was needed to keep the company going. A.D. convinced two Saint John men, Messrs. Knight and Prime, to put up $20,000 each to keep the firm afloat. A new company, McCain Prime, was formed, with Prime, Knight, H.H. and A.D. McCain as equal partners. By 1914, H.H.'s debts were paid off, and A.D. bought out Knight and Prime.

A relic of the family's hay crisis, McCain Prime still exists, a subsidiary of McCain Foods Inc. But the most significant vestige of the financial disaster has become the McCain credo: pay your debts before you pay yourself. In fact, the hay fiasco with its lesson about paying creditors has become, perhaps, *the* single defining event in the family's financial history, and can ignite strong feelings in McCains thrice-removed from it. "These guys worked for 13 years, not me, worked for 13 years to pay off those goddamned bills," says Harrison McCain. "The rest of us have taken strength with banks ever since, from that. You get a reputation for paying, even if it hurts. It was 13 years without any wages."

By 1910, H.H. McCain had built another storage warehouse near the CPR tracks in Florenceville, but the advent of the automobile and the growth of the railroad gradually lowered demand for hay. In 1910, H.H. and A.D. started a new venture, the McCain Produce Company. They, like other produce suppliers in the area, needed a new export crop, and found it in the potato.

Potatoes grow exceptionally well in the rich soil of Carleton County. By 1915, potatoes had become the most important cash crop in New Brunswick. The province's farmers grew almost 218 million litres of spuds that year on 16,187 hectares of land, most of it in Carleton County. Production reached a high of 545 million litres of potatoes in 1920; many of them were exported to the U.S. The second decade of the twentieth century saw several large produce companies in the area, including McCain Produce Co.—run by A.D. after the death of his father in 1920—peg their hopes on potato exports to the United States and the West Indies.

In 1922, however, the American potato market collapsed when Congress passed the Fordney-McCumber Tariff, which slapped a 50-cent-per-barrel tax on potatoes imported into the United States. Heber Hatfield, whose son Richard would one day become premier of the province, led a consortium, including A.D. McCain, to offset the loss of the American potato market by selling to Cuba. "Every winter, with $15 in his pocket, Heber left Hartland in his car to seek export contracts," wrote Richard Hatfield's biographers. "Peddling potatoes along the East Coast, he would drive all the way to Florida and catch a boat to Cuba."

Once the Cuban market was established, two groups of potato producers colluded to raise the market price in Cuba while lowering the price paid to New Brunswick growers. (The first group consisted of Guy G. Porter of Perth, Heber Hatfield of Hartland and C.E. Gallagher of Bath. The second group, headed by A.D. McCain, included Fred Pirie of Grand Falls and Henry Phillips of Pembroke.)

Gordon's McCain family history cheerfully notes that "competition in the produce field was lively, with B.F. Smith at Florenceville, the Bohans at Bath, Heber Hatfield at Hartland, Jim and Guy Porter at Andover, and Fred Pirie at Grand Falls, all in the same business." The truth is that competition was long dead. The two groups agreed on prices to be paid to local potato growers, while working together to squeeze the maximum amount from their Cuban buyers. The dealers reaped tremendous profits. One testified before the federal Combines Investigation of 1924 that he and another dealer made $15,000 from one deal alone. A.D. testified that in a year when farmers were getting 60 cents to one dollar a barrel for their potatoes, "Roughly speaking, I would say I had a profit of 40 cents a barrel, likely, on that." Farmers before the Combines investigating committee testified that because of the low prices they were being paid, 10 per cent of farmers had been forced off their land.

"It is evident to me that the potato situation in New Brunswick is absolutely controlled by the shippers, and that potato growers receive practically no benefit from market advantages," said L.F. Burrows, of the province's Department of Agriculture.

In 1925, the Combines Investigation wrapped up, with the registrar concluding that the two groups had indeed colluded to fix prices. Such a conclusion was hard to evade, when even one of the producers involved in the combine, Guy Porter, testified that: "If there hadn't been collusion, I might call it, between McCain and myself we couldn't have raised the price nohow."

The registrar stated: "The evidence establishes various agreements, arrangements and combinations at different times, fixing a common price and preventing and lessening competition in and substantially controlling the transportation, purchase, sale and storage and otherwise restraining or injuring trade or commerce in potatoes, to the detriment of or against the interest of the public."

However, charges could not be laid because the investigation was never formally completed. In his submission to the Minister of Labour, the registrar chose to report that one witness, who was living in Cuba, could not testify, and that this witness was "essential to the completion of the investigation."

According to Harrison McCain, however, A.D.'s seed-potato business was so small, collusion among similar-sized potato shippers amounted to practically nothing. "I'll tell you how my Dad's business was run," he says. "There was the boss, like my Dad, and the bookkeeper. And sometimes, a secretary, called a stenographer. That was it. That was the whole administration. The rest of the businesses, the guys that were in the deal, would have been run the same way. So a combination of three or four of those fellas to buy together and ship together wasn't any earth-shaking deal."

Large business or not, the fact remains that farmers blamed the colluders for driving them off their land. The McCain name was already beginning to wield power in Carleton County.

CHAPTER TWO

Boys Will Be Boys

THEIR PORTRAITS HANG IN THE KIND OF LARGE, GILT FRAMES usually reserved for dead politicians or living heads of large corporations; but the faces in these large canvases show nothing of pride or overbearing ego. A.D. McCain and his wife, Laura, their eyes the size of nickels, gaze at visitors as they pass through the small foyer of the Andrew and Laura McCain Library on McCain Street, just around the corner from McCain Produce Co., Florenceville, which would be more aptly named McCainville.

Even if the McCains had not funded this library in honour of their parents, you get the sense that the villagers would have hauled up some monument to them anyway. A.D. may have been accused by the Combines Investigation of fleecing local farmers, but you rarely hear people in these parts carp. Instead, you hear "his word was his bond" or "A.D. was honest as the day was long."

Mary Walters, a retired telephone operator who has lived in the house almost directly behind the McCain Produce Co. since 1911, recalls that long before the big houses on McCain Hill were built, before prosperity came and people had two cars parked in the driveway, when people lived in shacks and relied for help on the community, not government, the McCains were building their reputations as benevolent capitalists who cared about their village.

When farmers were hurting during the Depression, Walters says, A.D. dipped into his own pocket. Sometimes, if a farmer could not supply the quantity of potatoes he was contracted to sell to McCain Produce, A.D. would allow the agreement to slide. And the influence of Laura, who later became known in the town as Mrs. A.D., was at least as strong as her husband's. She was the town cheerleader, personally begging a schoolteacher "to do something, anything" to help lagging students pass their provincial matriculation exams, so the boys could get jobs. Though they lived through a time when nothing came easy, their library portraits sport aw-shucks-it-was-nothing looks on their faces.

On September 19, 1916, A.D. McCain celebrated his thirty-eighth birthday; but for a man whose family was traditionally prodigious in producing offspring, it was not momentous. He was now one of the oldest bachelors in Florenceville—and with good reason. H.H.'s "hay crisis" of 1902 left A.D. virtually broke for the next 12 years, and his determination to pay off all of McCain Produce Co.'s debts meant that A.D. delayed getting married and raising a family until the company was in the black. "He always said he couldn't get married because he couldn't afford to," says Wallace. "He had to pay off the bills."

A.D. was always impeccably dressed; even when he was visiting farmers, or negotiating a deal in a potato house, he wore a three-piece suit and spats. He had a pair of sleepy, heavy-lidded eyes—the eyes of a gambler, someone who would stake the farm on some future windfall—and a perfect poker face. He never smoked or swore, and it is said that liquor rarely passed his thin, tight lips. He could make himself so quiet you didn't know what he was thinking. "He was a quiet man," recalls A.D.'s second-youngest son, Harrison. "Just a straightforward man. Quiet, reserved, unemotional. Didn't brag, didn't complain: things going good, didn't do any bragging; going bad, didn't do any complaining. Just keep right at her."

Just as he had learned to shut up and wait for the right business opportunity, so A.D. seemed prepared to wait forever, if necessary, for love. Forever eventually came in the form of Laura Blanche Perley, an attractive 26-year-old schoolteacher from Maugerville who could spin energy like a dynamo into those around her. She was hired in 1916 to teach at the Florenceville Superior School, a stone's throw from A.D.'s father's home on River View Drive.

A.D. believed that a good businessman should take an active interest in the education of the village youth, and was therefore a member of the local school board. Laura was an employee of that school board. The daughter of a Tory MLA, a graduate of Mount Allison University in Sackville, New Brunswick, she, like her new suitor, was dedicated to community service: capable and independent, she would rather die than simply stay home and keep house.

The two tireless, happy workaholics were made for each other, except for their family histories: A.D. was a Baptist, from a long line of Liberals; Laura, an Anglican, from a family of dyed-in-the-wool Tories. Laura could accept A.D.'s political loyalties, but she refused to become a Baptist. "When A.D. and Laura were engaged," says Laura's daughter-in-law, Margaret McCain, "they were driving along in the buggy one day and Andrew says to Laura, 'When are you going to make a date for your baptism?' And she says, 'I beg your pardon? I've already been baptized.' And he said, 'You haven't been immersed, so it's not sufficient.' So she says, 'Well, in my book it is. And if that's a requirement of marriage, there will be no marriage. I will promise you one thing: You can go to your church, I will raise your children in your church, and I will go to it whenever there is time left over.'"

A.D. accepted Laura's conditions, and the two were married on October 2, 1918, a couple of weeks after A.D.'s fortieth birthday.

By the wedding day, Florenceville had grown into a bustling little village with four stores, three churches and a hotel owned by A.D.'s uncle, William L. McCain. The St. John River divided the town: East Florenceville had become the area's business hub when the railroad was brought down the east bank of the river in the late 1800s. Across the covered bridge on the hilly west side was Florenceville proper, where the McCain family built their stately homes. That built by A.D.'s father, H.H., is now owned by his great-grandson, Michael McCain, the former CEO of McCain USA who was fired by his uncle Harrison. About 150 metres up the road, on the left side, sits A.D.'s modest, two-storey home, overlooking the river and East Florenceville.

In A.D.'s day the Trans-Canada Highway was only a gleam in some bureaucrat's eye, but the CPR linked Florenceville with St. Andrews and its ocean port to the south, and with Edmundston to the north, with railroad links across Canada. Potatoes were loaded from the field into boxcars manned in winter by workers tending sheet-metal woodstoves to keep the potatoes from freezing.

Between 1919 and 1930, A.D. and Laura produced six very different children: Marie, Andrew, Robert, Eleanor, Harrison and Wallace. Marie, the eldest, was quiet and timid. Andrew and Robert were staid types. The younger sister Eleanor was the family firebrand—quick-witted, funny and talkative. Harrison inherited his father's staccato voice and his mother's boundless energy; and Wallace, the youngest, was the family jokester. A strict work ethic was instilled into all the children, and mediocrity was not tolerated. If one of the boys needed straightening out, it was Laura, not A.D., who would administer the punishment. "At home," Andrew once told a reporter, "if I got in trouble at school or something, and needed a good tanning, it was Mother who would give it to me. I don't think Dad ever laid a hand on me. But you knew. He just had to say one word, and you knew."

There is no denying, however, that it was Mrs. A.D. who not only ruled the McCain family, but was the matriarch of the entire Florenceville community. "She was a very strong, dynamic woman," recalls Margaret McCain, who later became her daughter-in-law. "She was a force in the community. She ran her own little social service agency, and she ran her own private real estate agency, but most of all she was the spiritual conscience of the community."

That is not to say that A.D. was not obeyed. Wallace remembers his father's gaze becoming so stern at times, he could rule with just a look. "Dad was a very strong-willed man," he says. "But quiet. I never heard him raise his voice around the house in my life. Half of us yelling at each other and raising hell, [but] he never raised his voice, never put a finger on us. Nothing. But if you did something bad, Mother would dish it out. He never did. But I tell you, if he spoke . . ." Wallace snaps his fingers in mid-sentence for effect. "[You] got with it. He just had that respect, I guess."

• • •

By the 1930s, Florenceville, like other small communities, was losing much of its workforce. People were abandoning their farms and moving to the big industrial cities in central Canada or the United States. Many went to Detroit, where Henry Ford was paying assembly-line workers five dollars a day. In New Brunswick a skinny man with a face like a hawk, named K.C. Irving, was thriving. As North America sank into its worst economic depression ever, Irving bought up vast holdings of timber, lumber yards and a string of gas stations stretching across the Maritimes.

Back in Florenceville, A.D. McCain was struggling, against the Depression and restrictive potato tariffs abroad, just to hold on to the family business. In 1927, following the United States' lead, Cuba slapped a tariff on Canadian potatoes, in retaliation for Canada cutting back on imports of Cuban cane sugar. (In 1926, prior to the tariff, Canadian shippers sold 109 million litres of potatoes to Cuba. In 1936, shippers sold only one-tenth of that amount to the Cubans.)

In 1938, A.D. joined a delegation of Maritime potato growers in lobbying the federal government to negotiate away the Cuban and American tariffs. The delegation argued that there was a danger that many potato farmers would be forced off their land if Canada did not act soon. Before the government acted, however, the country was plunged into World War II, and potato growers and producers were called upon to feed thousands of hungry troops in Europe.

It was here that A.D., unlike his father, missed the technological gold ring. Just as a new method of compacting hay had to be invented to feed the horses during the Boer War, so the Allies needed to transport vast amounts of food in the smallest possible space to their soldiers on the front lines: thus dehydration. But the potato smarts seemed to belong to two of A.D.'s former co-conspirators of the 1920s, Heber Hatfield, now a Tory MP and owner of New Brunswick Potato Products Ltd. in Hartland, and Fred Pirie, head of Pirie Potato Products up river at Grand Falls.

Potatoes would be peeled, cut and boiled. All their moisture would then be sucked out in a hot-air tunnel by two large fans. By the end of the process, 75 kilograms of potatoes would be reduced to seven kilograms. Sealed in tins, they were shipped overseas to military cooks, who brought the potatoes back to their original volume and weight (and, theoretically, to their original taste and texture) by soaking them in water.

The war had created a boom for potato growers. In 1943, New Brunswick potato farmers brought in a harvest worth $20 million, their best year since before the damaging foreign trade tariffs of two decades past. And if a local farmer managed to have a bad year or two, A.D. was always there to buy the property.

"A.D. bought farm after farm after farm after farm," says 85-year-old Mary Walters, who played the organ at A.D.'s funeral in 1953. "One day my father asked A.D., 'Why do you buy so many farms and grow potatoes, when you know that farmers need the money and they want to grow the potatoes?'

"A.D. said, 'I'll tell you why. I used to contract for potatoes with this certain farmer, who would deliver them when I called for them. And once when I called, he didn't have any. He told me that somebody else had given him a better price. I'd have shipments going to South America and Cuba—and

I'd call for potatoes and they wouldn't be there. So I buy farms because I'll always have enough potatoes to sell.'"

• • •

All six McCain children went to the Florenceville Consolidated School, where their mother used to teach. The school, which burned to the ground and was rebuilt twice in Laura McCain's lifetime, was a three-roomed affair, which served grades one through four in one room, five through eight in the second, and nine through eleven in the third. It had all the modern conveniences of its time: running water, flush toilets, an auditorium, a chemistry lab and a household-science room where farm girls were taught to cook, sew and keep house.

In the 1930s and 1940s, Florenceville farms were not yet mechanized, and few families could spare their children for schooling beyond the fourth grade. In 1939, Andrew, Robert and only six others graduated from high school. Wallace's graduating class of 1947 totalled three, yet there was no doubt in Laura McCain's mind that all her children would attend school through grade 11, and go on to university, as she had done.

Later, Harrison reflected that this urge to have all the McCain children university-educated was endemic. "Everybody wants their kids to be more educated than they," he says. "Particularly the closer you are to the date of immigration, the stronger the drive will be that those kids are going to have something better. That's why they left home. Would you leave home in Scotland, Wales, or Germany, or any place, and end up in some hick place like this, trying to cut the woods and build a farm, and growing crops to feed your family? Farming then was not selling for cash, it was living off the land. And educate those kids, definitely. That's why immigrants today are still the lifeblood of the country. They're the strong people. They all work hard."

This drive may have given the McCains academic ambitions, but they were treated no differently than other local children. A distant relative, Fred McCain (a great-grandson of William McCain, the eldest of the three McCain brothers who emigrated from Ireland in the 1820s), was principal of the Florenceville school in the late 1930s. Fred says that all the children inherited the work ethic shared by their parents. "They didn't get into any trouble, I know that," says Fred. "They weren't brought to my attention by the other teachers, which speaks well for their behaviour."

Nor did A.D. and Laura treat them differently from the rest of the community. They received nothing for free, except the luxury their father never enjoyed—the opportunity to attend university. Marie went on after graduation to study at Mount Allison University and later married Dr. Jed Sutherland, a Woodstock dentist who would become a partner in her younger brothers' frozen-food venture. Eleanor studied at McGill University in Montreal, taught at a private school in Florida, and in 1954 married an Oxford graduate named Patrick Johnson, who would later become headmaster of Upper Canada College in Toronto. Only Andrew did not graduate from university. He made two short, unsuccessful attempts—at the University of New Brunswick and at Acadia—but the call of the plow was too strong, and in 1941 he became McCain Produce Company's field manager.

The closest any McCain came to fulfilling A.D.'s dream of becoming a doctor was Robert. He completed three years of pre-med at the University of New Brunswick and had just launched into his medical studies at Dalhousie University when he was conscripted into the Canadian armed forces. Robert's ambition to become a surgeon was dashed when he lost the use of an arm after a mortar exploded near him during a routine artillery practice in Sussex, New Brunswick. After his war service, Robert, like his brother Andrew, returned to Florenceville to help run the family business.

• • •

Throughout their school years and into adulthood, it was the two youngest McCain brothers, Harrison and Wallace, who stood out. David Watson, a retired local woodcutter who grew up with the brothers, says that Mrs. A.D. seemed particularly devoted to Harrison, and that he received more motherly attention than Wallace. "I used to walk home from school with Harrison, and Mrs. A.D. would call us in and she'd quiz us as to which one was the sharpest on our math tables," says Watson. "She'd have him right up on the table. And he was quicker than me most of the time."

Indeed, Harrison led the school both academically and in athletics. A quiet child who loved to read, relatives remember the most likely place to find the young boy was sitting in a chair in the corner of the room with a book. Harrison read anything he could get his hands on. "I cleaned out all the library in Dad's house—and the neighbour's, Mrs. Stickney. She was a school teacher and had a nice little library. I read all that," he says. "And then I joined the New Brunswick Library in Fredericton. And they used to send me two or three books at a time. They'd have a list, and I'd order books off them—novels, histories, biographies—whatever I wanted to read. I remember my mother one time thinking that I was reading books that were far too adult for me. Anyway, she wrote a letter to the library down there, saying, 'Would you kindly take a look at this, and not send those off to [my] son.'"

His graduation picture shows Harrison wearing an itchy wool suit, high, starched collar, skinny tie and an almost glum expression. The official photograph of the Florenceville High School softball team (for which he was a fair-hitting shortstop) taken a year earlier, shows Harrison, his arms folded proudly across his thick chest. His eyes are confident, his lips are pursed into the smirk of a boy who is very sure of himself. In his Florenceville High School softball sweater and neatly pressed pin-stripe pants, his full head of hair combed back, he is the spitting image of his father, a young man with the whole world in his vision.

Harrison's grade 11 teacher, Miss Helen Somerville, now Mrs. William Depow, recalls Harrison having a sense of destiny. "I thought Harrison was the type who might lead the province," says Depow, who, in those days of multi-grade classrooms, also taught Wallace that year, even though the younger McCain was two grades behind. "Harrison was so clever, and a real gentleman, you know." Harrison, she says, set the tempo for the classroom, sitting in the front row and chastising Wallace, a back-row regular, when he got out of hand. "He used to be the leader in everything. Just every avenue, he was a leader."

Back then, she says, Harrison showed an uncommonly strong interest in politics, and she had the boy pegged as a future Liberal premier. When the provincial Tory leader and good old boy from Carleton County, Hugh John Flemming, made a run for premier, Mrs. Depow told the class that she intended to support him. Harrison, a Liberal like his father and grandfather, jumped up to debate the matter. "Harrison didn't like that I was going to vote for Hugh John very much," says Depow. "He said I should vote for the Liberal candidate." Indeed, the theme of Harrison's valedictory speech in 1945, she says, was why people should not vote Flemming for premier.

Whereas Harrison is remembered as a child who realized early on that a quick sense of humour would gain him popularity, those who knew both brothers say that Wallace was simply ordinary. Tall and rangy, Wallace, like his brother, found time for sports, and playing right wing for the Florenceville High School hockey team. But he never stood out like Harrison did. Although he may have seemed plain to friends, within the family Wallace was something of a rebel. When he was asked to describe his mother's influence over the children, Wallace replied: "She didn't rule me, but she ruled the roost."

Wallace needed constant prodding to finish school. In fact, he did so poorly in high school that Mrs. A.D. had to enlist Dorothy Stickney, a retired army major and tutor, to crack the whip. Wallace and other failing students would stay late after school each day with Stickney, who worked the boys like young men in a platoon. "She'd put on a teapot and get out the cigarettes, and say, 'Now we're going to get down to business,'" says Wallace's wife, Margaret. "So they'd smoke, drink tea, and do math. Wallace at first hated her, but by the end of the year they became bosom buddies—and they remained bosom buddies the rest of her life. He adored her. He completed his provincial exams with first-class honours. And he always said she taught him to smoke."

Harrison's and Wallace's legendary closeness did not

develop until university. Until then, their two-and-one-half-year age gap meant that they moved in different circles and shared few experiences. "I was his kid brother," says Wallace. "Really just a young brat." And like most brothers, the two had their scrapes.

David Watson remembers one of their pugnacious moments, when Harrison and Wallace were in grade school: "We used to drive down through the village with a horse and sleigh in the wintertime," says Watson. "We drove ourselves to school. We'd be going through the village, and if it was convenient, or if the other children in the village had an opportunity, they'd run and jump on the sleigh and ride on into school. Except we'd attempt to trot the horse so we wouldn't get overloaded. Well, one morning Harrison and Wallace were both making for the back of the sleigh to catch on and get a ride, and in their effort to get on, Harrison happened to bump Wallace and knock him down. So Wallace fell down and walked to school, while Harrison got the ride. When Wallace got into school, he just laid into Harrison. He was so mad he put the slap on him. He immediately started to slap him and hit him. Of course, Wallace was such a young kid, Harrison didn't pay any attention."

Perhaps one of the reasons Harrison and Wallace would become such close brothers later was born of necessity. Because the McCain home was too small to accommodate two parents and six children comfortably, the boys and girls had to double up in beds together. Until they moved out and went to university, Harrison and Wallace shared the same bed. "There were two double beds: Harrison and I had one, and Andrew and Bob had the other," says Wallace. "I slept with him for 20 years."

The McCains never lavished their children with spending money. Like the rest of the local children, if they wanted money, they had to earn it. "We had a pleasant life," remembers Harrison. "When I was a kid, my Dad was not rich. We had enough to eat, and we were comfortable and so forth, but definitely not rich." Harrison, always the salesman, earned pocket money selling magazines and newspapers on weekends. In the springtime, he'd sell Easter cards and garden seeds. "There was no favouritism showed to them, nor would their mother have wanted it," says Ernie Stickney, a former Florenceville mayor who went to school with both Harrison and Wallace, graduating with Harrison in 1945. "Harrison and Wallace took their knocks along with the rest of us. They didn't have two cents in their pockets, just like me. They didn't have any more than the rest of us."

Stickney has known the McCains all his life. When he was a boy, his mother did housekeeping chores for Laura McCain, known in Florenceville as "Mrs. A.D." He was a schoolbuddy with Harrison and Wallace and remained friends with them long after the boys became frozen-food moguls. In 1985, when he was recuperating from surgery in a Saint John hospital, Stickney got a phone call from Harrison.

"Harrison said, 'When you're ready to get out of the hospital, I'm going to fly down with my plane, pick you up, knock the cap off a bottle of rye, throw it out at the Saint John airport, and we'll throw the empty bottle out in Florenceville.' And when I was ready to leave, I called for Harrison, but he was in England. So I called Wallace and told him about his brother's promise. And he said, 'Is that right? Well, I'm just leaving here myself for England, but I'll call the pilot and tell them to get it all arranged. And you call the switchboard at the plant tomorrow morning and they'll tell you what time the plane will be there.' So the next day they picked me up, put me on the airplane, and flew me home. That's the kind of people they are. Very generous."

The McCains had a little farm near H.H. McCain's property on River View Drive—a couple of cows for milking and a team of work horses. "Harrison and Wallace looked after those horses, and they had the cows to milk every morning," says Stickney. "In the spring of the year, the ditches along the town roads had to be cleaned out. The town would hire a bunch of young fellas to shovel the ditches, and Harrison and Wallace were out there shovelling, too. There was nothing lazy about either one of them."

Wallace later admitted that he detested the farm chores his father forced on him. "Dad had a strong work ethic," he says. "Mother did too. And we were brought up that way. I remember we worked in the summertime—just as soon as you were old enough to do anything, you worked. You worked in the hayfields, you worked in the fall, picking potatoes. I always had a cow when I was a child. I would have been eight or nine, or ten, something like that. Dad would buy us a cow, and we milked the cow. You got paid for the cow with the calf. If you wanted to sell it, it was yours. Bob had one. I think Andrew got off the hook because he had heart trouble. Harrison had one too, and I had one. Harrison finished school before me, so Dad felt that I could keep two. So I had two for the last three years of high school. I walked from home about three-quarters of a mile to where the farm was and milked that damned cow. I learned to swear milking the cow. In rain or snow, the cow's in the pasture, never find the cow. It was nothing like it is now, where you have a cow and put him in the barn and feed him. It was hard work."

After graduation, Harrison went to Acadia University in Wolfville, Nova Scotia, where he made a half-hearted attempt at fulfilling his grandfather's dream of a McCain doctor. Harrison received passing grades in his pre-med courses, but his marks were not high enough to get him into medical school —a very fortunate ending for a natural-born salesman who would make millions of dollars selling french fries. "I didn't get into medical school, and that was a great blessing," he recalls. Although Harrison finished with a Bachelor of Science degree in chemistry and economics, Mr. A.D. was not pleased that his son would not become a doctor. "He was very, very, very disappointed," says Harrison. "And cheesed off."

Wallace followed Harrison to Acadia, where Wallace's extra-curricular antics at the Baptist university became legendary. Wallace was more likely to have a drink in his hand, or a girl on his arm, than his nose in a book. According to one family joke, Wallace wallpapered his dormitory room with labels from bottles of Seagram's VO. "He majored in sowing wild oats," his wife Margaret says flatly. "You know, he was straight off the farm, and he came into this big, wide world, and let it all hang out."

At Acadia, Wallace fell in with a crowd of battle-hardened World War II veterans who were keen on both completing their educations and having a good time. "They were men, they were not boys," says Wallace. "And they raised hell. So I had some problems with the disciplinary side of my time at Acadia, to say the least. No studying—that was the bottom line. In those days, it was alcohol. I drank a lot. But the funny part is, I always had a hangover, and I think that kept me from becoming an alcoholic."

Wallace spent two years there, flunking courses and partying, before both he and the university agreed it would be best that he not return. He went back to Florenceville in 1949 and announced to his parents that he was giving up college. Wallace had spent his summer holidays in the University Naval Training Division, and had decided on a career in the Navy.

"So I said I was going to go to the Navy," Wallace recalls telling his father.

Mr. and Mrs. A.D. were not amused.

"Forget the Navy," his father shot back. "Now you're going to university and get your degree." And that was the end of the argument.

"It wasn't *if* you were going, it was *where* you were going," says Wallace. "So when Dad had spoken, I thought, 'I'd better go.' And I changed my ways a bit."

Wallace spent a make-up summer at the University of New Brunswick, and then transferred to Mount Allison University, where he graduated in math and economics—and met his future wife, Margaret Norrie.

Born in 1934 in the backwoods of northern Quebec where her father, James Norrie, was a successful mining engineer, Margaret was raised to be a strong, independent woman like her mother, Margaret Fawcett Norrie. James Norrie, who was instrumental in the discovery of gold in the Abitibi and Malartic regions of Quebec, died when Margaret was 11 years old. Her mother, who never remarried, moved back to the family farm in Truro, Nova Scotia, and raised her children alone. And children came first in the Norrie household. "My mother was very much a hands-on, loving, caring, supporting woman," says Margaret. "It didn't matter what we did, we were validated and supported. And loved and nurtured and affirmed."

Margaret's mother, who later became a Liberal senator, invested time in her children: she made them hot lunches when they came home from school, and went out of her way to drive them to piano lessons, hockey games—whatever the children were involved in. "And when she was in the Senate," says Margaret, "she attended every birth, she was there for every child, every grandchild. She was just a very hands-on mother and a great parenting model. I grew up in a family where trust was a foundation in the relationship."

Margaret attended Havergal College, the exclusive girls' school in Toronto, where she skipped two grades and ended up a freshman at Mount Allison at age 15. That was the year she met Wallace. "He lived in town, not in residence, because he thought he wouldn't be tempted to become involved in some of the residential activities," she says. Although Margaret and Wallace met briefly at a dance during initiation week, they didn't see each other for another four years.

"I graduated in 1954, and it was just a month or six weeks later when Wallace happened to be in town. He was working for Thornes Hardware, and he was on a sales trip. He ended up in Truro on a Sunday night, didn't know anybody, and called me. I remember being apprehensive, because I was still a young girl off the farm, I was still pretty young, 19 years old. And I still saw him as a man of the world, and I was on guard. But I realized that I didn't have anything to fear. He was a proper gentleman; he came to pick me up that night in a suit and a tie. There was nothing to do in Truro on Sunday night, except have coffee. The other common activity was parking in the cemetery—and I didn't particularly want to park in the cemetery."

Their first date was uneventful, except that Wallace's innocent sense of honesty immediately impressed itself on Margaret. He was so open he almost embarrassed her. "I could see, even then, a man I could respect. I was as pure as the driven snow, and I'm not bragging, because things were different in the 1950s. But he had sown his wild oats; he had a past life. And one night he had to tell me everything. It was all spilled out. He sat there telling me about a life I didn't know existed."

Wallace was accepted by Margaret's mother the night he showed up at their door in a suit and tie, but it took several visits to Mrs. A.D.'s home in Florenceville before Margaret was accepted by the old McCain matriarch. On one overnight visit to Mrs. A.D.'s—Margaret and Wallace slept in separate bedrooms—Wallace made the mistake of bringing Margaret home after midnight.

"I was upstairs trying to get to sleep, and somehow through the register Mrs. A.D.'s voice came up through the pantry," says Margaret. "She's berating Wallace for getting me home after twelve o'clock at night. She was saying, 'Don't you know that a woman's resistance is lowered after twelve o'clock?' I remember being upstairs thinking, 'Oh dear, what does she think of me?' There was no question I was being interrogated when I went there. And then she went to my Aunt Nita at a Women's Institute convention, and said, 'Nita, who is this young woman Wallace is seeing?' Aunt Nita and I were very close, so she got a good report."

One year after they began dating, Wallace and Margaret were married. "We were out one night, and he said, 'Remind me to tell you something this evening.' And I said, 'Tell me now.' My curiosity was piqued. Later, I asked him what he was going to tell me. 'I just thought I'd tell you that we're going to get married,' he said. So that was my romantic proposal."

Harrison's introduction to his future wife, whether you prefer Harrison's version or his sister-in-law's, was certainly more romantic. Harrison says he met her through a blind date arranged by Wallace. According to Nancy McNair Moody, however, Harrison met her sister Marion "Billie" McNair, at a Mount Allison University dinner in 1951. Billie attended the dinner with her father, who was then Premier of New Brunswick. Nancy says that Harrison spied Billie from across the room, and sent his introductions through a waiter. "You are the most beautiful woman in the room," read Harrison's note to Billie. "Can we meet for a date?"

Harrison wasn't exaggerating Billie's beauty—soft, sweet features and a broad, stunning smile. Billie McNair would have stood out anywhere. As a child, however, Billie was often mistaken for a boy—which accounts for the nickname she was given at the age of three. "I took her out to the barber shop, and the barber thought she was a boy," says Nancy. "And he put her up in the chair and was cutting her hair like a boy's. And you know, she was going to be called William had she been born a boy. So when we went home, my Dad said, 'Well, I guess we'll call her Billie now.'"

Born in Fredericton in 1929, Billie is always remembered by relatives as shy and withdrawn. After Billie's birth, her mother, Marion Crockett McNair, was hospitalized for what was called post-partum psychosis. Billie's father, a former Rhodes Scholar who became Premier of New Brunswick in 1940 and held office until 1952, when he was defeated by

Hugh John Flemming, could not spend as much time as he would have liked with his four children, and they were raised largely by household staff.

Billie went to public schools in Fredericton, but completed high school at Mount Allison University's private boarding school for girls. She later received a fine arts degree from Mount Allison. Harrison and Billie were married October 4, 1952, at St. Andrew's Presbyterian Church in Fredericton.

• • •

Acadia may not have been the place for the McCains' higher education, but it was a proving ground for many successful New Brunswickers, and an ideal place to build connections and networks. At Acadia, Harrison and Wallace became friends with two of the three Irving boys, Arthur and Jim, sons of New Brunswick industrialist, K.C. Irving. It would be a turning point in the McCains' young careers, eventually leading to senior management jobs with K.C. Irving.

After graduation, the two boys shunned Florenceville, believing that they were cut out for something better than shipping potatoes to South America. Wallace did try working for his father's company, McCain Produce, for three months. "I didn't like the style, I just didn't like it," he says. Harrison spent his first year out of university as a salesman for a pharmaceutical company, Mowatt and Moore, in Montreal. Then he was offered a job in the Irving empire.

Harrison recalls how it was luck that got him the job. "I was home on holidays, and Jimmy [Irving] dropped into my Dad's," says Harrison. "And I just happened to be there. I think we had lunch and we were sitting there talking, and I got a letter. [It] was from my boss in Montreal. I opened the letter, and enclosed was a cheque for—I don't know, two or three hundred bucks, four hundred bucks, something like that—two months pay. Jimmy was just astounded. The boss had written me a letter . . . I was really doing a good job, and he wanted me to have a bonus, a non-structured bonus. Jimmy was mightily impressed, and he got the impression that I was the best salesman. Why would they be mailing cheques out, unsolicited? I know he went home and told his Dad that. 'Harrison is getting these unsolicited cheques. He's such a good salesman, they're just sending him cheques from the office.'

"So in jig time, Mr. Irving was on the phone to me. He said to come on down and work for them. I said no. Negotiations went on and on, and to make a long story short, they finally made me an offer I couldn't refuse."

In 1951, at 24 years of age, Harrison became Irving Oil's sales manager for New Brunswick, P.E.I. and Newfoundland. Harrison eventually worked on the top floor of the Golden Ball Building on Union Street in Saint John, in a large office just four doors down from K.C.'s. Although Harrison never reported directly to K.C., they often travelled together on business trips. Harrison learned that while K.C. was a hard-driving business man who appreciated hard work, he also had a playful side. "He was a good fella to work for," says Harrison. "He had great energy, wonderful energy. Never got tired. Good fun, too. Just laugh all the time. He was full of stories, jokes, making fun of people and things. We used to have a good time."

One quality Harrison learned to respect in K.C. was his keen attention to detail. "Mr. Irving was a great stickler for a lot of detail," he says. "He had a huge amount of detail in his mind. Like he'd say, 'I don't know if I'm buying that ship. How long is that ship? Oh, it's too long. You can only get a ship 258 feet long through the St. Lawrence Seaway.' His mind was full of all these pieces of commercial information, from which you could measure stuff, get some idea about things. He had a huge fund of information." Ironically, former Irving employees would say that attention to detail was an attribute K.C. saw in Wallace, not Harrison.

Still, it was not uncommon for Harrison to work 16- or 20-hour days, which put him in good standing with his boss. George Urquhart, who owned a propane business, lived above Harrison and his wife Billie in a flat on beautiful, tree-lined Manawagonish Road in West Saint John during the 1950s. Urquhart recalls that, like everyone else who worked closely with K.C., Harrison was worked to the bone. The best time he seemed to have outside the office was when his father-in-law, former premier John B. McNair, would drop by and Harrison would have his friends over to say hello. "He had a great rapport with Billie's father," recalls Urquhart. "They got along real well and Harrison was so proud of him." But the visits with his famous in-law became fewer the longer Harrison worked for Irving. Harrison was on the road with K.C. constantly, dealing with customers and governments. "He always kept an extra bag packed, just in case," Urquhart recalls.

K.C. expected absolute devotion from his upper management employees, and Harrison gave it to him in spades —and liked it. "There was this incredible work ethic," says Urquhart, who later sold his propane company to Irving and went to work for the old man. "You had to work, or at least felt you had to—and you did. And you were always looking carefully into things and you learned to make decisions quick and, hopefully, right. And you learned to have a real good memory, because if you couldn't remember, it was just too bad."

Harrison was determined to learn everything he could during his five-year apprenticeship with Irving. "He had a great admiration for K.C.," says Urquhart. "And he had the greatest admiration for the style of K.C. The main thing he learned there was that you had to put in long hours and hard work to succeed." Harrison also learned never to underestimate anyone—especially not his enemies. "That's one of the features I saw in him back then, and I think it's continued ever since. He never, in all the years I've known him, ever downplayed anyone, never even privately."

Wallace's first job after university was flogging bug spray for Green Cross Insecticide. His territory included the St. John River valley from Saint John to Edmundston, which brought him one day to Thornes Hardware, the Saint John–based store owned by K.C. Irving. "I called on Thornes because they weren't selling the line," says Wallace. "I made four or five calls, and then I got a call from the purchaser at Thornes, and he said he wanted to see me. And I thought, 'Great, he's going to give me the order.' But when I went to see him, he hired me."

Thornes was a hardware store, but also sold everything from marine supplies for Bay of Fundy fishermen to industrial supplies for Irving's subsidiaries. Wallace became the store's general manager, in charge of Thornes' 143 employees and its sales reps in the Maritime provinces. When Wallace arrived, the store's catalogue and pricing system was an antiquated shambles. "We worked practically every night for a year on that catalogue," recalls Gus Higgins, a former purchasing agent with Thornes, who says that "Wally" was a perfect team leader, involving everyone in the decision-making process. "He got along with everybody. He had a knack for talking with everyone, didn't matter who you were. He would even talk with the truck drivers."

Even then the brothers had formed their distinct business styles. Harrison was the ebullient, glad-handing visionary—a man in charge, while Wallace was introverted, with an enormous capacity for detail. These very different qualities were united in K.C. Irving. Like Harrison, he could be outgoing and ruthless; like Wallace, he was a stickler for minutiae. Yet former Irving employees say that when the brothers left K.C.'s organization in the mid-1950s, K.C. was more saddened by Wallace's departure: he appreciated Wallace's talents more than Harrison's.

Bev O'Keefe, who worked with both brothers for Irving, recalls K.C. speaking fondly of Wallace during one of the late-night reminiscing sessions during which the old man would unwind.

"K.C. was the kind of fellow," says O'Keefe, "who never got up too early in the mornings, you know. He'd come to work about 9:30, a quarter to ten. And on the road he was the same way. And he always had something for you to do at six o'clock in the morning and then he'd meet you about 9:30. And of course, six o'clock at night didn't mean anything to him. He'd work until maybe nine or ten o'clock. And he was always the type of man that when the day was done, he wanted to slow down and relax. And he'd do that by reminiscing. Or he might occasionally call his wife,

Hattie, and he'd say, 'Jim and Jack are with me, and I got O'Keefe and a couple of others, maybe we could come to the house and have some dinner.' Jesus Christ, you knew that was going to last until about twelve or one o'clock and it was going to be all business. But he liked to reminisce. Back in those days, it was before they had fax machines. You had to send cables. And Christ, didn't it take him 20 minutes to work out a three-line cable. There were about three or four in the room and he'd get all their opinions, but he ended up doing whatever he wanted to do, but that would have been about eight or nine o'clock at night and that was the method he used to slow down. Or he'd want to talk about something.

"And I guess I had just come in off the road and I had been up in the St. John River valley, and he asked me what was going on, how much new business I got that day, how many new accounts. 'What's this service station doing?' And he asked me if I had seen Harrison and Wallace McCain recently. 'You know,' he said, 'They were two great boys. But I took it pretty hard when Wallace resigned. I really regretted that.' Wallace made a tremendous contribution to the hardware business. When Wallace left him he was handling all of Thornes in the Maritimes, as well as Irving's hardware stores in Quebec and Ontario. It was very evident that Wallace was going to become one of the chief CEOs in that business. He said, 'Wallace was a tremendous loss to our group. He had great business judgment and he knew how to control his employees and receivables, managed payables the way I like them managed. But I could see that if their business was to be successful, Wallace had to join Harrison, otherwise, it could never get to be where they are heading.'"

● ● ●

A.D. McCain died on a cold February day in 1953. He was 74 years old, but had business on his mind right to the end: he was planning his first trip to South America. Millions of kilograms of McCain seed potatoes had been sent there since the late 1800s, but the potato buyers had always come to Florenceville, staying at the old hotel once owned by A.D.'s Uncle William, on the east side of the river. Breaking with family tradition, Harrison and Wallace decided not to help run the family business after their father's death, but to continue to work for Irving.

A.D. died without a will, leaving the opportunity open for a family war over his assets. But Mrs. A.D. would not tolerate family dissension—only later would the McCain name become synonymous with the word "feud." After A.D. died, recalls Harrison, "somebody said to my mother, 'You'll have a terrible time with these six kids, dividing up the estate, because there's no will and there's going to be an awful fight.' And she said, 'There will be no such thing. These children are not scrappers. They're not scrappers, they're a family that get along well together. They will not fight about that.'"

Harrison pauses several seconds for effect. "She was right *then*," he laughs.

Indeed, one-third of A.D.'s assets went to his wife and the remaining two-thirds were split among his six children. Most of A.D.'s holdings were in land, potato contracts, the McCain Produce Co., and some stock in Algoma Steel, where he made most of his money.

"That old fellow didn't make his money in the potato business, that's for sure," recalls an old family friend. "The potato business was a means, over the course of the year, of

41

creating lots of cash. It's a buyer's business. He bought and sold stuff, and brought in all the cash, and then settled up with the farmers in the spring of the year. He had all that cash to use."

A.D. had used the cash from his potato business to earn a tidy fortune on the stock market. He bought all the shares he could in Algoma Steel, and never looked back. It was 1935 and the son of a Bathurst carpenter, Jimmy Dunn, had just become the largest shareholder of Algoma, the northern Ontario corporation that had gone into bankruptcy. "There was a broker in Fredericton who phoned A.D. one day and said, 'You mortgage your home and buy all you can buy,'" recalls distant relation Fred McCain. "He bought all that he could at the time, on the strength of that fella's advice." Miraculously, Dunn brought Algoma Steel back to solvency soon afterwards with a whopping new government contract for steel rails, and Algoma's stock went through the roof. "I think it split twice," says Fred McCain. "I don't think A.D. ever sold any." When A.D.'s estate was settled, the boys decided not to cash in any of the assets, but save them in case they needed seed money for their own business.

The running of the family company fell largely to brothers Andrew, Robert, and, surprisingly, Mrs. A.D. The 62-year-old widow, who had been deliberately kept in the dark about the business affairs by her husband, suddenly sprang into action as the company president. Local legend has it that Mrs. A.D., realizing that the only way to learn about the potato business was to work in it, drove to the McCain Produce Co.'s office every morning and didn't quit until late at night. While Mrs. A.D. had her hand in the business, reports of her involvement in the family company have been exaggerated, says Harrison. "She didn't run it, my brothers ran it. She was the type who would go over there a little bit and give them a little free advice," he says. "Stir up the pot."

Mrs. A.D.'s efforts, however, did not go unnoticed by Wallace. "I didn't really realize Mother was strong until after Dad died," he says. "She would have been known today as a very, very strong feminist. Without any question. Dad never talked business in the house, but after Dad died, Andrew and Bob were working in the produce company and she moved in."

No matter how hard Mrs. A.D. and her two sons worked, however, the fact was that potatoes were not commanding the price they used to, neither domestically nor in the foreign markets. By the 1950s, mechanization, which had been slow in coming to New Brunswick, meant that fewer local labourers could count on jobs every year working the potato fields. Fred McCain, who was then the local MLA, said that all of Carleton County was on the verge of collapse.

The area had tried, unsuccessfully, every way imaginable to turn their potatoes into profit. There were ill-tasting dehydrated potatoes, potato starch and potato feed; but none brought the profits their inventors had predicted. No, Carleton County needed a new idea, or the region was doomed—and the young McCain boys figured they had hit on it.

CHAPTER THREE

The Fries
that Bind

HOW THE MCCAINS GOT INTO THE FROZEN FRENCH FRY business is as well-worn a tale as you might hear at the Florenceville IGA, where the frozen food section is an icy McCain monument: french fries, pizzas, vegetables, juices, cakes, complete dinners, and every other freezable food the McCains produce. Any shopper will tell you how Robert McCain visited frozen-food plants in Maine, and a light bulb clicked on in his brain. He came home and talked younger brothers Harrison and Wallace into going into the frozen-food business. Florenceville's local heroes not only made good, but more importantly, made it on their own.

However hard they were capable of working, the McCains were not innovators. Indeed, marketable frozen food was invented before Harrison and Wallace were in diapers. Between 1912 and 1916, Clarence Birdseye, a Brooklyn-born naturalist and inventor, joined a fur-trading expedition to Labrador, where he was struck by the fact that natives could keep quickly frozen meat in the ice for long periods of time without its losing texture or flavour. This was the problem with frozen food and refrigeration in general. Commercial freezing kept foods from going bad, but sapped meats and vegetables of flavour. Defrosted foods became a pulpy mass. The problem was ice crystals. The slow freezing of the day allowed the water in the food to form into crystals, which tore apart the cell walls. But the food that was flash frozen in the arctic retained its freshness and flavour because ice crystals were not given time to form.

Birdseye, it is said, buried a load of vegetables in the Labrador ice one year and, on his return a year later, found them agreeably edible when defrosted and cooked. Eureka. He returned to the U.S., armed himself with $7 worth of brine, some ice and an electric fan, and created arctic-like conditions by circulating brine mist around food at -43°C. Rather than taking the usual 18 hours to freeze, the food froze in 90 minutes. When defrosted, it tasted absolutely fresh.

He formed Birdseye Seafoods Inc. in 1923 and, a year later, General Seafoods Co. of Massachusetts, with the idea that if you offered quality frozen food, refrigerating companies would improve their product to meet consumer demand— which is exactly what happened. Birdseye's company was selling a variety of frozen foods by 1929, when it was purchased for $22 million by the Postum Cereal Co., later General Foods Corp. By 1934, General Foods-Birds Eye was selling 80 per cent of America's frozen foods.

Birdseye's process, by which food was frozen between two super-cold metal plates, was a boon to both farmers and food processors. Farmers had been at the mercy of seasonal price swings and the risk of crops rotting before they reached market. One of the early beneficiaries was the Florida citrus industry, which produced more than 54 million litres of frozen orange-juice concentrate in 1949, thanks to quick-freezing and refrigeration. But the new industry was not without risks. In order to ensure that every package of frozen food arrived in the consumer's kitchen with its quality intact, transportation required minute attention. In 1947 alone, 200 U.S. frozen-food companies went bankrupt.

The key to bringing frozen food to New Brunswick was Premier Hugh John Flemming, the man Harrison once urged his teacher not to vote for. According to Cy Sherwood, a former agriculture minister in Premier Flemming's government of the 1950s, the tale of Robert's seeing the frozen-food future makes a good story, but is not very accurate. As Sherwood tells it the provincial government, desperate for local job creation and an outlet for Carleton County's potato surplus, lured the McCains into the french-fry business with government grants and loan guarantees. "They didn't come to us first," Sherwood says. "We went to them." The McCains, he says, showed smarts not in concocting the business, but in accepting the government's hand-outs.

The 1950s were indeed dismal for potato farmers in Carleton County. Jobs were scarce and farmers received only about 50 cents per hundredweight for their crop. The county had few business prospects, a shrinking potato market, and mechanization was replacing seasonal workers. Potatoes were being exported, processed and shipped back for sale to the people who grew them.

"We needed an employer and we needed someone to save the potato industry," says Fred McCain, a member of the provincial legislature at the time. "If the McCains hadn't come in, we'd have been in hell at best."

Hugh John Flemming's Tory government decided that New Brunswick's potato crop would bring in more money if one of the American food processing giants opened shop in the province. Not only would there be a guaranteed market for New Brunswick potatoes, there would also be spin-off jobs in the processing plant. And so, in March 1954—almost three years before the McCains opened their frozen-food plant in Florenceville—Premier Flemming concluded debate on the provincial budget with a 10-point industrial development plan that included plans to entice investors to establish "fast freezing plants" along the St. John River Valley, "thus providing alternative markets for farmers owning rich potato land," Flemming told the legislature. "Results in Carleton County last year provide encouraging possibilities. I am sure that all will agree with me that the matter deserves and should have, all possible encouragement, since we must be sending a great deal of money out of the province for food products which could be grown and processed here at home."

Naturally, Flemming, being from nearby Juniper, preferred that the plant be in Carleton County, which he and Fred McCain represented, but Sherwood says that none of the American corporations would bite. Americans were eating about 6 kilograms of frozen food a year, but per capita consumption in Canada was only a bit more than one kilogram a year. What market there was, the Americans argued, could be serviced from the U.S.

Flemming's government, hungry to create jobs, produced studies showing that Canadian consumers would eventually follow the American lead in frozen foods.

About this time, Harrison, 28, and Wallace, 25, two of the hottest managers in K.C. Irving's quickly growing industrial empire, were starting to change. They began to spend less and less time cursing, swearing and partying, as former co-workers describe the brothers' after-hours antics in Saint John, and more evenings entertaining dreams of empire building.

After all, this was 1955, the year a Chicagoan named Ray Kroc opened his first McDonald's hamburger stand in Des Plaines, Illinois.

Whether Harrison and Wallace planned to go into business together after their stint with the Irvings is a contested issue. Wallace says they always planned to start something together; Harrison, however, says he first set out on his own, and only later asked Wallace to join him in the frenchfry business.

In any event, Harrison was the first to resign from the Irving company. "The job was pleasant, the pay was good, so it was hard to leave," says Harrison. "I thought there'd be an opportunity show up some day and I'd just seize the opportunity, get onto something else. And one day, it dawned on me—that wasn't going to happen. I had to just make it happen, so I quit."

Harrison says that Wallace only fit into his plans later. "Wallace at that time, wasn't . . . going into business with me," he says. "That wasn't part of any plan. Later on, after I left, we talked about going into business together, and we looked at a couple of deals together, but I was working at it full time without pay. I wasn't representing the two of us. I paid my own bills, he wasn't paying half. Looked after myself . . . he was on the fringe of the deal, you know."

However, Margaret McCain, Wallace's wife, remembers that from the time she met Wallace, in 1954, the brothers planned to become partners in business. Harrison and Wallace owned a world of possibilities in their heads. There was nothing, she says, that they weren't prepared to conquer—including their old boss, K.C. Irving. "When I first started going out with Wallace, on our first date, he and Harrison had already decided on going into business together," she says. "It was not a question of if. It was a question of when, where, what." A year later, Margaret remembers, Harrison told them he would quit his job and devote six months to researching business opportunities. He would then discuss them with Wallace.

Harrison quit his job at Irving Oil in the fall of 1955, and spent a month in Florida, selling Christmas trees. "I took a load down to Florida, [and] we stayed for a month," recalls Harrison. "I think I had three or four hundred dollars in my pocket when I left, and I had three or four hundred dollars in my pocket when I came back. It didn't cost me anything."

The months after Harrison returned from Florida were hectic, recalls Margaret. "Every single night when Harrison was home and we were free, we went over to their house in West Saint John because they had a baby, and Billie and I sat while they talked and they explored," she says. The brothers first considered a dry-cleaning business in Truro, Nova Scotia. The prospect excited Margaret, as it would mean moving to her home town. Another idea was opening a hardware store in Amherst, Nova Scotia. This, too, was shot down. "I was heartbroken, because that was only an hour from my home town," says Margaret, with a hint of sadness still in her voice. The brothers even considered buying seats on the Montreal Stock Exchange and going into the brokerage business, but the idea that troubled Margaret most was a half-baked plan to compete with K.C. Irving. "That almost gave me a heart attack," she remembers. "I had confidence in them, but not that much."

While the two men discussed their dreams, their wives did what wives were expected to do in the 1950s: made coffee and kept their mouths shut. "Billie and I talked about recipes . . . I had no kids, so what else could we talk about? So we sat like good little girls off in the corner, while these two did their thing."

The McCains, perhaps with the later exception of Wallace, never questioned such absolute patriarchy. Later, family friends would use this McCain attitude to explain why neither Marie nor Eleanor were asked to join the brothers' venture. The McCain view of women's role was precisely what the burgeoning fast-food companies were portraying to their customers. "Give Mom a Night Out," and "Give Mom a Night Off" were McDonald's advertising slogans at the time: food companies sold the same view. It wasn't that mom was overworked, but hey, why bother peeling, washing, slicing and deep-frying potatoes, when you can just pop our frozen fries in the oven. Geez mom, now you can cook and entertain hubby's friends at the same time.

In the 1950s, *I Love Lucy* featured Lucille Ball as a modern American housewife desperately trying to create a role for herself outside her husband's shadow. When Lucy and Desi divorced, Lucy was working and raising Little Ricky all by herself on *The Lucy Show*. And when she didn't have time to cook, Lucy could always feed the kid frozen food, made piping hot in the oven. Television, divorce and the pressures of modern life made America ready for frozen food.

But Canada? After Flemming's government failed to entice U.S. food processors to Carleton County, they approached the McCains. For Harrison and Wallace, the timing of the government offer was perfect, although the idea of producing frozen food seemed less so. "I didn't think it was any earth-shaking idea," says Harrison, "but I had nothing to do since the fall before, and I was quietly desperate." The government persisted and invited Robert McCain to tour a Birds Eye plant in upstate Maine. "There were several people that prodded them a little bit, and encouraged them a little bit," recalls Sherwood. "Certainly as a government, and as a department, we opened up every avenue we could in researching markets and researching processing techniques and things like that."

Robert soon convinced his two younger brothers of the proposal's viability, arguing that a locally owned company could do well, considering that Carleton County farmers were already selling their produce to be frozen—by Birds Eye, in Maine. "We pinched the idea," recalled Harrison. "There was nothing particularly brilliant about it. Birds Eye were in Caribou, Maine, and they were taking New Brunswick peas, then processing them, then shipping them back across the border for sale. So we thought: 'Why can't we do the whole process within the province?'"

Why not indeed? Margaret was appalled at the prospect. "I said, 'I'm 21 years old,'" she recalls. "'Do you mean I'd have to move to Florenceville? I just moved from the country—and I don't want to go back to it.'" Wallace suggested that if the company succeeded, they would probably move to Montreal or Toronto within a couple of years. Wallace then gave his notice at Thornes. He and Margaret packed up their Saint John home and moved to Florenceville in June 1956. Harrison and Billie arrived in August.

The only snag was money. Start-up costs, from construction to workers' first couple of months' wages, were estimated at $600,000. Harrison and Wallace each invested $30,000 from their inheritances; Andrew and Robert kicked in $20,000 apiece, for a family total of $100,000. A $150,000 loan was ponied up by the Bank of Nova Scotia; the rest, the brothers figured, would have to come from elsewhere.

"We began cogitating about this," remembers Sherwood, in his King's County drawl. "We were talking with Bob, Harrison and Wallace, and one of the boys in the Department of Agriculture was well acquainted with A.D., their father. And I know that our conversations with them stimulated their interest." More stimulating than the talk, however, was the loan the provincial government was willing to underwrite. It was extremely rare that governments assisted in starting up businesses back then, but Fred McCain insists that Premier Flemming agreed to put politics aside. "They weren't political supporters of mine, but that made no difference," says Sherwood, a lifelong Tory. Says cousin Fred McCain, also a Tory: "They never voted for me, either. But they got the money because we needed their plant as badly, or worse, than they needed us."

The McCains received two guaranteed loans: $280,000 to get McCain Foods Ltd. started and $140,000 to set up Carleton Cold Storage Ltd. As the McCains estimated the cost of constructing the 2643-cubic-metre cold storage plant was $260,000, the federal government agreed to give the brothers an $87,000 grant.

Now the public had to be sold on the idea. In March 1956, at a meeting with provincial agricultural department officials and representatives from the Maritime Board of Trade and the New Brunswick Federation of Agriculture, Robert set out his brothers' plans to buy not just potatoes, but peas, blueberries, strawberries, and anything else Carleton County farmers could coax from the soil.

Everyone at the meeting immediately saw that the McCains were on to a good thing. New Brunswick produced only a small fraction of its fruit and vegetable needs—Saint John alone had imported $75 million worth of processed vegetables in the past five years, vegetables that could have been grown and packaged in Carleton County. The plant was also badly needed by local farmers, who would have a steady, reliable market for their crops.

While the McCains were seriously considering building the plant, Robert told his eager listeners, a number of surveys had yet to be completed. Maritimers, he said, would first have to be "educated" to buy local products, particularly frozen ones. The scheme, he pointed out, was risky, it might never get started.

What the McCains didn't mention was that they had a site picked out, on an old cow pasture less than four hundred metres from the McCain Produce Co. building on the east side of the river. Building plans had been drawn up and they were only weeks away from drilling wells to supply water for the new cold storage plant and processing factory.

Harrison told Carleton County Council in June 1956 that the plant would not be built unless the McCains received generous tax concessions. He talked of the company's ushering in a "new era of prosperity for New Brunswick" and that the plant would process enough french fries to feed the entire Atlantic provinces in just two weeks. The county's potato crop was a "liability, rather than an asset," Harrison reminded the councillors, but cash-crop contracts for peas, strawberries and potatoes, he said, had already been negotiated. Fifty workers—one shift for 11 months of the year— would be hired as soon as the plant opened. But the food processing industry was highly competitive, and the McCains could not operate without a tax break.

County councillors could not afford to say no, and voted to give the McCains every tax concession they lawfully could. Harrison had learned K.C. Irving's lessons well.

• • •

Construction of the plant began in August 1956, and was completed that November—Wallace oversaw the buildings' construction and installation of the frying and freezing equipment. The brothers formed Opco, or "Operating Company," an umbrella firm under which McCain Foods, Carleton Cold Storage and future McCain subsidiaries would operate. In January 1957, packages of french fries bearing the now-familiar McCain logo, with a star dotting the "i" in white script on a black background, began rolling out of the plant.

The official opening took place in February. The ribbon-cutting ceremony attracted more than one thousand french-fry-munching visitors, including Premier Flemming and the federal labour minister, Milton Gregg, who snipped a 22-metre scarlet ribbon joining the food plant and cold storage building, and formally declared McCain Foods Ltd. and Carleton Cold Storage Ltd. open for business. "It is always thrilling to see our young men building something where there was nothing before," said an enthused Flemming.

Judging by a newspaper account of the opening cere-monies, the locals were as thrilled as the Premier. "Before the fluttering ribbon touched ground a rousing ovation went up from the huge crowd," reported *The Telegraph-Journal*. "Within minutes the entire length of ribbon was carried away in pieces by scores of souvenir hunters." Above the story was a photograph of the four McCain brothers and their mother, holding a box of McCain french fries. The 65-year-old Mrs. A.D., sporting a wide, flat-brimmed hat, horn-rimmed glasses, and a corsage the size of a Boston lettuce, looked rather like a gangster's moll surrounded by four good-looking, well-dressed G-men.

Inside the plant, the brothers relied heavily on the expertise of former Birds Eye employees. One was Olof "O.P." Pierson, who invented frozen french fries in the 1940s, at the H.C. Boxter Co. in Hartland, Maine. Pierson later became a United Nations food consultant, and helped establish potato processing plants in Poland, Brazil, Greece and Sweden. When he died in 1993, Pierson's obituary was carried in newspapers worldwide. The McCains also hired Franklin Hickling, a lifelong frozen-food man, a walking french-fry encyclopedia who was there when Birds Eye produced frozen french fries in Caribou, Maine, in 1947. "We froze the first [commercial] french fry that was ever frozen in the world," he remembers proudly. Hickling's career spanned five decades and the entire North American continent. "I froze blueberries, peas and beans in Maine, succotash and corn and lima beans in Indiana, strawberries in Arkansas, peas in Walla Walla, Washington, beans in Texas and tomatoes in New York, and baked beans in Boston," he boasts.

It was just as well. What the McCains knew about potatoes and produce had been handed down from their father; but they knew nothing about frozen food. "We put him [Hickling] in charge," recalled Harrison. "He made it. We sold it." Hickling recalls that in his first five years at McCain Foods, he was the only employee who had ever been in a frozen-food plant. "Harrison said that . . . he walked through a plant once," says Hickling. "And Wallace said that he didn't have that opportunity.

"Well, my friends over in the States, when I said I was going to get up and move to Canada, they said, 'Look, how crazy can you be?'" recalls Hickling. "They said, 'Those two kids over there think they're going to start up a frozen-food plant and compete with the giants that we have in the States today—they're crazy.' But of course, I was a born Canadian, so it was just like coming home.

"I thought I was going to have a real easy time," he says. "But I underestimated them greatly. They worked me nearly to death for the next 20 years. I couldn't build fryers fast enough."

According to Wallace, American frozen-food companies had been shipping inferior grades of frozen french fries to Canada as they had no competition. This made it easy for the McCains to gain market share with a superior product. "We didn't think the frozen french fries sold were good quality," Wallace says. "It was called 'oil-blanched' french fries. They were all white; they cooked white, and usually a french fry is dark in color. It was greasy, it had no flavour, and the texture was bad. So we said, 'Number one, the housewife wants a darker french fry. She doesn't want a white french fry.' So we started a fully fried french fry."

Hickling recalls that the McCains and their superior french fry caught the U.S. frozen food producers off guard. "The Americans figured," he says, "a couple of kids over in Florenceville going into the french-fry business . . . they didn't pay any attention to them [McCains] until it was too late. One day they woke up and said, 'Holy God, where's our sales all gone? Not only that, but those buggers are coming over to the States.' They bought three plants in Maine—in Washburn and Easton . . . they're the only people in the business there now."

It was truly a family business, with each of the four brothers responsible for an aspect of the company. "It is a rare thing," said a family friend at the time, "to see how each complements the other, particularly among members of the same family." Rare, indeed, as later events would prove.

Harrison was president of McCain Foods, Wallace vice-president and secretary-treasurer; Andrew, Robert, and sister Marie's husband, Dr. Jed Sutherland, were directors. Andrew and Robert were to run the company founded by their grandfather, McCain Produce Co., which would grow crops for the new processing plant and continue to ship seed potatoes worldwide. Wallace also became president of Carleton Cold Storage Ltd., which would freeze and then warehouse McCain Foods' frozen vegetables, and appointed two family friends, lumberman Sam Bell and potato farmer Eugene Brennan, to its board of directors.

Harrison and Wallace had learned a valuable business lesson from K.C. Irving: vertical integration. Irving owned the land on which the trees were grown, cut them down with machinery built and sold by an Irving company, shipped them to the Irving-owned mill on Irving trucks (which roll on Irving tires and are run with Irving diesel); there they were turned into high-grade paper for Irving offices, toilet paper and napkins for Irving gas stations and newsprint for an Irving newspaper. Vertical integration means keeping your money inside the company.

Andrew and Robert, of McCain Produce, would grow crops, fertilized by McCain Fertilizer, for McCain Foods, which would process them and transfer them frozen to Carleton Cold Storage. Later, the company would vertically integrate to an even greater extent, but while the company was in its infancy, the brothers relied on its own farmland as well as contracts with local farmers to meet production requirements.

The McCain farm consisted of 810 cultivated hectares, of which 324 were devoted to potatoes, 101 to peas, and another 101 to the grain that fed the McCains' 30 Holstein and 140 Hereford cattle. But this was far from enough to supply the processing plant for an entire year. Harrison contracted for a further 405 hectares of peas and 22 hectares of strawberries.

In the summer of 1957, the brothers learned the hard way about overproduction. That summer, the plant processed almost half a million kilograms of peas, more than the market could bear. Large pea crops in the U.S. and Canada forced the price to drop, and the McCains were faced with disaster. Rather than sell the peas at a loss, Harrison decided to hold onto them and wait out the market. His decision paid off the following year, when North American pea crops shrank and prices went through the roof. The McCains sold their stock at a good profit.

Just as the two brothers worked long hours for K.C. Irving, so they slaved for their new company. The pair traversed the Maritimes like a couple of Fuller Brush salesmen, sleeping in cheap motels and knocking on hundreds of doors. "They never quit," says Franklin Hickling, who worked equally long days for Harrison and Wallace. "I saw us work up to three o'clock in the morning in the offices, trying to figure out what direction we were going, what products we would plant. And then they'd take off the next morning and we might not see them again for two weeks. They'd just call in and tell me what products to do and what labels to put on, and away we'd go."

Most of McCain Foods' early shipments went to Montreal and Toronto, where some of the country's institutional customers such as hospitals, restaurants and hotels, were concentrated. The brothers' pitch had it that because their produce was both grown and frozen in New Brunswick, it was a fresher, better-quality product than the American competitions', which was often processed far from the fields. "I have heard it from experts in this field," boasted Harrison to a local newspaper at the time, "that local peas, for example, are of an exceptionally fine quality. Location of farms in the river valley, coupled with the cool evenings, helps bring them to the peak of flavour. And that is the stage [at which] we intend to get them from the fields and into the plant for processing. We make the world's best french fries here and stand ready to back this statement against anyone wishing to contest it."

CHAPTER FOUR

All Work and No Play

WITH THE CONFIDENCE THAT CREATES HELL-BENT DICTA-
tors and successful tycoons, 29-year-old Harrison McCain,
in debt for more than half a million dollars, with almost half
a million kilograms of unsold peas sitting in cold storage,
was unfazed. Short, thick, and built like a bulldog, Harrison
declared that his fledgling frozen-food company, built the
previous year in an old cow pasture in one of the poorest
regions of a chronically depressed province, would become a
giant. In just five years, he predicted, McCain's would employ
more than 200 people.

The year was 1957. The Soviet Union had just launched
Sputnik, television was everywhere, and streamlined cars
with wings and fins were rolling off assembly lines in
Detroit. The era's exuberance touched even Florenceville,
and Harrison wrote a memo predicting that his company
would "grow into a tremendous operation as the vegetable
garden of Canada, supplying the Central Canadian and perhaps even the Eastern U.S. markets." Yet years later, named
CEO of the Year by *The Financial Post Magazine*, Harrison
scoffed at the suggestion that he had a master plan back at
the company's inception. "Those guys who think they know
what they're doing when they start out," he laughed, "are
crazier than hell."

Harrison's self-assurance certainly seemed maniacal. At a time when most Maritime companies were content with prosperity at home, McCain's announced that anything short of national—and international—success would be failure. While Franklin Hickling saw to it that the potatoes kept rolling out of the McCain fryers, Harrison and Wallace launched into what they did best: selling. They knocked on doors and met with customers. No account was too small to receive the brothers' personal attention.

"It was all basic sales work," Wallace later recalled. "We called at restaurants, where they were still cutting their own french fries. We went after retail, but the big volume was restaurants; it still is—75 per cent or more. I called on restaurants from one side of the country to the other."

Although Harrison's official title became Chief Executive Officer of McCain Foods, and Wallace's, President, both functioned as co-CEOs. They established a tradition early on that neither could make a decision without the other's agreement. "In the early days," Wallace recalls, "we both did everything, and we overlapped everything. Except that he definitely looked after all the finance, and I leaned more to construction work, building the buildings. But we both overlapped: he did some of mine, and I did some of his."

In the public eye, however, there was only one CEO—and it was Harrison. Look at the top 200 Canadian companies in *The Financial Post Magazine*'s annual roundup, and you'll find Harrison, not Wallace, listed as the company's chairman. This perception did not go unnoticed by Wallace, who blamed it on Harrison's desire, when the company was founded, to grab the limelight. Wallace, a shy and sometimes inarticulate man, preferred that the company build quietly with little media attention.

"I probably got that attitude from Mr. Irving," says Wallace. "He never did any public relations, as you know. I didn't believe in that, and Harrison did. In fact, I think it was one of the major disagreements we had in our first 30 years; that was something we really, genuinely disagreed on. I had one or two interviews early, and I got my fingers burned a bit . . . I felt that news was bad for the company. But he liked it, he wanted to do it. He wanted to be in the front, but it didn't bother me.

"The perception was that Harrison ran the company. I'd run in to people, and they'd say to me, 'Oh, I see your brother is running the company. What are you doing with the company?' I probably had that question asked a thousand times in my lifetime. I'd say, 'I work here.' Sometimes I'd say, 'I run the peelers.'"

There was little time for the brothers to argue the point. Harrison and Wallace spent so much time on the road that they rarely spent back-to-back days in Florenceville. "The first years were nothing but difficulty," said Harrison. "Both Wallace and I were on the road the whole time. I was in Toronto, Wallace in Halifax. I can remember getting a phone call from him. He was jubilant. He had sold one account: things were that tough."

The only flaw in Harrison's grandiose plans was that Canada's frozen-food business was 10 years behind the U.S. In fact, "it was practically non-existent," says Harrison. Most grocery stores didn't even have freezer sections. "If it was a good supermarket," says Wallace, "it had a freezer cabinet, but it was only eight feet long. It usually had orange juice, peas and fish sticks. Not much." The answer, the brothers realized, was the catering market, which could drastically cut its labour costs by using frozen foods. In their cross-country trek to sell the caterers, they also lined up distributors to market their frozen products. The local marketers could then convince grocery retailers that frozen food was good for their business. The McCains' sales pitch worked so well that in both the company's second and third years of operation, in 1958 and 1959, additions to the cold storage plant had to be built to keep up with the orders.

"We built the market," says Wallace. "Actually, that's what made the company successful. There's nothing like being the first one in with a good product. You can't compare it with anything else. We started in the Maritimes, where we looked after sales ourselves, and we got a broker in Montreal, we had a couple of brokers in Quebec, and two or three brokers in Ontario. Then we got brokers in Manitoba, Saskatchewan, Alberta and the West. After a short period— I'd say in the early sixties—we switched from brokers to company salesmen."

Every year was profitable, and every nickel was sunk back into the company. "As with any small business growing rapidly, you bet the bundle every year, year after year. If you're wrong once, you're out," Harrison would say later. "We kept pushing the business as hard as we could, borrowing all we could, building and borrowing and building."

Harrison's prediction of McCain's growth wasn't quite accurate. By 1960, two years ahead of his 1957 forecast, McCain Foods Ltd. was employing 230 workers, and had also become one of the largest frozen-food processors in Canada. The McCains' product line had grown as well, from straight-cut french fries and peas to brussels sprouts, carrots, strawberries, broccoli, beans—everything Carleton County could produce. Even fiddleheads, a fern that grows wild along the banks of New Brunswick rivers, was packaged, frozen and sold.

Potatoes, however, remained the McCains' mainstay—fried, boiled, baked and roasted. In 1961, they bought a potato chip plant in Grand Falls, just up river from Florenceville, going head to head with their father's old rival, the Hatfields of Hartland, whose chips were already a mainstay in the New Brunswick market. Their venture into potato chips, however, turned out to be one of the few on which they lost money, and after only a few years, they sold the plant to Humpty-Dumpty, another east-coast potato chip manufacturer.

As Harrison and Wallace built their empire brick by brick, they became the saviours of Carleton County, bringing prosperity to an economic disaster area. There were some, however, who viewed the McCains in a sinister light, referring to Harrison and Wallace as "the Skinner brothers."

The loudest complainers were a small but vocal contingent of potato farmers who claimed that the McCains lived up to their potato contracts only when it suited the company. According to Harry Ebbett, a retired potato farmer from nearby Upper Kent: "It's not a contract. It is for them, but not for you. They can kill it anytime they wish. You take a load of potatoes in, and they just say they don't want them: 'They're not up to grade.' Or they'll lay them in storage and then ask you to bring them in. All kinds of ways."

Darrell McLaughlin, a former potato farmer and past director of the local branch of the National Farmers Union, says the McCains were a sometimes divisive force in the community, doling out largesse to friends, and scorn to others. "Some farmers [went] to school with Harrison and stayed buddies with them all along," says McLaughlin. "This pick and choose is one of the things that allows them to hold up certain producers to the community around them and say, 'Well these guys are making a good success of it, why can't you?' But they ignore the fact that . . . the average [potato] producer just doesn't get the chance to use those sorts of connections."

Nonetheless, the McCains were proud of the benefits their success brought to Florenceville. "It's a lot of satisfaction," said Harrison, "to have a large number of people working, and to drive around the countryside here and look at the quality of the buildings, the automobiles, the quality of life, and compare that with 25 years ago. I'm not suggesting we deserve all the credit for the change but we deserve some of it, and the difference is enormous. Twenty-five years ago, every building here leaned."

• • •

In 1964 the brothers discovered that a Centreville mechanic named Emery Thomas had invented a new type of potato harvester, and was building them in his backyard. The McCains liked the harvester so much they bought it, formed a subsidiary company, Thomas Equipment Ltd.— named in honour of its inventor—and hired Thomas to build the harvesters for them. "Mechanization was the way to go," says Wallace. "You should always, always, always get mechanized. In those days, you had to pick potatoes by hand, and a man named Emery Thomas built one of the first potato harvesters ever built. So we asked Thomas to make us four or five, and he said, 'Geez, it's too much for me. Why don't you buy the company?' So we bought it, and started to grow fast with it."

Now the McCains could sell seed and farm machinery to local farmers, process the vegetables, ship the finished goods by truck—and keep the money all in the family. Wallace denies, however, that he and his brother wanted to establish a vertically integrated company as their former boss, K.C. Irving, had done. "We never really attempted vertical integration," he says. "It's minuscule. If our father and grandfather had not been farmers, we probably would not have gone into farming at all. We had some farmland, and we bought more."

A year later the McCains cut out another middleman when they founded MacBan Equipment Ltd. (short for McCain Brand) to sell their harvesters, loaders and other farm equipment. That year they also incorporated Carleton Land Investments to oversee their vast tracts of St. John River valley farmland. The 80- x 32-kilometre potato belt, between Hartland and Grand Falls, grew spuds and other crops, as well as feed for the McCains' Holsteins, said to be among the best dairy cattle in the Maritimes.

The cattle and their farming operations were run by brothers Andrew and Robert, who maintained control of the original McCain Produce Co. Andrew and Robert remained hometown boys, sticking close to the land and the farmers there, supervising the company's field operations, in walkie-talkie contact with the plant, Robert's car and home, and the company trucks. "They were not in it [McCain Foods] from day one," says Wallace. "They were not asked to join, and they had no desire to join. Andrew and Bob looked after

Dad's business. I don't think our styles of doing business were the same."

In 1965, Harrison and Wallace bought into Day and Ross Ltd., a profitable trucking company, and then took over the firm, with Wallace as president. Now they were not only shipping their goods in their own trucks, they hauled for other businesses as well. That year, too, the McCains completed the final link in their vertically integrated company, incorporating McCain Fertilizer Ltd.

By 1966, McCain Foods Ltd. was 10 years old and one of the world's largest producers of french fries. The McCain group of companies were exceeding Premier Hugh John Flemming's hopes, and the government kept pouring in money to keep it that way. In 1960, the province guaranteed a $138,000 loan for a Carleton Cold Storage addition. And between 1963 and 1967, McCain Foods Ltd. received $3.3 million in guaranteed loans from the province.

As a testament to his confidence in McCain Foods' success —and to his remarkable braggadocio—Harrison arranged, in the mid-1960s, for Karsh, the renowned photographer, to make his and Wallace's portraits. This was too much for Wallace's wife, Margaret, who believed that Wallace and Harrison would be better off deflating their swollen egos than posing for Karsh. "I remember Wallace walking into the house, saying that he and Harrison were flying off to Ottawa to have their pictures taken by Karsh," says Margaret. "I was standing at the kitchen sink when he told me. I looked at him and said, 'Who the *fuck* do you think you are?' And he said, 'You know, you're right. I'm not going.'"

Perhaps Harrison, who went alone to be photographed, guessed correctly about their importance: McCain Foods did so well in Canada that they soon saturated the frozen-food market. Harrison and Wallace had single-handedly created consumer demand for frozen food in Canada; by the mid-1960s, they controlled the market. For many companies, this would have been reason to celebrate; but the McCains, who were raised by a father who shipped potatoes worldwide and were schooled at the knee of expansionist K.C. Irving, wanted other markets to conquer.

"There was a huge drive to push her," recalls Harrison of the company's growth years. "And there's a limit to how far you can push in New Brunswick, or in Canada."

The McCains' international expansion eventually grew from the east rather than from the west or south. In 1959, the British pea crop suffered a bad year. Because of Canada's preferred trading status with Britain, as a member of the Commonwealth, and because of the devalued pound, it became advantageous for a Canadian company to ship peas to the British Isles. That year, McCains sold 45.37 tonnes of frozen peas, worth about $50,000, to Smedley's, a British grocery retailer. Other modest sales followed, and in 1965, Harrison and Wallace realized that it was to Britain, not to the U.S., that their frozen vegetables could most success-fully be exported.

The U.S. frozen-food market was dominated by huge conglomerates—General Foods, Heinz and Libby's—and muscling in on their business would have been impossible. England, Europe, Australia—everywhere but America—were ripe for the picking, and seemed of little interest to the U.S. giants. "We said, the hell with it, we're going to England first," remembers Wallace, who also noted that because of their father's international seed-potato business, dealing with foreign countries was natural: "Shortly after we started, I guess in two or three years, we recognized that Canada had not that many people here, so we thought we had to do something outside [the country]. I think that wouldn't really be a natural instinct for people in those days. We heard all our lives about exports. Dad sold potatoes in Argentina, Venezuela, Uruguay and Cuba, and I heard the story about the famous hay in South Africa all my life. So that was the thing that made us go international."

With their propensity for eating chips with anything, British consumers, Harrison and Wallace figured, were the perfect object of their first international foray. In 1965, with British sales above the $1-million-a-year mark, the brothers hired Charles "Mac" McCarthy, a 28-year-old former production manager with a British frozen-food company, to sell the McCain brand out of his home in Grimsby, a small Yorkshire town 320 kilometres north of London. It was a tough job. England had virtually no fast-food restaurants, selling frozen food was pioneer work, and though the English loved french fries, chips that went from the freezer to the oven were a strange novelty.

In 1966, the McCains bought Caterpac Limited of London, one of England's largest importers of frozen foods. Founded about the time McCain's started operating in Florenceville, Caterpac bought food from Europe, the U.S., South Africa and Canada. Now that the McCains owned it, Harrison promised, McCain Foods Ltd. in Florenceville would provide as much of the company's import requirements as possible. Mac McCarthy was named managing director of Caterpac, which was moved from London to Grimsby, where port facilities were cheaper.

McCain's french fries were selling in England all right, but in bulk or with no-name packaging. The McCain name was known only to the distributors. But Harrison and Wallace wanted their name on every carton of food sold in the U.K. In 1968, the brothers changed the name of Caterpac Ltd., to McCain International Ltd., and announced plans to build a $2.6-million plant in Scarborough, England. The 8361-square-metre factory and 14 866-cubic-metre cold storage plant, completed in 1969, made it the largest french-fry producer outside North America. The McCains had been flogging their frozen chips in England for almost five years and it was time, the brothers reasoned, to establish themselves firmly in Great Britain. Said Harrison: "It is a necessary step to protect our hard-won position in the United Kingdom."

McCain's worldwide sales grew exponentially. In 1968, the company took in $30 million; in 1969, $50 million. By 1970, sales had doubled to $100 million. By the 1970s they had built such a strong financial foundation that the company catapulted into three continental markets simultaneously: mainland Europe, Australia and the U.S.

Harrison spent most of his working hours "thinking about deals, acquisitions or building something." Or recruiting top people for management posts. "How to recruit a guy—how do we get a guy doing better. Unfortunately, I have to go to damn meetings, read reports—a lot of things I don't like doing. The game is action, what's going on. There's something new all the time—buying companies, building factories, hiring guys, motivating people, seeing advertising programs, taking positions on commodities, borrowing money, settling lawsuits."

According to Joe Palmer, former head of the McCains'

trucking firm, Day and Ross, Harrison is the most disciplined man he has ever met, able to change his demeanour, from cocky and brash to quiet and dignified, to suit the occasion—and win the deal. Palmer recalled a situation from 1970 that illustrated how determined Harrison could be to win. It involved the purchase of a small Saint John trucking company that Harrison desperately wanted. An agreement in principle was hammered out, but when Palmer was in Saint John with the auditors and accountants to sign the deal, Jim Thompson, who was negotiating for the other side, suddenly upped the ante.

"Harrison worked on the deal for about three years," says Palmer.

I was in Saint John closing the deal with Jim Thompson. He was down to sign the final contract. We had the money all there, because Jim wanted his share in cash, and we had the cash there and four other shareholders. And Jim looked up and said, "I'm not going to sign unless I have that Lincoln of Harrison's."

I said, "You got it."

I phoned Harrison up later and he asked if I had closed the deal. I said, "Well, I've got some good news and some bad news; the good news is, we own the company."

He said, "What's the bad news?"

I said, "The bad news is, I had to throw in your Lincoln."

He laughed—he thought it was good. I got somebody to drive a red Volkswagen up from Saint John for Harrison and drive the Lincoln back down for Jim. That was about the time Louis Robichaud was beaten by

Richard Hatfield; it was just about a week after the election, and Harrison drove into Florenceville with this little red Volkswagen. And Fraser Stephenson, a long-time friend of Harrison's, a big farmer in the area, was at the gas station. He said, "Look at that. The Tories haven't been in power a week and [Harrison] McCain's already driving a Volkswagen."

It was also a time when they would secure their lock on the Canadian frozen-food market, revolutionize frozen french fries with an oven-baked product called Superfries, and expand their line to include pizzas and frozen juice. There were some duds—salmon pie, chicken and chips—but, for the most part, "We put money into areas where the industry was growing," said Harrison. "We don't get involved in melon balls. You people in Toronto can have all the melon-ball business. We want something where we can do good volumes." But one product is beyond matters of market share and margins: fiddleheads. "If they said tomorrow 'we're losing our shirt packing fiddleheads,' I'd say 'we're not quitting, just because it's New Brunswick.'"

By the 1970s, however, McCain Foods had grown into a giant, and they decided to split their responsibilities along geographic lines: Harrison became responsible for the U.K., Europe and their transport business in Canada; while Wallace directed operations in Canada, Australia and the U.S.

• • •

The McCains had entered Britain at just the right time. Fast-food restaurants with American-style food were springing up all over the country, and British consumers began demanding the type of American french fries the McCains were selling to restaurants. Larger supermarkets, with frozen-food departments, were steadily replacing corner grocery stores. Working the U.K. almost single-handed, Mac McCarthy had installed a distribution chain that covered virtually all of England, Wales, Scotland and Northern Ireland. Business in the U.K. was flourishing, but most of their sales still came from restaurants and institutions. The McCains' Scarborough plant doubled its 363-tonnes-day capacity; in 1972 the McCains opened a second french-fry plant, capable of processing 226,800 tonnes of potatoes a year, in Whittlesey, near Scarborough. Though their U.K. french-fry sales were on the upswing, the total frozen potato market had levelled out.

A breakthrough came in 1979, when the McCains launched Oven Chips. These french fries were fried in more oil than original McCain french fries, so they came out of the oven tasting as if they might have been deep-fried in a restaurant. An immediate hit when they were launched as Superfries in Canada in the mid-1970s, the McCains' British marketing staff were reluctant, at first, to introduce them to U.K. consumers. In the end, it took an executive order from Harrison to get Oven Chips onto the British market. "They told him for five years that it wouldn't sell there," recalls Wallace. "Finally, Harrison said, 'Go to hell and sell it.'" An instant best-seller in the U.K., in one year, sales of the new-fangled frozen french fry were twice that of all frozen potato products combined. McCain instantly became the country's leading french-fry producer. By 1982, a third U.K. plant, in Grantham, was built.

The McCain strategy in the U.K. was used in each country they moved into. First they developed a market by exporting their products. Then they flooded the country with distributors and sales staff who built up the McCain brand name. If all went well, the McCains constructed or bought a plant, and trained local people to churn out frozen french fries, pizzas, or whatever was popular in that country, and presto! McCain was suddenly part of the frozen-food landscape.

"We learned how to do it in Canada," says Wallace. "The technique we developed we used in England. We took a couple of sales guys from here and set them up in England . . . [it was] the exact same pattern there. Basically, in the areas we control—and when I say control, I mean the markets where we sell a majority—we started the business."

The McCains moved into Australia in 1968 with a simple sales organization that imported McCain frozen products from New Brunswick, and sold them to institutions and, later, grocery chains and restaurants. In 1970, the McCains purchased and expanded a frozen-food plant in Daylesford, about 80 kilometres from Melbourne. By 1975, they built another, in Ballarat.

But the McCains desperately wanted the European market, where frozen food was in its infancy. In the early 1970s, Europe was going through the same cultural revolution that swept North America 10 and 20 years earlier. Women were leaving the home to work, leaving less and less time to cook. "Peeling potatoes is such a mean job to do yourself," said Harrison. "A wife can't work all day and then prove to her husband what a wonderful cook she is." The McCains' marketing strategy was to convince European consumers that their products made life easier. Indeed, in continental Europe the oven french fry would be called 1-2-3, its very name resounding with ease and quickness.

They first moved into Holland, buying a french-fry plant in Werkendam in 1972. The Netherlands became McCain's European nerve centre. Centrally located on the continent, Holland was also a major potato grower, the quality of its spuds comparable with those of Idaho, Maine, P.E.I. and New Brunswick. They were such a hit with the Dutch that a second plant was built in Lewedorp in 1973 and a third, in Hoofddorp, was completed in 1978.

From their Dutch plants the company exported french fries to Belgium, Germany and France. Only the names were changed to suit the market into which they were being exported. (In France, they were called, not surprisingly, Pommes Frites; in Germany, 1-2-3 Frites or 1-2-3 Chef-Frites, with the fries' relatively low fat content—either six per cent or three per cent, depending on the variety—emblazoned on the bag to attract increasingly weight-conscious German consumers.) Some product lines, however, were developed to suit local tastes. Germans, for example, could buy McCain's schnitzel and chips, "mit dip-sauce."

The one constant was the McCain logo, with its eight-pointed star. This posed problems, particularly in Germany, where local marketers said that the Germans could not pronounce "McCain" and advised the brothers to change the name to something more linguistically palatable. But George McClure, the company's vice-president of corporate development and the man responsible for launching the company in Europe, disagreed: "If you can sell something called Blaupunkt in Canada, you can sell McCain in Germany." Indeed, Harrison talked like an excited kid about the McCain brand name: "It's well-known in Rotterdam, London, Hamburg,

Leeds and Milan and all those places. I get a kick out of that."

One of the McCains' boldest moves of the 1970s was their unlikely venture into Spain, where there was virtually no french-fry market. In 1976, McCain Espana, S.A., was formed and a french-fry facility built in Burgos, near Madrid. McCain in Spain rhymed all right, but could the McCain marketers convince the Spaniards to eat french fries? They began with the country's hotels and restaurants. Spain was a leading tourist centre, and the company argued that visitors from Europe and North America would want a side order of french fries with their meals, even when abroad. Once a distribution system was in place, the natives could be educated in the ways of french fries. However long it took the Spanish to acquire a taste for french fries, the factory would be a good investment, giving the McCains access to North Africa and the Middle East.

By 1975, the McCains were successfully conquering Europe, and turned their attention to the United States. Europe and Australia "were much easier pickings," as Wallace put it, but the odds against making a serious dent in the saturated American market were high. "But we had a tremendous amount of expertise to offer to keep our production costs down and because of our proximity, we understood the American market."

Even though the biggest markets were in the Northeast, most of the large American potato processors were located in the potato-growing states of the Western U.S. They therefore had to transport their frozen food as much as 5000 kilometres to the country's largest concentration of consumers. "Maine's location, near the most populous area of the country, gives it a shipping advantage to markets as far west as Missouri and as far south as Miami," said Wallace. "We can ship product into New York City for more than three cents a pound less than the cost to most western processors." So the McCains built in the Northeast—just across the New Brunswick border in Maine.

Their first french-fry plant was purchased in 1975, in Washburn, Maine. They bought another the following year, in Easton, about 16 kilometres from the Washburn plant. The McCains modernized both plants at a cost of $12 million, and spent $2 million more, in advertising and promotion of the McCain brand name. The bulk of their initial sales, however, would come from producing private-label products for large grocery chains, rather than going head to head with H.J. Heinz Co.'s Ore-Ida of Idaho, or Lamb-Weston of Nebraska. "We didn't expect to sweep all before us," said Wallace. "But we have done more than anyone predicted, insofar as our production has increased every year and the plants are profitable."

While they were busy buying up the world, the McCains never forgot Canada or New Brunswick. In 1971, they completed construction of a new plant in Grand Falls, which would produce not only french fries and frozen vegetables, but the McCains' growing line of pies, cakes and other desserts.

"We were reaching the limits of explosive growth with potato products within the borders of Canada," said Wallace. "That caused us to make important investments in other frozen product lines." In 1974, they went outside the province, buying Bilopage, a Quebec-based meat-processing firm. In 1976, they built a pizza plant in Grand Falls. "Despite suggestions that the brand name McCain did not suggest a rich,

Italian flavour, the pizza has become the best-selling label in Canada," said Wallace. They also invested a lot of money in research and development, particularly in the testing of Superfries, the fully fried frozen french fry which would revolutionize the french-fry market around the world.

Meanwhile, their trucking firm, Day and Ross, had become one of the largest transport companies in Canada, with annual revenues of close to $60 million. By the end of the decade, the McCain group of companies had annual revenues of $360 million.

The brothers also showed they had business savvy playing the stock market. In December 1978, they bought 25 per cent of Commerce Capital Corp. Ltd. of Toronto, when its stock was trading at $7 a share; in four months, they pocketed $1.2 million profit when they sold their Commerce Capital shares for $9 each to Eaton/Bay Financial Services Ltd.

One investment that would prove ironic later was the McCains' attempted buy-out of Canada Packers, the meat-processing giant, in 1979. Harrison and Wallace dearly wanted the company, and paid $21.4 million in an initial grab for 12 per cent of Canada Packers' shares. "I was impressed with its size, I got carried away with its size," recalls Harrison. "It was a very big deal for us." But W.F. McLean, whose family and friends were majority shareholders in the company, saw a McCain takeover coming, and refused to give the brothers a seat on the board of directors. Rebuffed, the McCains sold their Canada Packers stock in 1985 for $53.6 million.

"It was a blessing in disguise, that they didn't like us," says Harrison. It was just too tough for us. But if we would have got deeper in that company, it would have taken a lot of borrowing power from us, and would have kept us from more attractive things in other parts of the world."

In 1990, Maple Leaf Foods took over Canada Packers, and five years later, after he was ousted from his executive post at McCain Foods by Harrison and his nephews, Wallace bought more than half of Maple Leaf's stock and became its majority shareholder.

• • •

In the early 1980s, Harrison broadened his already grandiose vow to conquer Canada. "Our strategy," he said, from his large Florenceville office overlooking the St. John River, "is to grow in the packaged goods business and the road transport business in Canada, and to dominate the potato-processing world."

Diversification into a number of key areas was necessary to achieve Harrison's domestic goals. McCain-owned Day and Ross Inc. entered the courier business, buying up Sameday Right-O-Way, and the school and charter bus sector with its purchase of Bustrax Division. McCain Refrigerated Foods Inc. bought up three Ontario cheese producers, marketing the cheese under the McCain brand, and selling it to McCain Foods for their Deep and Delicious pizzas.

One of McCains' most successful products of the 1980s was most unlikely—fruit juice. What made McCains' juice unique was its packaging and a quick-sterilization process that did not involve freezing or chilling. The juice, packed in boxes called tetrapaks, could be kept for a long time outside the refrigerator. Today the juice box is a staple of most schoolchildren's lunch boxes, but early in the 1980s, it was revolutionary.

In 1980 the McCains bought Toronto's Sunny Orange Company from American shipping tycoon Daniel K. Ludwig, and in 1981, acquired Niagara Food Products from the Weston Group. In 1983, the McCains opened an $11-million juice plant in Grand Falls.

The juice caught on in Europe, Canada and Australia, but try as they might, McCain's marketing people in Great Britain couldn't give the stuff away, even though other McCain products, such as frozen pizza and desserts, were almost immediate hits in the U.K. In 1984, the McCains opened a fish-processing plant in Hull, and in 1988, acquired two dairies, one in Scotland and the other in Wales, to produce cheese for their frozen pizzas. That year they added another pizza factory to their U.K. base when they bought Tolona Pizza Products Ltd. in East Pimko, near Liverpool.

By the end of the decade, the McCains were the number one frozen-food processor in the U.K. Prince Charles, on a royal visit to the Maritimes, insisted that he knew the McCain company and that clearly, it was British. When New Brunswick's minister of agriculture demurred, Harrison sided with the Prince: "By God, we aren't a Canadian company in England. By God, we've got six factories in England. We employ 1,500 people there. It *is* a British company as far as the British are concerned, and as far as Prince Charles is concerned. So that's that."

Not everyone, however, was expected to claim McCains as family. France was one market the McCains figured they might never crack. Yes, the French loved their frites, but frozen ones? "One might say we are pioneering the development of french fried potatoes in France," joked Wallace in 1981 at the time of the opening of their $27-million french-fry plant in Harnes, although the McCains knew the French were ready. The McCains had used their tried and true strategy of opening a distribution centre, flooding the country with imports, and then determining if and where a french-fry plant was viable.

The Harnes plant—and McCain Alimentaire, as their company is called in France—did so well that by 1986, the company was supplying three out of every 10 kilograms of french fries consumed in the country. The retail market for frozen frites had quadrupled in five years, to 22,000 tonnes annually. The fries were selling so well that the McCains purchased the french-fry company, Beau Marais SARL in Bethune, and in 1988 announced a $33-million project to double production at Harnes. Before the decade was over, McCains controlled 90 per cent of France's french-fry market, worth $800 million a year.

Gradually the McCains became the number one producer in just about every country of Europe, and built up their success Down Under as well. They brought frozen pizza to Australia in 1979, and in 1984, purchased a vegetable-processing plant in Smithton, Tasmania; two years later, they expanded it into a $13-million french-fry facility. In 1987, they acquired the Australian frozen-food company, Chalet Foods. The McCains moved into New Zealand in 1990, buying Alpine Foods Ltd., of Timaru. In 1992, they took over Safries Pty. Ltd., a frozen food producer with plants in Penola and Millicent.

In the U.S., however, the McCains still lagged behind the giant processors such as Ore-Ida. In 1985, they decided to spend more time and money on developing the market— and went on a spree. That year, they spent $5.5 million improving their Easton plant. In 1987, they bought another plant in Maine, formerly owned by competitor J.R. Simplot Co., in Presque Isle. They also bought two potato plants, in Othello, Washington, and in Clark, South Dakota. They bought Ellio's Pizza Co., of Lodi, New Jersey, which they later renamed McCain Ellio's Foods, Inc. In 1989, they spent $50 million doubling the Othello, Washington, plant's capacity.

They also bought into the U.S. juice business, purchasing processing plants in Chicago and in Taunton, Massachusetts. They first called their juice company McCain OJ, but later renamed it McCain Citrus Inc. In 1988, they picked up Dell Products Corp., of Hillside, New Jersey, and announced the construction of an $8.1-million juice-production facility in Fontana, California. In 1990, they acquired the frozen juice concentrate assets of Cliffstar Corp., of Dunkirk, New York, transferring production to Hillside, New Jersey, and Chicago.

A little more than 30 years after the brothers launched McCain Foods Ltd. in 1957, they had plants in nine countries. Their expansion was spectacular. The company's growth was like a tiny snowball rolling down a steep slope: growing, losing its shape and becoming an avalanche. In 1985 the McCain group of companies topped the $1-billion sales mark, and approached $2 billion in sales by 1990.

The company's head office, however, remained in snug Florenceville. The McCains clung to the image of a company run by two happy brothers from a friendly village in New Brunswick. Harrison and Wallace worked as a team; they were friends. Although Harrison's official title was CEO, and Wallace's, President, the two functioned as co-CEOs.

Traditionally, every decision was made by consensus; they rarely had board meetings. "I can only recall two," said Harrison in 1983. "But maybe there were three. I don't think I was at any of them."

By the end of the decade, however, it was clear that neither McCain Foods Ltd., nor the McCains, were one big happy family. There would soon be board meeting after board meeting, as Harrison and Wallace fought over who would control the company when they were gone. In the 1970s, local farmers cursed the McCains and their success, saying the brothers and all their money had somehow robbed Carleton County of its neighbourliness. The quest for better potato crops and material wealth pitted farmer against farmer. Harrison and Wallace would prove themselves not immune to competitiveness and aggression, as they attempted to first control the frozen-food world, and later, themselves.

McCain's success, Harrison liked to say, came because the company was privately owned, with none of the burdens of complex, corporate decision-making processes. "I feel sorry for people who run public companies," said Harrison, his words ringing with unconscious irony. "If they make a mistake, they have to wash all that dirty linen in public."

CHAPTER FIVE

Politics as Usual

EARLY IN 1968, GORDON GIBSON, A FORMER ASSISTANT TO the federal Minister of Northern Affairs, had been crisscrossing Canada trying to raise support and campaign money for a relatively young and politically inexperienced Liberal leadership candidate, Pierre Trudeau. One February day, Gibson was at one of his more unlikely stopping places— Florenceville, New Brunswick. There, he was told, he would find two young, successful businessmen who would likely offer both money and time to the Trudeau campaign. Gibson knocked on the door of Harrison McCain's big white Cape Cod house and explained the reason for his visit. Would he and Wallace work for Trudeau, Gibson asked Harrison. The brothers didn't need much convincing. Harrison, impressed by Trudeau's "fresh thinking and style," had already made preliminary calls indicating that he was willing to work for the future prime minister.

The meeting between Gibson and Harrison had been arranged by Trudeau and Louis Robichaud, who was then premier of the province. "I called [Trudeau's] office, and didn't get a very good answer, the person I talked to didn't know much about the deal," says Harrison. "So I called Premier [Louis] Robichaud. He said, 'No, no, Harrison, we don't want you to support Trudeau. We want you to support

Winters. Robert Winters is the guy who can run the Liberal Party, he's a great friend of New Brunswick's, and he's the guy.' Well I said, 'You can do what you want to do. I'm not doing that. I'm supporting Trudeau.'"

Wallace was recruited as Trudeau's campaign manager for New Brunswick, and Harrison became Trudeau's chief fundraiser for the Maritimes. In the months leading up to the leadership convention, Harrison and Wallace put so much time into their political work that some at McCain Foods felt they were sacrificing the business for Trudeau. "Harrison, I think, spent I don't know how long—I would say a couple of months at least, maybe more—in Montreal, as manager of Trudeau's campaign," says Fred McCain, the brothers' distant cousin and former Member of Parliament for Carleton County. "Their business was growing, and then everything came to a standstill because the brothers weren't around to make decisions."

Gibson, who would become Trudeau's executive assistant, and later, leader of the British Columbia Liberal Party, remembers Harrison and Wallace working hard right up until convention day. "My most vivid memory of them was on the floor of the convention itself. Each one of them wore an enormous, green stove-pipe hat. They were very, very efficient in shepherding the New Brunswick delegation, moving them around to appropriate demonstrations. They really put a lot of energy into it."

Their early support and hard work for Trudeau was repaid in spades. The brothers—particularly Harrison—established important contacts in the federal government. "Trudeau, I've heard him say it publicly, that I was his first supporter in Canada," says Harrison. "I don't think that's true for a minute, but I was one of them." The day after Trudeau was elected prime minister, a factory-floor story has it, Harrison walked into his office and told his secretary to "get Trudeau on the phone." For years, he kept a signed portrait of the former prime minister on his desk, and he remains friends with many former Trudeau aides, most notably Jim Coutts, Trudeau's former principal secretary.

Gordon Gibson remembers that it seemed unlikely that Harrison and Wallace would latch on so early to the up-and-coming candidate for leader. "Trudeau was considered the guy to watch, but he certainly wasn't considered the front runner," he says. "There were the heavyweights—I don't think Winters had entered the race yet—but there were a number of big names there and he was just one of them, and he was the stranger of them. He wasn't the natural place for these guys to go."

Yet Harrison and Wallace were relatively young up-and-comers themselves, who shared with Trudeau a slight, left-of-centre Liberal philosophy. Indeed, the McCains had been Liberal almost since their arrival in Carleton County. Ever since H.H. McCain, the founder of McCain Produce Co., was elected to the New Brunswick legislature in 1895 and 1899, a McCain has run on the provincial Liberal ticket. H.H.'s son, A.D., ran for the provincial Liberal Party in 1916, in one of the most hotly contested by-elections of the time. The Tory government of George E. Clarke was awash with scandal—one of his ministers allegedly received kickbacks from a contractor hired to paint the province's steel bridges. But Carleton County was a Tory stronghold, and despite the Liberal Party's throwing all of its resources behind them, A.D. and his running mate, George Upham, were defeated by 550 votes.

All four of A.D.'s sons would grow into the Liberal mould. Robert, who sat, at different times, on the school board, the hospital board and the county council, made a stab at a seat in the provincial legislature, running—and losing—on Premier Louis Robichaud's ticket in 1960. Brother Andrew had been the treasurer of the New Brunswick Liberal Party.

Even Fred McCain, a distant cousin and political black sheep—a hated Tory—became one of the riding's MLAs in the 1950s. Later, Fred was elected to the House of Commons.

Although no one among the current generation has expressed any interest in politics, the McCains remain staunchly Liberal. Not surprisingly, Harrison and Wallace, the two most successful McCains, have been the family's most prominent and influential party members. They even married Liberal: Harrison to former New Brunswick Liberal Premier John McNair's daughter Billie, and Wallace to Liberal Senator Margaret Norrie's daughter. They were early supporters of Louis Robichaud, who seemed to come out of nowhere to beat the Tory government of Hugh John Flemming in 1960. Robichaud and the McCains have remained close, Harrison being most active in Liberal Party politics. "Wallace was never the politician," says Robichaud. "Harrison was. He wanted his brother [Robert] to run in 1960. Then he wanted his brother Andrew to become treasurer of the party. He's very influential."

Robichaud credited his victory at least partially to the backing of K.C. Irving, who would later unleash his powerful, family-owned newspapers on the premier after Robichaud changed the province's tax laws in his famous Equal Opportunity program.

Now a Liberal senator, Robichaud recalls, "The McCains went ahead with the philosophy of sharing. He [Harrison] wants to make money of course, and he did, but his interest in the country is number one. He understands the situation in Canada. But the Irvings . . . I couldn't—conscientiously, politically, philosophically, Liberally—couldn't agree with K.C. Irving. He was of the philosophy of one other person from New York, Leona Helmsley, who believed only poor people pay taxes. He made five, six, seven, eight billion dollars within a lifespan. When somebody pays his fair share of taxes, it's awfully difficult to make that amount of money."

The McCains, on the other hand, says Robichaud, "are good corporate citizens of New Brunswick. They paid their own way."

That assessment was not shared by the late NDP leader, David Lewis, who devoted a couple of pages to McCain Foods' adeptness at hustling government grants in his book, *Corporate Welfare Bums*. Indeed, the McCains learned very early in their careers that low-interest loans or grants were available for the asking.

At the inaugural meeting of the New Brunswick Industrial Development Board in October 1956, the McCains had the honour of receiving the board's first loan: $280,000 for the construction of the McCain Foods plant; and $140,000 for the construction of their cold-storage subsidiary, Carleton Cold Storage. Both loans were for 20-year terms at five per cent interest per annum. When they wanted to expand Carleton Cold Storage a couple of years later, the brothers went back to the Industrial Development Board, who gave the McCains an additional loan of $57,500. In June 1959, they were given a further $100,000 loan from the government board, which noted that this would be the "final instance" in which they would consider loan applications from the McCains. The government's self-imposed cap on McCain loans, however, went unheeded. Less than a year later, in April 1960, the McCains asked for and received an additional $100,000 loan for yet another expansion to Carleton Cold Storage. Between 1956 and 1960, the McCains received $677,500 in provincial loan guarantees—and that was in the reign of Hugh John Flemming, a Tory premier.

The McCains had only just begun. Between 1960 and 1967, under the administration of Harrison's old friend, Liberal Premier Louis Robichaud, McCain Foods and its subsidiaries received at least $3.2 million in loans from the province. Even the Tory Premier Richard Hatfield, whose father Heber once competed against—or colluded with—their father A.D. in potato exports, guaranteed $5.2 million in loans for the McCains in 1971. But the biggest payoff came after the election of Pierre Trudeau, whom the brothers had so aggressively helped to win the Liberal Party nomination.

When the Trudeau government launched the Regional Development Incentives Act in 1969, the McCains were given the Act's first Department of Regional Economic Expansion (DREE) grant, for $2,925,000. And there was more where that came from.

One of the men responsible for deciding whether the McCains would get DREE grants was George McClure, DREE's director of programs for the Atlantic Region. Between December 1969 and June 1970, while McClure was a DREE director, the McCains applied for three DREE grants totalling $7,772,221, for projects including the construction of a $5.6-million plant in Grand Falls, New Brunswick, and a $400,000 expansion of McCain's Florenceville plant. In August 1970, McClure left to work for McCain Foods, where he served as Harrison's assistant. By the end of the year, DREE had awarded McCain Foods every penny they had applied for. McClure was later promoted to managing director of McCain Europa, where he was responsible for setting up french-fry plants in Holland and Spain. In the 1990s, he was given a seat on McCain's family-controlled board of directors.

DREE granted the McCains another $600,000 between 1977 and 1978, but the big DREE payoff came at the end of the 1970s, when the McCains decided to move into Western Canada.

The high cost of transporting refrigerated frozen food thousands of kilometres to Western Canada had made the brothers shy away from invading the Prairies and beyond. With a little government money to sweeten the deal, however, the McCains chose Portage La Prairie, Manitoba, a small town west of Winnipeg, as the ideal location for their Western Canadian base. Situated in the heart of Manitoba's potato-growing region, Portage La Prairie was close to railroad lines, opening up western North America, Japan and the Pacific Rim as well.

The McCains planned their new factory, and headed off to the government for help. DREE coughed up a $2.4-million grant, and the Manitoba Development Corporation threw in a $7-million loan; this $9.4 million was more than 60 per cent of the $14 million cost of the plant. When the McCains found structural changes were necessary to get the facility built, another $4.1 million was made available to them in loans and grants by the Province of Manitoba and DREE for a new water-treatment plant to accommodate the factory. A $436,000 water supply line from the new treatment plant to the reservoir was paid for by the city of Portage La Prairie and the provincial government. A massive plant, occupying 11 hectares, was completed in 1979 at a cost of more than $14 million, virtually all of it in government grants or loan guarantees.

The McCains began drawing criticism for their ability to raise a lot of public money from governments to subsidize their highly profitable businesses. And as their success grew, so did the perception among farmers in their home county that the brothers were taking advantage of them. The loudest critics were the McCains' own workers, who pointed out that, despite their millions in profits, the McCains paid only five to 10 cents an hour above the provincial minimum wage. Farmers, particularly in Carleton County, grumbled that the McCains controlled every aspect of the potato-growing operation, and were driving down the price of potatoes by buying up all the good farmland in the county. Publicly, the brothers said they owned 1,756 hectares of farmland in the St. John River valley, but a 1980 National Farmers Union study claimed that the McCains owned at least 4,673 hectares, almost triple the amount the brothers claimed to own.

Harrison counters by stating that it was his family's right to buy any land they could pay for. His company got grants and loans—"huge ones," he admits—because they deserved them. The money invested by the government, he adds, gets re-invested in the community many times over. "We've never been hassled by the government," he said. "We *are* hassled by anybody who wants to criticize us on the basis that 'You have these government grants, therefore, you should be paying the farmers more money, or doing this or not doing that.' They forget that you don't get a government grant because you're a good fellow; you get it because you promise to perform by supplying a certain number of jobs.

"That was a very good investment for the government and for us both. The government had their money back in jig time. Just jig time, you understand me? Between seven and eight hundred people work [in Grand Falls] now . . . there were hundreds of people working there for 15 or 20 years. And those are all people who pay taxes, instead of collecting income, if you know what I mean.

"[The grants] are not sufficient. Did General Motors decide to move to the Maritimes to collect a grant? Why doesn't Stelco come down and collect these 'huge government grants?' Who else do you want to name? The Ford Motor Company? General Electric? Why don't they all come down and get these great grants? A grant only goes towards compensating. It doesn't pay the bills. Even in Ottawa they don't understand that. It's a long story."

What Carleton County farmers did understand was that, by the time the McCains incorporated Foreston Seed Co. Ltd. in 1968, they couldn't spend a dime without a few pennies trickling back into the McCains' pockets. The McCains bought more than half the county's potato crop each year. Potatoes were either grown on McCain land, owned by Valley Farms Ltd., or contracted out to local farmers. The potatoes were more than likely purchased as seed from Foreston Seed Co., grown in soil enriched by McCain Fertilizer Ltd. They were harvested by machinery built by

McCain-owned Thomas Equipment and purchased at a MacBan sales agency, and were stored at McCain's Carleton Cold Storage, shipped to McCain Foods Ltd. for processing, or sold fresh to McCain Produce Co. Processed or fresh, the potatoes were shipped to market in McCain's Day and Ross trucks. Those being shipped overseas were hauled to the McCain's seaside port, Bayside Potatoport Ltd., in St. Andrews, from which McCain International Ltd. would export them worldwide.

The McCains underwrote loans to farmers who could not pay cash for their $30,000 or $40,000 harvesters, holding the farmers' potato crop as collateral. Once they were in debt, potato growers could be locked in an endless cycle of planting and harvesting just to meet their payments. It was like the old story of owing one's soul to the company store.

"We have become virtual serfs, the very condition our ancestors came here from Europe to escape," said one farmer. As early as 1971, wrote Wilhelmine Thomas of Hartland, in *Maclean's*, the McCains had killed the once-rich community spirit in their hometown:

> Florenceville is no longer a village but a booming town, could be an affluent suburb of Toronto, swimming pools and rock gardens. Here, McCain Foods operates a frozen-packaging and dehydration plant. Materially, it would seem the people who work for McCains are better off. They have car payments and TV payments, and every house, trailer and shack boasts a snowmobile. But money as well as land has shifted hands. Progress has poked its nose into New Brunswick.

• • •

After french fries and pizza pockets, the two things the McCains are famous for among New Brunswickers are swearing and die-hard Liberalism. "They could curse," says Robichaud, who saw both qualities first-hand. "But . . . it was not meant to be malicious." Wallace's wife, Margaret, has tried unsuccessfully to break her husband of the profanity habit. "I've always said that Wallace is bilingual," she says. "Unfortunately that means English and cursing." For Harrison, politicking and swearing seemed to go hand-in-hand. Mixing his rapid-fire delivery with well-chosen profanities kept people off guard. "Harrison just fires bullets at you, he puts you on the defensive all the time," says Don Marmen, an ex-department manager at McCain Foods' Grand Falls plant who does an expert imitation of his former boss's speaking style.

Marmen, who was also coach of the McCains' senior league hockey team, the Florenceville Potato Kings ("What else?" jokes Marmen about the name), left McCain Foods in the mid-1980s to pursue a career in provincial Tory politics. He recalled his last meeting with Harrison, who apparently bore no grudges about an employee making a run for the Tories. "I met with Harrison for about three-quarters of an hour," says Marmen, who was unsuccessful in his bid for a seat in the legislature. "And after we made our deals and shook hands, he says: 'Listen Marmen, you're a good fellow, and I wish you luck. But we don't want any special fucking favours, we just want our fucking share.'"

Because of Marmen's interest in politics, he saw Harrison's and Wallace's political sides more than others. "I remember a provincial Tory leadership convention one year, when Hank

Myers sought the leadership. Hank had been Minister of Agriculture during the last two years of Hatfield's tenure. One of the things that the McCains don't like is a bullshitter. And they have a way of finding out if you are one or not. And I think they find that in this world of ours, there are a lot of bullshitters. Harrison asked me one time about Myers. And I have to say, that among politicians, Myers is a very straightforward and sincere fellow. And Harrison was very glad to know that. And I know that when Hank sought the leadership, Harrison said, 'You let me know, I'm going to get some money for you.'

"I was working with Hank at one point, and things weren't getting off the starting gate that well. And Harrison called one time and said, 'What the Christ is going on over at that fucking campaign of yours? Jesus Christ, where's your fucking fundraiser? I haven't heard anything.' Here's a guy calling you up to give you shit *and* a few thousand bucks. You don't often hear that."

Marmen, who described his career at McCain Foods as that of a "lowly department manager," saw a lot of the McCains because he managed and coached the Potato Kings. "Harrison certainly called Pierre Trudeau up more than Wallace," says Marmen. "Wallace loved the conventions—it was like the hockey games, he went there to get away from it all. Harrison told me one time, that politics for him [Harrison] was just a game, just a hobby. Wallace, the only time I ever heard of him getting involved in anything like that was when there was a leadership convention. Harrison . . . kept close ties at the top."

Harrison clearly relishes playing a role in national politics. In 1991, for example, he gave up several days out of his normally hectic schedule to join "The Group of 22," a group of politicians and business leaders who gathered in Montreal to discuss Canada's future in the wake of the failure of the Meech Lake Accord. Among the participants were Jean-Luc Pépin, Hugh Segal, Allan Blakeney, Bill Davis and Maurice Sauvé. "I saw Harrison in a group situation where he was not a chief executive," says David Cameron, who wrote up the group's final report.

He wasn't in negotiations. He was in a group situation looking at broad policy proposals in a kind of self-appointed, mini-Royal Commission. And he was working in an area that he knew very little about, which was constitutional issues, relations between French Canada and English-speaking Canada. So it was not a field he had spent a lot of time on . . . [but] he was clearly sufficiently concerned about it to spend a big chunk of his time working on it.

In that context, I found him quite delightful. He was very sharp. And you could tell he had a fairly short fuse, although he had it under control. But he'd find sometimes what would appear to him to be interminable discussions that didn't land up any place as people were searching their way through the nature of the problem and how to make proposals in respect to the problem. There's a lot of futzing around that goes on, because these things don't lend themselves to crisp, clear, border-defined analyses and choices. Occasionally his face would get a bit red, and he would say, "Come on, we've got to move on, we've got to decide on this stuff." His whole impulse is to action. It's "let's do it." But if the choice isn't clear, you can't do it, until you know what it is you want to do. But he participated very effectively as a member of the group, he listened to other people and what they had to say. He didn't try to dominate the discussions. He would ask pointed questions. I thought he was a very acute observer of the group dynamic. Nobody could be unaware that he was in the room, but he was not trying to take over, or he didn't monopolize the floor. He listened carefully and was very intelligent in his comments. He was learning as much as he was teaching. I liked him very much. I was glad he was in the group. I thought he was an impressive man. He was dealing with people like Bob Blair and Blakeney and Pépin, who had been beating around that bush for a long time. They knew, I'm sure, more than he did. And he's smart, and acute, and would recognize that.

Wallace, on the other hand, slowly moved away from politics after helping to raise funds for the Trudeau leadership in 1968. In 1970, he even supported Richard Hatfield, a Carleton County neighbour—and a Tory.

"I vote on the basis of, a: I am a Liberal," says Wallace. "I call myself a Liberal. That's number one. But number two, the difference between Liberals and Conservatives today, is there's not much difference. There's no difference, as far as I'm concerned. So I look at the leader. If I have strong feeling to that leader, whether he's Liberal or Conservative, I vote that way. Apart from that, if the leaders are both the same, I'll look at the local candidate. If they're both the same, I'll vote Liberal."

Whether they were backing a Liberal or a Tory, the

McCains always defended their right to a chunk of government assistance to help their company grow. After all, they argued, the corporate handouts were available to all. Only they didn't take too kindly to government-backed competitors—such as Cavendish Farms—muscling in on their turf.

CHAPTER SIX

The Great Potato War

TRUE, NEW BRUNSWICK HAS BEEN CONSISTENTLY POOR and unsophisticated since the big shipbuilding companies of the nineteenth century weighed anchor and set sail for other shores. Yet, the province has spawned more than its fair share of industrialists. Perhaps the province's poverty breeds virile individualism. During the first half of the century came Lord Beaverbrook and Sir James Dunn, men from small, depressed towns in the interior, who battled their way to the top of the heap. The latter half of the twentieth century belonged to K.C. Irving. His name dominated New Brunswick from industrial Saint John in the south to the rural north shore. The corporate empire Irving built, from his home town of Bouctouche, touched almost every aspect of provincial life. When he died in 1992, Irving owned, among many other assets, the largest oil refinery in Canada, a shipyard, a fleet of oil tankers, service stations and convenience stores, one-tenth of New Brunswick's land, pulp and paper factories, bus and trucking companies, television and radio stations, and newspapers. One of the hallmarks of K.C. Irving's private empire is secrecy. Today, one in 12 New Brunswickers works for an Irving-owned business, whether he or she knows it or not.

By the time the McCains started making their mark as upstart empire-builders in the 1960s, Irving owned pretty much everything but the province's trucking and food businesses. Those concerns were left to the McCains. The two families divvied up the province. Their businesses operated along parallel lines, and each side respected the other's territory. Both understood that the Irvings would mind their own business as long as the McCains minded theirs.

Ask the McCains or the Irvings if they have been fighting a war for the past three decades and they'll probably deny it. Employees of their companies, however, say the only disputable issue is who started it.

"There was no feud that I knew about," says Harrison. "If there was, it was one-sided. But they are competitors of ours, so we have to look after our interests. And what they do, if we don't consider it fair or right . . . we'll scrap with them."

A former Irving Oil sales manager says it all began in 1974, when the McCains revoked a products agreement with the Irvings. The 40-year contract locked their trucking company, Day and Ross, into purchasing their fuel and truck supplies from Irving. The McCains, he said, figured they could get a better price from Petrofina, later Petro-Canada. "That did it," said the former Irving man.

"Oh, there's a McCain-Irving feud all right," says a retired senior manager, who spent 25 years working for the McCains. The Irvings fired the first shot, he maintains, in 1972, when they crossed the line and started a trucking firm, Midland Transport Ltd. Maybe so, but the cancellation of McCain's fuel contract for Day and Ross made the Irving patriarch livid. It touched off a corporate battle unrivalled until the Harrison-Wallace feud over their own company.

Day and Ross Co. Ltd. was founded in 1950 by a couple of Hartland natives, Elbert Day and Walter Ross. They had one truck and a load of ambition. Like Harrison and Wallace, they were pioneers, running the company out of an Irving gas station which they ran for K.C. in Hartland. Trucking freight over the Maritimes' rough roads was unheard of at the time. Most companies shipped their goods by rail, trusting trucks only for short-haul deliveries. Day and Ross were considered cowboys, their drivers rolling all night long, curling up in the cabin for a couple of hours' sleep when they found a quiet stretch of road.

Most of Day and Ross's early contracts came from local potato shippers, willing to gamble on the newfangled mode of long-distance transportation in order to save a bit of money. The problem was finding customers with loads to ship into the Maritimes, which would make the round trip profitable.

"The first years we had to buy a lot of our loads to bring back, because they didn't trust the trucks. We used to buy cement and haul it down here and sell it. Sell it by the bag, just to make trips," said Day. "Eventually we got people to trust us, I guess, and then we started to get loads."

After their first year of operation, Walter Ross decided the trucking business was not for him, so Day and his wife Margaret bought him out; but the Day and Ross name stayed. The Days spent the next 10 years working 16 hours on good days and around-the-clock on bad ones. They lived from invoice to invoice. "I was the last one who got paid," said Day. "I took what was left, and it wasn't very much, back in those days. We used to work all day and then load a load of potatoes. My brother and I would take it up to Montreal during the night, crawl back into the back end of the trailer and have a sleep, and then load it out and come home."

Day came to hard work early. Born on a Hartland potato farm, Elbert was forced to take over the family operation when his father died young. He sold potatoes to the McCains, whose hard-working ways Day learned to respect. "I can remember being in a restaurant in Saint John and Harrison come in with a bag of frozen french fries to see if he could sell them to the restaurant," said Day. "He himself. He started out the same way we did."

By the late 1950s, Day's one-truck operation—"Our first tractor-trailer was only 26 feet long. Just imagine,"—had grown into a fleet of up-to-date refrigerated trailers. But the long hours took their toll, and in 1959, Day invited another Hartland potato farmer, Joe Palmer, into the firm. Palmer has a reputation for not mincing words. When the Day and Ross headquarters in Hartland burned to the ground one year, the trucking company's office employees were temporarily moved to the McCain building in Florenceville. There, Palmer, unconcerned that he might anger the McCains, told a reporter, "We were as welcome as a skunk at a garden party."

Although Day will not say how much he received for his trucks, a big part of his decision to sell his part of the business was that he was plumb tuckered out. "I got tired working night and day."

Day went back to farming, became a potato supplier to the McCains, and never looked back, although he admits to feeling a lump of pride in his throat whenever he sees an orange Day and Ross truck speeding along the Trans-Canada Highway. "The name's going. They're in the U.S. and Canada, and I feel good about it. Because if it hadn't been for me starting it, people wouldn't have all these jobs. There's thousands of people working for them now."

Palmer bought out Day in 1963, but his acquisition left the company short of cash. In 1964, when Palmer wanted to build a Day and Ross transfer station in Hartland, he went to Irving for money. Palmer won't say exactly how much the Irvings loaned him, except that it was "much higher" than the $20,000 many locals suggest. In addition to repaying the loan, Palmer shook hands on a 40-year products agreement, under which Day and Ross was obligated to buy fuel, crankcase oil—everything to keep their trucks running—from Irving.

By 1965 the two largest trucking firms on the east coast were Day and Ross and Maine Maritime Express, and the McCains hired both to haul their frozen foods to the big markets in central Canada. Day and Ross, who were licensed to ship west only to Quebec, hauled their products to Montreal. Maine Maritime, one of the only east-coast trucking firms licensed to ship to Ontario, delivered their frozen foods to Toronto. According to Palmer, when Maine Maritime got into financial trouble in 1965, the McCains were forced to buy the company to ensure these shipments could get to Toronto.

The only problem, says Palmer, was that the McCains didn't trust Maine Maritime's management, and needed someone with experience to run their new company. They offered to buy out Day and Ross, merge it with Maine

Maritime, and have Palmer head up the expanded firm. Day and Ross doubled in size.

"The McCains had money and no management, and I had management but no money, so we merged the two companies," said Palmer. "Harrison and I spent a week in Oakville, Ontario, working out the details. After we shook hands on the deal, he went and fired the manager of Maine Maritime and put me in charge. About three days later, there was a big railway strike right across Canada, and it was about two weeks later before I got my eyes closed and went to sleep."

In 1972, the Irvings bought out a number of small carriers in New Brunswick and merged them into a company they called Midland Transport Ltd. The McCains were not happy. "When Irving went in the trucking business, that hurt," said Palmer. Harrison told Palmer to cancel the 40-year products agreement. "I went to Arthur [Irving] and told him I wanted to break the contract," said Palmer. "And he agreed. We didn't go to court or anything. It was a gentleman's agreement."

During the next several years, however, the relationship between the two empires became anything but gentlemanly. The McCains resented the Irvings' decision to go into trucking; the Irvings were rankled by the McCains no longer buying Irving oil. "I think with the Irvings or the McCains, there's bad blood when they lose business of any nature," said Palmer. "You'd fight it just like any other business deal. If you're in business, you try to fight anyone who tries to get in on your territory. It's like drug dealers, the only difference is in business you work hard to keep your competitors out, but in drug gangs, you shoot them."

Palmer insists, however, that the McCain-Irving feud did not affect the families' personal relationship. The McCains, for instance, would dump abuse all over Irving Oil, but would say nothing bad about Arthur. "It only upset them in a business sense," said Palmer. "Mr. Irving thought the world of Harrison McCain. When Harrison worked for him in the 1950s, Mr. Irving put Arthur under Harrison for training. Harrison today will tell you that Mr. Irving is one of the smartest people he ever met. I went to Mrs. Irving's funeral with Harrison, and I was at Mr. Irving's funeral with Harrison. And I want you to know that we were treated like royalty by the family."

The McCains and Irvings had strong personal affinities, but their business feud went ahead full bore. The straw that broke the camel's back came in 1977, when Harrison helped rescue a tiny lumber company from bankruptcy. The mill belonged to Harrison's old friend, former premier Hugh John Flemming. The Flemming-Gibson Lumber Co. was located in Juniper, a tiny hamlet about 50 kilometres east of Florenceville. The small sawmill had been founded by Flemming's father, James Kidd Flemming, a fiery orator from Woodstock, dubbed "the silver tongue." Flemming senior, who spellbound his audiences with his fancy clothes and good looks, was premier of New Brunswick between 1911 and 1914. Alas, his good fortune did not extend to his Juniper sawmill. One of the area's permanent, part-time industries, it was open for business when there was money, closed when times were bad, and an erratic source of employment for more than three hundred workers. Future Tory strategist Dalton Camp, from nearby Woodstock, worked a couple of summers at the Flemming-Gibson mill in his youth. "I got

22 cents an hour, and worked five-and-a-half days a week," he said. "I remember Hugh John used to walk around the place in these white suits." Along with his father's good political fortune and penchant for dandyism, Hugh John also inherited James Kidd Flemming's on-again off-again sawmill. By 1977, J.D. Irving Ltd., which owns most of the Irving family's vast timber holdings in the province—including much of the timber land around Juniper—set a death watch over the Flemming-Gibson Lumber Co.

K.C. Irving had a winning strategy for taking over failing businesses: he'd wait until the company hit rock bottom, swoop in, and buy the assets at bargain-basement prices. The Irvings circled like buzzards, but Flemming was adamant that the mill not fall into Irving's hands. According to a family friend, Flemming enjoyed telling how he called in political IOUs to keep the mill from Irving. The former Tory premier first approached Premier Richard Hatfield, who politely declined to help. "I remember talking to Mrs. Flemming just like it was yesterday, about how Hugh John could not get over how Richard had turned him down," said Jackie Webster, a long-time friend of the Flemmings. If a fellow Tory wouldn't help, Flemming would go to a Grit— a Liberal who had money, and owed Flemming a favour.

After all, Premier Flemming's government had put up half a million dollars to get McCain Foods Ltd. started up. Now it was time for Harrison to pay back. Former Day and Ross chief Joe Palmer said that he and Harrison discussed how the McCains could help out Flemming on a trip home from Newfoundland in the McCain corporate jet. "We both knew Hugh John very well," said Palmer. "He had lost the company and it was available to anybody. But we weren't thinking about that as much as the three hundred jobs that were lost." Harrison agreed to help out the lumber company, and began a confidential financing scheme that, by 1979, got the company back on its feet. Harrison and Palmer sold shares in the mill, which eventually became Juniper Lumber. Bev O'Keefe, a former manager of both Irving and McCain companies, took 85 per cent of the company. The other 15 per cent went to the McCains.

Bev O'Keefe, who still runs the Juniper Mill, admits that Irving was certainly ticked off at the McCains for keeping Juniper Lumber out of his grasp. The Irving-McCain feud started, however, "when Harrison rescinded Day and Ross's fuel contract with Irving." O'Keefe does a lot of business with the Irvings these days and may be loath to criticize; but most others close to the Irvings believe that Harrison's bailout of Juniper Lumber was what caused direct reprisals from the Irvings. Trucking, after all, was a sideline for the McCains. Frozen food was their baby. And K.C. was known to go to great lengths to punish disloyalty—especially from competitors. Was Irving angry enough to march off to P.E.I., buy a frozen food firm, and kick the McCains right in the french-fry market? J.K. Irving, the senior brother who oversees much of the Irving empire, refused to be interviewed, but an employee at the Irving's Golden Ball Building in Saint John said, "It sounds like something the Irvings would do."

• • •

By the mid-1970s, the Canadian frozen-food industry was no longer enjoying exponential expansion. It had matured, and was growing at a sedate two to three per cent a year.

Even the McCains were operating their Canadian plants at only 63 per cent capacity. This made K.C. Irving's decision to move into the frozen-food business even more puzzling. Yet, in the late 1970s, the Irvings set their sights on C.M. McLean Ltd., a relatively small frozen-food outfit based in New Annan, P.E.I. McLean's had sold blueberries, peas, frozen vegetables and french fries under several brand names, including Seabrook Farms, since 1962. It had scored some minor victories in a mini french-fry war with the McCains in the 1970s; but by 1978 the company was on the verge of bankruptcy. "The McCains were extremely rough competitors," said Mitch McLean, the son of founder C.M. McLean, and now general manager of Northumberland Ferries Ltd. in P.E.I. "They kept the price of french fries down, and we couldn't make any money."

McLean had been an Irving Oil executive from 1955 until 1965, when he returned to P.E.I. to help his ailing father run the frozen-food business. McLean's had been steadily losing sales to McCains; and in 1977, the year Harrison McCain helped Hugh John Flemming rescue his mill, the Irvings gave Mitch McLean a much-needed injection of cash. But by 1979, McLean Ltd. wasn't able to pay some of its potato farmers and the business was in trouble again. The word went out that the company was for sale to the right buyer. So it was no surprise when Mitch and the Irvings began studying McLean's books.

"Basically, we sold the business because interest rates were going up and, quite frankly, for the company to stay in the business took considerably more cash flow than we had," said McLean. "So the Irvings took it over. It was a mutually agreed thing. That's as simple as it is. But the interesting thing is, the day the Irvings bought the company, Harrison put the price of french fries up."

Today, Wallace admits that perhaps the biggest mistake he and Harrison ever made was not buying the company from McLean before the Irvings did. "The government urged us [to buy McLean's company]," says Wallace. "The government would have given it to us, if we would have taken it. One of our biggest mistakes was not taking it."

The Irvings jumped at the chance to get even with their former employees, says a former Irving executive. Irving bought the C.M. McLean company in the summer of 1979, but in typical Irving fashion, kept the takeover secret and rushed away from reporters seeking to confirm the buyout: "We're in the business of growing trees in northern New Brunswick," said K.C.'s son, J.K. Irving, at the time. "Gosh damn it, can't you fellows leave us alone and let us run our business?"

But there were warning signs that the Irvings were about to make a move into spuds. They owned 405 hectares of excellent farmland near St. Quentin in northern New Brunswick, and could easily clear hundreds more. The Irvings had even seeded 81 hectares with buckwheat, a crop commonly planted to prepare raw farmland for vegetable crops. By 1980, however, not only had the Irvings purchased C.M. McLean Ltd., they were ready to stand and fight the Florenceville brothers for the Maritime frozen-food market. The Irvings owned hundreds of convenience stores throughout the Maritimes, so they were well placed. In the past they had ordered their stores not to stock competitors' products, and they could ensure that the Irving stores wouldn't stock the McCain line in their freezer cabinets.

The McCains and the McLeans had tangled before. Always a distant second, McLean decided in the 1970s to pursue the profitable, yet less prestigious, institutional markets for frozen food. McLean's believed they had made the right decision when they became a french-fry supplier to McDonald's, but according to C.M. McLean's son, the contract with McDonald's never created the significant sales increase McLean expected. The fast-food giant, he said, didn't buy nearly as many french fries as they had suggested they would.

But what upset the McCains was McLean's decision to cancel its Seabrook Farm brand name in favour of the McCain sound-alike name, McLean. The McCains launched an $8-million lawsuit against McLean, alleging the small P.E.I. firm's new McLean packaging was a rip-off of their own. Even the lettering, they claimed, was almost identical to that on the McCain logo. The McCains argued that the McLean products were so similar to their own, grocery-store shoppers would not be able to distinguish between the two labels. The issue was settled out of court in the summer of 1980, when the Irvings decided, on the advice of the Toronto-based advertising firm Vickers and Benson, to change the brand name to Cavendish Farms.

It was a name designed to evoke wholesome images of Anne of Green Gables, healthy P.E.I. potato fields, and the legendary Cavendish beach resort area; but it made the McCains see red. The Irvings immediately launched a million-dollar advertising campaign to familiarize shoppers with their new label. They also dropped the price of Cavendish Farms french fries, forcing the McCains to do the same or lose sales: with global assets in the billions of dollars, the Irvings had no immediate need for profits. Although executives of both the McCain and Irving companies insisted there was no bad blood, a former Irving executive said that Cavendish Farms' strategy at the time was to hurt the McCains, at whatever the cost.

"Cavendish Farms is a very small part of the Irving global situation," said the former Irving manager. "If they made or lost money it didn't make a difference. What it did to the McCains was important. The price wars cost the McCains a lot of money, and Cavendish Farms is still doing that today."

The McCains fought the Irvings every step of the way. In 1980 they sued Cavendish Farms in the Federal Court of Canada, alleging that the Irving-owned company violated patent rights on a french-fry slicing machine that shot peeled potatoes along a fast stream of water through a series of cutting blades. The so-called "water knife" had been invented by two Americans, who sold the U.S. rights to giant potato processors Lamb-Weston Inc. of Oregon. The McCains argued that they owned the Canadian patent rights to the device and asked that the court order the Irvings to stop using it. The suit was dismissed, but a victory by the McCains would have left the Irvings with millions of kilograms of potatoes and no cost-effective way to slice them.

Back in P.E.I., the Irvings' feud with the McCains took its toll in unexpected ways. Farmers were initially excited about the Irvings purchasing the old McLean plant, and credited Mitch McLean with giving the plant a future. "Mitchell McLean did wonderfully well," said one potato farmer. "He developed the McLean plant to the point where it was a real going concern and growing. He was the first one to take the plant and really run it well. He deserves the credit for developing that plant so it became a real attractive buy for the Irvings." Soon, however, they grew to mistrust the Saint John–based conglomerate, for, along with the plant in New Annan, the Irvings picked up 809 hectares of prime P.E.I. farmland. Not surprisingly, the Irvings wanted more land and in 1981 attempted to add 2428 hectares of potato fields to the company holdings. With 3237 hectares, Cavendish Farms would be able to supply 20 per cent of its potato needs from its own farms. Island farmers smelled a rat. If the Irvings got the land, they protested, Cavendish Farms could drive down potato prices and force them out of business. "If they buy up our land," protested one farmer, "we've had it." Even the local Roman Catholic Church proclaimed "Land Sunday," and urged its parishioners to support the farmers against the Irvings.

It was a 1972 law, requiring cabinet approval of any non-resident's purchase of more than 4.05 hectares of P.E.I. farmland, that saved the farmers from the Irvings. The Tory government of Premier Angus MacLean denied the Irvings exemption from the law; but the province's action just made the Irvings try harder. In 1987, amid threats by the Irvings to pull out of the province if the government continued to stonewall them on the land purchases, P.E.I.'s Land Use Commission denied a further request from Cavendish Farms to buy the 2428 hectares of potato land.

The Irvings tried just about everything to buy P.E.I. potato land, including slipping in through the back door. In April 1990, the provincial government discovered that K.C. Irving's granddaughter, Mary Jean, and her preacher husband, Stewart Dockendorff, had purchased some 8,094 hectares of prime P.E.I. potato land in their own names and through Indian River Farms, a company the Dockendorffs had set up to grow crops for Cavendish Farms. The provincial government ordered Mary Jean and her husband to divest themselves of this land. Weeks later, the government of Premier Joe Ghiz amended the province's Land Act to require all corporations wishing to purchase more than 2.02 hectares of land to apply for cabinet approval.

Meanwhile, Cavendish Farms ventured into markets that were traditional McCain strongholds. When the Irving-owned company began selling its french fries in the U.S., the McCains howled to the American trade authorities. The McCains' subsidiary company in the U.S., McCain Inc. of Washburn, Maine, accused the Irvings of dumping. They told the International Trade Commission in Washington that frozen french-fry exports by Cavendish Farms were being sold at less than fair market value, thereby hurting McCain sales. The trade commission dismissed the McCains' complaint; however, fair trading was a weapon they would wield again and again against their New Brunswick confrères.

The McCain-Irving war turned ugly early in 1989, when the Irvings, who had captured a respectable 30 per cent of the Canadian french-fry market, decided to build a mammoth, $80-million potato processing plant in Summerside, P.E.I. The Cavendish Farms plant would be the largest frozen french-fry factory in the world—and a staggering display of corporate overkill.

News of the planned mega-project was delivered to Harrison over the telephone by Peter Van Nieuwenhuyzen, a P.E.I. potato farmer. The McCains were building ultramodern plants all over the world for roughly $25 million, less than one-third the Irvings' estimate for Summerside. After hearing about the Irving proposal, Van Nieuwenhuyzen had called Harrison to ask why the McCains were not also interested in building a plant in P.E.I. Harrison told Van Nieuwenhuyzen that the McCains were interested in expanding onto the island, although they had never considered it. The truth was they were deathly afraid of the size of the plant. They estimated that the proposed Cavendish Farms facility would be able to churn out 80 per cent of the frozen french fries needed for the Canadian market. In reality, the plant's capacity was 250 million kilograms of potatoes a year, more than the entire Canadian market could absorb. Cavendish Farms would have more than enough capacity at Summerside to service their American market as well.

Worse, the McCains argued, the Irvings were going to build it with up to $65 million in government subsidies. Summerside, which was going to lose 1,300 jobs when the federal government closed the local Armed Forces base in 1992, would need a major employer to fill the job vacuum. The provincial and federal governments began scrambling for prospective investors just when the Irvings decided it was time to turn up the heat under the McCains. Cavendish Farms promised that it would hire up to 300 people at the new plant if both governments came through with subsidies.

The McCains fought back, launching a massive media blitz that attacked both the size of the plant and the amount of government subsidies earmarked for its construction. "It was crazy," remembers Wallace, "because the government was going to pay half the bills. Don't you think that would have been a disaster? It sure would have. It was a bad decision.

It would have ruined the potato business in Canada and a quarter of the United States. It was a bad deal, that's why we fought it."

Harrison, too, is still easily rankled over the proposed Cavendish Farms plant. "We had two factories here in New Brunswick not at capacity," he recalls, "and Irving had one factory in P.E.I., and they were going to build another huge factory, largely paid for by the government, against businesses that were already established and going. And where was the business going to come from? It was not going to come from God. It was going to come from guys already producing it."

Not only would the enormous plant flood the Canadian market with cheap french fries, the McCains maintained, it would be seen by the U.S. as an unfair subsidy in breach of the Canada-U.S. free-trade agreement. The U.S. would impose countervailing duties against all potato processors, including the McCains, who exported their products to the U.S. In an ironic twist, the McCains, who had rabidly fought against the free-trade agreement, hired Simon Reisman, the man who negotiated the deal, to fight the Cavendish Farms subsidy. "Such a scheme is insane," said Reisman. "It will be seen in the U.S. as the most blatant kind of bad trades practice."

In just one week, the McCains' screams of protest had reached the ears of Ottawa politicians, who began to reconsider subsidizing the Irving plant. To encourage Ottawa and Charlottetown to turn their backs on the Irvings, the McCains said they would build a $36-million french-fry facility in Summerside and create 169 jobs, if plans to subsidize the Cavendish Farms super-plant were halted. McCain officials admitted they didn't need the plant and hadn't planned to expand onto P.E.I., but "this thing was a speeding freight train and our objective was to derail it," said Archie McLean, a McCain senior vice-president. The McCain offer was a "defensive" measure, he said. The McCains would fund the entire construction of the plant without government subsidies. The only condition was that the P.E.I. government would build a $14.5-million waste-treatment facility, for which the McCains would pay a user fee.

The McCain proposal, which promised job creation without direct government funding, struck a pleasing note with federal politicians, who quickly cancelled their deal with Cavendish Farms. The Irvings countered by announcing that while they would cancel plans to build the $80-million super-plant, the company would spend $30 million to upgrade its existing plant—if it got the same, $14.5-million waste-water facility the McCains were promised. Meanwhile, just to make sure the McCains got the message that they were not wanted on the island, the Irvings began buying up potato farms around the proposed site of the McCain plant, in an effort to cut them off from nearby potato supplies.

The McCains, who never really wanted to build on P.E.I., believed they had scored a victory against the Irvings. After all, they had successfully scuttled construction of the mega-plant. They barely had time to congratulate each other, however, when the Irvings announced that Cavendish Farms would build another plant, smaller than the cancelled Summerside facility, yet still in the super-plant league—a $50-million monster. Moreover, the Irvings promised, they would build it in Grand Falls, New Brunswick, right across the street from the McCain plant.

The prospect of an Irving plant in Grand Falls was inconceivable: it was as if a satanic cult had calmly announced it was building a cathedral to the Antichrist next to the New Brunswick Bible Institute in Hartland. Moreover, the Irvings promised they would build it in the good, old-fashioned, Maritime tradition: with government subsidies.

The Irvings were wrong if they thought, after the announcement of the proposed Cavendish Farms plant in Summerside, that they had seen the McCains go ballistic. Only now did the McCains show just how adversarial they could be. The Florenceville potato kings let loose Simon Reisman, along with his fellow free-trade negotiator Gordon Ritchie. Again they attacked the Irving proposal on the grounds that it would invite countervailing duties from angry American protectionists, particularly in Maine. Ritchie reported that the proposed plant, with its $29 million in provincial and federal subsidies, would likely flood the Maine market with frozen french fries, severely undermining potato producers there. "The result would almost certainly be a very nasty trade dispute very probably leading to a substantial countervailing duty against production not only of the proposed plant but of other plants in the region and across Canada," wrote Ritchie.

Being dutiful American corporate citizens as well as patriotic Maritimers, the McCains made sure Maine governor John McKernan and Maine senators George Mitchell and William Cohen were informed of the proposed Irving plant and subsidies, along with estimates of the unfavourable impact it would all have on the state's potato market. (In the 1980s, Maine potato production dropped by 10,927 hectares, a slump, Maine farmers like to believe, caused by increased imports of Canadian potatoes.) The governor and both senators sent angry letters to Prime Minister Brian Mulroney and Premier Frank McKenna, and a full-scale free-trade war erupted. Maine's political leadership threatened Canada with heavy potato tariffs if the Irving plant in Grand Falls materialized.

Senator Mitchell wrote to U.S. trade representative Carla Hill, urging her to halt the subsidies promised to Irving: "Potato processors in Maine simply cannot compete with Canadian processors whose costs are so heavily subsidized . . . If left to stand, subsidies such as these will further erode the U.S. manufacturing base by encouraging firms to locate in Canada where they can enjoy substantial competitive advantage."

New Brunswick premier Frank McKenna responded to Governor McKernan, arguing that the subsidies to the Irving plant would consist of job-training grants, a waste-water subsidy and $10.5 million in tax credits. These did not, McKenna stressed, justify trade sanctions from the U.S., and his government was "determined to move forward with this project."

McCain vice-president Archie McLean dubbed the Irving proposal "economic insanity," to which Cavendish Farms spokesman Robert Bonnell countered that "the only madness is in the minds of the McCains." Robert Irving, K.C.'s grandson and Cavendish Farms' manager, suggested that the prospect of countervailing duties was simply a McCain ploy to protect their turf. "We do over 50 per cent of our sales in the U.S.," he said. "So we would take a major risk ourselves if we did anything that would cause a major countervail concern in the United States."

In the end, however, it was all for nothing. In the fall of 1991, Robert Irving announced that Cavendish Farms had cancelled its plans to build in Grand Falls because of poor market conditions. He denied that tariff threats had anything to do with the decision. "The slowdown in the economy this past year, in terms of the recession, has caused many of the markets where we sell our products to have less demand," he said. "Because of the softening and increased competitiveness out there, we felt the timing wasn't appropriate."

The McCains built their plant on P.E.I., and the Irvings eventually expanded theirs. As of 1995, the McCain plant was producing 1.13 million kilograms of french fries a year; the Cavendish Farms plant 2.72 million kilograms. Both plants are expanding, which means better prices for P.E.I. potato farmers.

"It was one of the things people in Prince Edward Island were looking for to round out the potato economy," said Harry Fraser, the P.E.I.–based editor of *Fraser's Potato Newsletter*, an authoritative publication on the potato-growing industry. Fraser, a fast-talking storehouse of Maritime potato lore, was born in Woodstock, New Brunswick. The son of a potato farmer and shipper, Fraser grew and sold potatoes to the McCains before he moved to P.E.I. in the 1960s. He talks lovingly of Prince Edward Island's excellent soil and climate conditions, which make for great potatoes.

"There's no rocks here, no bruising. And the red soil doesn't hurt at all. It makes for a nice-looking potato," says Fraser, "and despite all that, we never had potato processing, or mass production of french fries on Prince Edward Island, before Cavendish Farms. That was one thing that was missing. Here we were, producing the best potatoes in

Canada. This little island is number two in the whole world in potato exports."

Fraser said the McCain-Irving dispute has developed into healthy competition. "There's probably more competition coming right up than there has been at any other stage," he said. "Both the McCains and Cavendish Farms are expanding right now, and land base here is not getting any better."

Local farmers, he said, have buried any ill feelings they may have had toward the Irvings, particularly K.C.'s granddaughter, Mary Jean, who still runs Indian River Farms and sells at least part of her crop to Cavendish Farms. "I don't have any problems with them," said Fraser, "especially with Mary Jean, because she's up-front, honest, and is just a fabulous gal. She's very well liked by the island farmers. I know she sells some potatoes to Cavendish Farms, but she has her own deal. She's making her own way."

Harrison says that while McCain Foods, like many companies, are getting fewer government loans and subsidies these days, the Irvings are still living off handouts. "The subsidy deal that was endemic in those days, all around the world, isn't much today," he says. "It's just as old-fashioned as high-button shoes. So P.E.I., for example, giving Irving a big subsidy for building a potato storage plant last year [1994], that's just outrageous. Every farmer in P.E.I. is building storages, and not getting those kinds of grants . . . The Irvings don't need to borrow from P.E.I.—P.E.I. should be borrowing from the Irvings."

CHAPTER SEVEN

All in the Family

IT WAS THE SPRING OF 1990, MONTHS BEFORE WALLACE would appoint his son Michael CEO of McCain's U.S. operations, one year before the McCain family would become key players in the company through Harrison's Board Expansion Proposal and unite against Wallace. Yet, even then, as Margaret McCain sent invitations to the McCain brothers, sisters and cousins, asking them to attend Wallace's sixtieth birthday party at their vacation compound on Round Hill in Jamaica, the divisions in the family were deep and intractable.

John Ward is a Chicago-based family-business consultant, whom Wallace had hired in the late 1980s to help heal the growing split between himself and Harrison, and in the larger McCain family as well. Ward figured that what the family needed was a big, happy McCain reunion. Wallace's birthday, on April 9, happened to fall on Easter weekend that year, and Margaret planned dinner-dances, games and tournaments designed to bring the family—particularly the younger generation—together. The compound in Jamaica, she thought, would provide a perfect backdrop for the reunion: she and Wallace had a five-bedroom house and a four-bedroom guest cottage. Overflow guests would be put up in private cottages.

Round Hill, which attracts celebrities from Paul McCartney to U.S. television journalist Diane Sawyer, has a golf course, private beach, tennis courts and swimming pool. What could be better than a weekend of family fun and frolicking, particularly at Easter, a time for a resurrection of family love? Margaret, who holds a degree in Social Work, and keeps current in the field with a small library of psychology books, talked about the family need to bond, to "re-glue" itself.

The only problem with ideas out of text books is they sometimes don't work in reality. Nevertheless, oldest sister Marie accepted the invitation; so did Eleanor and her husband, Patrick Johnson. Harrison, Billie, their two sons Peter and Mark, and daughter Anne said they would come, as did two of Andrew's children, Nancy and Stephen. Everyone else sent their regrets, including cousins Allison and Andrew.

Despite the lack of support for the reunion, Michael suggested that everyone attending submit several humorous reasons why they loved Wallace. At Wallace's birthday dinner, they would put on a show: 60 reasons why they loved Wallace were then tossed in a hat, which was later passed around the table. Each McCain was then to reach into the hat, pull out a why-I-love-Wallace slip and read it aloud.

Margaret said she loved Wallace because "you have saved me so much time and energy all these years by leaving every closet and cupboard door open in case I might want something in a hurry."

When Harrison's turn came—he was fifth—he stood up, put on his glasses, grabbed the back of his chair, and launched into a five-minute eulogy, which completely destroyed the mood. Eleanor, who was torn by the two brothers' fight, shot up next, uttered a dozen words no one could catch, and then plopped back down again. By the time Billie's turn came, it was black comedy at its best. Billie stared down into her lap as she spoke, as if afraid to look up.

Nonetheless, Wallace and Margaret got the message: they were not wanted by the family, and they could not put the McCains back together again.

• • •

There were no fireworks when the McCain family began to split. Like fine china, they just cracked. The cousins, nieces and nephews finished high school and went on to different universities, different careers and different friends. But some in Florenceville claim that the family began to become unglued when Mrs. A.D. died in 1982.

Mrs. A.D. not only ruled the family, she presided over the town. "Mrs. A.D. was the matriarch of the local Anglican church," says Stephen Morris, a communication-arts instructor at the New Brunswick Community College in Woodstock. Stephen's father, Carl Morris, is McCain Foods' vice-president of manufacturing. Stephen and his brothers grew up with the McCains, first in a little house next door to Robert's in East Florenceville, and later across the road from Harrison and Wallace on River View Drive. Stephen lives in Centreville now, a tiny village a few kilometres west of Florenceville. "To this day, people say that if she was around, she'd cuss these boys," he said.

"Mrs. A.D. was sort of a maternal figurehead," says Barb Carter, a Florenceville High School English teacher with a sandpaper voice like a drill sergeant's. Grey-haired and gritty, she can quote Shakespeare, but prefers her discussion raw and to the point. Former students remember her as their "cool English teacher," who would invite her favourite students over to her house after school to drink beer and smoke. She has lived in Florenceville for years and knows the McCains intimately.

"The boys would fire someone and the poor wife would come to Mrs. A.D.—and they'd be employed again. She was a very compassionate person."

And as long as Mrs. A.D. was alive, there was a focal point in the family, a reason for big Sunday dinners. She would not permit dissension in the family ranks, and no one dared cross her. Mrs. A.D. was so powerful, Margaret—a strong woman herself—remembers questioning Mrs. A.D.'s authority only once. "She was taking Eleanor Johnson's two boys, and was picking up our two boys, to go swimming at Harrison's house," Margaret recalls. "I said, 'Gran, who's going to be the lifeguard?'

"She said, 'Well, I am.'

"I said, 'But you can't swim.'

"She said, 'That's all right. If they get into trouble, I'll find somebody that can swim. I'll be there.'

"She was so insulted—because I was questioning the quality of care she could give her grandsons."

If Mrs. A.D. wanted to criticize anyone in the village, she would write them a letter, mark "Personal and Confidential" on the envelope, and drop it in the mail—even if the villager being reprimanded lived across the street. "I saved one that she wrote to Wallace because he was 'working Scott too hard,'" says Margaret. "So Wallace got a 'Personal and Confidential.' She said that Wallace was going to 'destroy Scott's industry and ambition.'"

When she died, she left a vacuum so large that nobody—

not even Harrison—could fill it. After her funeral, except for the annual McCain picnic in July, the McCain family never got together again.

The people of Florenceville looked on with awe as the cracks began to undermine the family that had been such a powerful force in the community for so long. "This airing of dirty laundry is just not typical of the family at all. It's just not done," says Barb Carter. "They would have done well to have re-read Macbeth before all of this. They didn't plan for the business."

Stephen Morris, who watched the rise and fall of the McCains first hand, says that, in retrospect, if you took away the McCain millions, you'd find a family just like any other. "You know, it's like any family, I guess. They're human. I wouldn't say the McCains were well-to-do when we first came here in 1963. But then they became very nouveau riche. Getting caught up in all those things. That was something I could never understand, because when you got right down to it, they were still farm boys, still put their pants on one leg at a time, just like everyone else. You're not talking about the Bronfmans, where there's generations of it, or the Kennedys; it's the McCains, where two generations back Mr. A.D. had come close to bankruptcy a couple of times.

"They're just a normal family, with the same screw-ups as everybody else. They just have to play the game a little more high profile than anyone else . . . They made their millions, they climbed the ladder." Morris laughs sarcastically, "Gosh, isn't it too bad that everything else fell to pieces around them?"

When Mrs. A.D. died, it is generally agreed that

Harrison became the family patriarch. If any of the McCain boys were social climbers, it was Harrison who played the game best. Harrison was the first of the brothers to build a massive house on River View Drive, overlooking the McCain fiefdom. And he married up. Marion (Billie) McNair, daughter of former premier John McNair and graduate of private schools, brought a love of classical music, fine art and literature into a community where the most popular music was Gospel, and where the Bible might be the only book in many a house.

"Harrison is the most interesting man you'd ever meet," says Barb Carter, who refers to him fondly as The Lord of the Manor. "He has a tremendous amount of energy, and he's well-read, well-travelled. I've attended dinners at Harrison's with people *I* wouldn't have to dinner. You know, the local farmers."

"The family that had the boarding-school values would have been Harrison's family," says Stephen Morris. "I remember when I was growing up that Scott and Michael were down-to-earth people and their parents were just down-to-earth people. They were people like us. The Harrison McCain family was sort of snooty. I mean, Margaret played piano for me at the music festival, whereas Billie, when you went up to the house, there was one room in the house you were allowed in. The rest of the rooms, you didn't go near. And of course, she was the daughter of the Premier. You can find pictures of her fishing salmon up at the old American Salmon Club . . . when those sports owned the province."

Harrison lorded over everyone in town, becoming infamous for his overbearing ways. One Sunday a new McCain employee and neighbour of Harrison's was making a racket cutting his grass. Harrison walked over to the man's fence and said, 'Excuse me, but I don't want you to mow your lawn on Sunday.' On another occasion, Governor General Jeanne Sauvé was a dinner guest at Harrison's house. It also happened to be Hallowe'en. Harrison heard that one of his close neighbours was going to have a party that night. Harrison knocked on his neighbour's door and told him he didn't want a party going on while the governor general was dining. "He said, 'Look, I'll give you another house for the night down the road,'" recalls a resident. "He made him move his party. It's hard to say 'no' when your boss is standing on the other side of the fence."

Sometimes Harrison would turn his imperiousness on his family. He would even berate Billie in public. "He would say things to her in front of people and embarrass her," said a former employee and friend of Harrison's. "She was isolated from the community because she never knew when he would show up and tell her to go fuck herself. I've been at a few dinner parties where things weren't going well, or something wasn't served properly, and Christ he'd take it out on her. He'd give her shit in front of maybe half a dozen people. By Jesus, if I did that to my wife, she'd hit me with a goddamned baseball bat so fast it wouldn't even be funny."

Stephen Morris received several personal doses of what he calls Harrison's badgering. "He roughed me around a little," says Stephen. "He chased me around, threw me around a bit. Talked about 'fucking good manners,' things like that."

But Harrison pushed Stephen a little too far at a Christmas party at Stephen's parents' home several years ago. "Me and my brother used to spend a couple of hours at the beginning of the evening, doing door duty. And Harrison came in one time—I have longish hair—he comes in and he started throwing money at me. 'You need a haircut,' he said. 'You need a haircut.'

"He just started throwing money at me, and I'd pick it up and say, 'No, no, no. That's okay.'

"So he says, 'What's the matter, not enough?' He pulls out his billfold and flips some more money at me.

"I said, 'Look, thanks a lot, but I don't need it.'

"He says, 'No, no, you take it, you need a haircut.'

"So he goes in to the party, and I had two hours to think of a comeback line. And I used to work for Day and Ross, and I didn't anymore. So he's going out, and I grabbed his hat and I tucked the money in his hat, and I gave it back to him and said, 'Thanks very much, but I don't need this.'

"He said, 'No, no, no. You need more.' And he started pulling the wallet out.

"And I put my arm around him—which he hates, okay? he sort of shuns physical contact—and I said, 'Look, maybe you don't realize this, but I don't work for you any more, and because I don't work for you any more, I can afford to get a fucking haircut anytime I feel like it.'

"He just sort of had this blank look on his face. He said, 'Touché' and left."

• • •

Barb Carter has taught just about every McCain who went through Florenceville High School since the early 1970s. "I met a lot of them—tons of them, all over the place," she says. "The three sets of parents that I know did a damned good job with their children. If they weren't family, they'd be the best of friends, I'm sure."

The 1975 edition of the Florenceville High School year-book says that Harrison's son Peter was nicknamed "Padré." Like his father, Peter was a quiet kid and a big reader; perhaps the name was intended to invoke images of studiousness. "Peter was different," says Carter. "He was a reader, and more aloof. [But] if you're talking about raw intelligence, he probably has it. Peter has the brains."

But "Padré" was not a name Stephen Morris, who was a friend of Peter's right through university, remembers. Peter, he said, had more than a passing acquaintance with the bottle. "Put it this way," he said, "Pete's nickname when he was young was 'Wild Man.' Suffice it to say that a lot of people have 'I saved Pete McCain' stories."

Stephen's younger brother, Alan, who was the same age as Peter, recalls, "We were both readers. We both read a lot, and I remember sitting down and talking with Peter for hours. Peter was an interesting guy, he was. He was smart, very interesting. And of course, very eccentric."

But Peter could also be cruel, Alan remembers. "Peter hated to lose. I like basketball, and he had a basketball hoop at his house. And I remember we played basketball and he would always have games like, 'If you lose, I get to spit on you.' And I suppose all kids do it, right? But to me, that was very strange. You couldn't just lose, there had to be a consequence of losing."

One day Peter and Alan were boxing in Alan's basement. When Alan walked away after laying out Peter several times, Peter chased him up and down the street on a go-cart, trying to spear him with a ski pole. "He was trying to run me down in this friggin' go-cart and ski pole. But all I had to do [to avoid him] was step off the road. But he kept trying. And when I look back, I think, that was a pretty crazy way to be. He did not want to lose: 'If I lose, you're going to pay.' I remember going home and telling my mother, 'these people are nuts.'"

Another thing that made Peter "eccentric" was that he had access to handguns, particularly a .357 Magnum that he and Alan would use to shoot potato barrels. "I remember going shooting with Peter when I wasn't very old—could you picture two 15-year-olds with a .357 Magnum? Shooting potato barrels? I remember . . . marvelling at the fact that the hole at the front of it was this big," he says, making a circle with his thumb and finger the size of a dime, "and the hole at the back was like this," spreading his hands about 30 centimetres apart.

Peter later went to Trent University in Peterborough, Ontario, and Dalhousie University in Halifax, graduating with a B.A. and an M.B.A. At Trent Peter became involved in student government and was briefly attracted to socialism. "You know, Pete, he is just one of the most well-read people that I have ever been with," says Stephen Morris. "I remember at Trent University he was into political science really heavily. He won a seat on the student senate . . . One of the things I remember him saying was 'My old man says this is the perfect time for me to be a communist, when I'm at school.' That kind of attitude. We used to sit around and talk about Che Guevara and the Chicago Seven and Jerry Rubin and Abbie Hoffman, and existentialism."

Peter worked at the Florenceville factory or in the crop fields in the summers and later worked in sales, in Newfoundland and Toronto, before becoming his father's executive assistant, vice-president and then president of McCain

Foods International, Inc. Peter's young adulthood contrasted that of his father's. Whereas Harrison was driven by ambition to succeed, Peter nearly destroyed himself with alcohol. For fear of Harrison's wrath, McCain family members will speak only anonymously about Peter's drug and alcohol abuses; but Peter, said one McCain, thought nothing about smoking pot on the McCain plane, en route to a sales conference in Newfoundland. At one point in the 1980s, Peter was even admitted for alcohol-abuse treatment at The Donwood Institute, one of Toronto's top drug and alcohol treatment centres. He has since been rehabilitated.

Peter's older brother Mark is now a business analyst with McCain Foods. Because he was sent away to private schools at the age of 12, few people in Florenceville know him. According to McCain family insiders, Mark was sent to boarding school because he was too much for Harrison and Billie. He was sent first to Upper Canada College, where his uncle, Patrick Johnson, was headmaster. After a year he was asked to leave. "He did get booted out," says Stephen Morris. "And how do you manage that when your uncle is the headmaster?" Mark was transferred to Lakefield in Peterborough, and finally graduated from the University of New Brunswick in 1977.

Mark returned to work summer jobs at McCain companies. A former manager of Thomas Equipment, the McCains' farm machinery subsidiary, recalls, "Mark worked one summer for me. For about three or four weeks. He worked on the production floor, a labourer. And work started at seven in the morning and he'd show up at 9:30. Finally I called him in one day and said, 'Lookit, Mark, that's not the way we function here. If you want to continue working here you show up at seven in the morning and work 'til five at night, like everybody else, and if you don't want to do that, don't bother coming back.' He didn't come back." For twelve years after graduation Mark worked as an investment broker in Toronto, then returned to McCain Foods at their Toronto offices, in 1990.

• • •

If Harrison's family was uppity, Wallace's were the other side of the coin, down-home and friendly. Wallace preferred hunting moose to reading, and while Billie drove a Mercedes, Margaret—known to everyone in Florenceville as Margie— drove a Pontiac station wagon to transport her children and their equipment to hockey practice. Margie was raised on a farm in Truro, Nova Scotia, and though she, like Billie, attended private schools, the people of Florenceville say that Margie never lost touch with everyday folks. One of Margie's favourite hangouts was the lunch counter at Buckingham's, Florenceville's family-owned five-and-dime store. Until she became Lieutenant-Governor in 1994, Margie played organ every Sunday at the local Anglican Church.

"Margie would go and bang that damned piano at the church, for God's sakes, and she would get up and do those damned concerts and stuff, that no one in their right mind would ever do," says Barb Carter. "When Margie was made Chancellor of Mount Allison, she got all involved in that. Somebody forgot to tell her that she was just a figurehead."

Harrison is renowned for his quick temper, but Wallace has his moments as well. "Wallace has a very short fuse," says Carter, "whereas Harrison was more methodical—but equally ruthless. Wallace fired his pilot one day after he tried to land in cloudy weather and knocked one of the wheels off the plane trying to land in Florenceville. I lived next door to the pilot, so I know. The plane was forced to land in Fredericton. Wallace fired the pilot in mid-air, on the way to Fredericton . . . Harrison would have fired him too, [but he] would have waited."

Wallace and Margie's first son, Scott, was born in 1956, the year Wallace quit his job at Thornes Hardware in Saint John and moved back to Florenceville to co-found McCain Foods. Scott grew into a six-foot-five-inch regular guy who is respected by everyone in the county. Scott is the McCain whom the feud has not touched. Everyone, including Wallace-haters, loves Scott, who seems to lack any capacity for vindictiveness. "Scott is just a hockey-playing, beer-drinking boy," says Stephen Morris. "And as close to a homey you'll ever get around here."

Carter remembers Scott doing well at school and, later, at university. Like his father, Scott was known at McCain Foods as someone who kept an eye on the details. Although he didn't rise as fast as his younger brother Michael, Scott eventually became vice-president of production, never lording it over his employees.

"One time he was calling a shift back to work [after a layoff], and he got on the phone and started calling people," says Stephen Morris. "And he called one woman and told her what was going on, and she said, 'Who should I say was calling?' And he said, 'It's Scott McCain, but you better tell him it's Bud Cox, the shift supervisor, because they won't come in for me.' He is so humble and down-to-earth."

Scott's brother Michael was born in 1958, with a middle name—Harrison—that his mother would later regret. Michael was always tall and, although not quite as big as Scott, seemed to possess a great capacity for punishment. Alan Morris remembers an incident on the school bus one day.

Hazen Hunter used to live down the road, and Hazen was kind of a bully. I remember Hazen thumping Michael, really roughing him up. And I remember Michael saying, "Come on, do it again. You think you're a big man? Hit me again. Come on, hit me." And here's Hazen, thumping Michael, and Mike is just laughing. "Come on, do it again." I remember thinking, 'Geez, this guy's got a lot of balls.' He was actually laughing at the guy. I think I had a new respect for Michael after that. He made this guy look incredibly foolish.

Morris says that Michael's personality contrasted sharply with that of Harrison's son Peter, who is one year older than Michael. Peter, he says, used to call Michael "Dim," after the big, half-witted character in Anthony Burgess's novel, *A Clockwork Orange*. "Michael was never really a social animal," recalls Alan's brother Stephen. "Not really great with handling people. Really, really smart boy, but not people smart. He really didn't understand anything about human relations, about the subtle art of management. He was like a bulldog."

Academically, however, Michael was anything but dim. In the 1975 edition of the Florenceville High School yearbook, there are more pictures of Michael than of any other student. There's Michael, a long-haired version of his father, a defenceman on the Florenceville High School hockey team, and in the school's drama club. Michael was also on the debating team, which was coached by Carter. "Mike was a great debater," she says. "He's very fast on his feet. He was very confident—but I don't mean cocky."

Michael's self-confidence was so great that it was a match for Harrison's. "He and I had personality clashes as far back as I can remember," says Michael. "Look, let's call a spade a shovel: I'm a reasonably assertive individual myself. And I had a reputation of being that way—and that's something I'm not always necessarily proud of, it's something I have to deal with and try to harness. But Harrison McCain looks for a certain type of individual to be underneath him, and I don't fit the bill. If it's the middle of the day, and he says, 'It's dark out,' he expects everybody to say, 'Yes, yes, yes. It's dark out.' But I say, 'No, no, no. It ain't fucking dark out. The sun's shining clear.' I refuse to acquiesce to anybody. What did the scorpion say to the frog? 'It's my nature.'"

The McCain who would later become the centre of his father and uncle's feud seemed to have been fast-tracked all his life. Although New Brunswick high schools end with grade 12, Michael went straight to Mount Allison University after grade 11. "Michael was so far ahead of his class," remembers an old family friend, "the president of the university [Mount Allison] said, 'You're doing this fella a disfavor keeping him here. Either ship him off to Harvard or to the University of Western Ontario.'" He went to the University of Western Ontario, where he earned an M.B.A.

"He was a very good student," says Barb Carter. "Michael was sort of groomed for the business. I guess it was understood for years . . . that Wallace's boys, specifically Mike, were interested in the business, while Harrison's children weren't. At all."

Michael was not only anxious to join the family company, he saw himself as a natural successor to Harrison. He played the heir-apparent role so well that he even bought the old, run-down house once owned by McCain Produce Co. founder H.H. McCain. "It hadn't been lived in for 15 years," says Michael. "It was literally falling in. I bought it as a shell and had to rebuild the whole thing."

The day he graduated from the University of Western Ontario, Michael decided he should lay his cards on the table, and inform Harrison of his ambitions. "I think that might have been one of the mistakes I made," says Michael. "The first thing I said to him was, 'Oh, by the way, just so there's no misunderstanding, my ambition is, some day, to have your job.'"

However lofty his aspirations, Michael was keenly aware how difficult his rise to the top would be. His first job at McCain Foods was tarring a roof; he was 14 years old. He spent subsequent summers performing a variety of production-line work. His early mentors were his father and McCain Foods vice president Archie McLean. Both constantly reminded Michael that his name alone would not guarantee success. Michael recalls.

My father's very first conversation with me was, 'Because your name is McCain, everybody is going to approach you on the basis that you were given everything that you have. And there is only one way to get over that: you've got to figure out who is the hardest worker on any crew that you work on—and you've got to work harder than the hardest person . . . ." He gave me that lecture not once, but, Jesus, a hundred times. And you know what? He's right. The first thing people will look at is your name on the stationery . . . . You could walk on water with the decisions that you make. But if you do it in a shortened work day or with less sweat on your brow, you'll have a goddamned hard time getting anybody's respect. But if you work harder than anybody there, you'll get the respect soon.

Archie McLean's advice to Michael was more succinct: "Just because your name's McCain," Michael remembers him saying, "doesn't buy you a cup of coffee. You've got to fucking work." Alas, Wallace and McLean did not counsel Michael on how to deal with fellow McCains—particularly Harrison. It became apparent to Michael, as early as 1982, that Harrison would stonewall his career plans. "I knew at that time that Harrison and I got along like oil and water," says Michael, "and that would probably impede any ability in me. My mother desperately wanted me to get out of the company. She told me for 15 years, 'You aren't going anywhere with Harrison McCain. So get out, don't work here.' That was my view as well."

At first Michael considered doing a little moonlighting until he founded a full-time business of his own. "I remember it was a summer day," says Michael, "and over a drink I told my father, 'Jesus, you know, I'm thinking about starting up a business on the side.' He looks at me, and says, 'The fuck you are. I'm going to tell you something: we have a strict policy in this company—no moonlighting. You either work for me or you work for somebody else or yourself. But you don't do both, so *nyet*.'"

Although they each owned a sixth of McCain Foods by

way of the $20,000 each contributed to their brothers' venture in 1956, Robert and Andrew H. McCain are generally known as the poor McCains. They ran McCain Produce Co., the seed-potato business founded by their father and grandfather, remained farmers all their lives, and never moved up to McCain Hill, where Harrison and Wallace and their executives erected lavish homes.

Robert married Rosemary Baird, the daughter of a Saint John doctor, and seemed content to live in his brothers' shadows; he died of kidney failure in 1977. "Robert and Rosemary's family, I suppose, was less conventional, less academically inclined than the other families," says Barb Carter. "[Robert's son] Andrew graduated," she says, clasping her hands in mock prayer. "Thank you Jesus, he did. He was one of those people who I prayed to God made 50 on his departmental exams. Little Andrew was probably the only McCain who knew he was a McCain. The other children didn't seem to be aware that they were."

Andrew had a younger brother, Kirk, who died in 1982 in a car accident while a student at Humber College in Toronto. Kirk and his sister Mary McCain had been adopted by Bob and Rosemary. They had talked about adoption for a long time, but never followed through until Wallace and Margaret came home from Halifax one day with a 12-day-old baby girl they named Martha. Bob and Rosemary seethed over the adoption. They ignored Martha, even when Wallace and Margaret brought her to their house. One Christmas, "We sat her in a crib by the tree, and they just pretended she didn't exist," said Margaret. "She did not exist for them."

A year later, Bob and Rosemary adopted two children, a boy and a girl called George and Darlene. Bob and Rosemary changed their names to Kirk and Mary. Kirk died in a car accident. Mary was never involved in the family business.

Right from the start, says Barb Carter, Andrew, who would later become chairman of the Holdco board, knew the family had money, and realized he wouldn't have to work very hard to live comfortably. "He had some kind of shop in Woodstock, somebody said, I don't know—a radio shop or something. Who the hell would know? But whatever it was, you want to be damned sure there was a lot of money behind it. You see, Andrew didn't have a lot of friends around here like the other kids did."

The "radio shop" Carter refers to is a Woodstock Sam the Record Man outlet, which Andrew ran for a few years. "He ended up buying his own stock," says Alan Morris. "He probably has the best record collection in the county—and he bought it all from himself."

Alan and his family spent their first few years in Florenceville living next door to Andrew's parents' home. "The first job I ever had was working for Bob," says Alan. "He had a huge horse barn across the road—racehorses. Horses were his passion. And I shovelled shit for Bob. But it was really nice because I got to hang with Bob. He was a really nice guy. I really thought a lot of him."

Because Andrew was two years older than Alan, and because the Morrises soon moved to River View Drive, Alan did not get to know Andrew until the early 1980s, when they were both in their twenties. However, Alan's older brother, Stephen, shared an apartment with Andrew in Fredericton, while Andrew was trying unsuccessfully to get a general arts degree at St. Thomas University. "I lived with him for a year off-campus," says Stephen. "I went to UNB and he went to St.

Thomas. He did very poorly there. I remember him getting pissed off and leaving a course one time because someone had made a disparaging remark about the McCain family . . . After that he went to the Nova Scotia Agricultural College in Truro. And he left there to become a salesman for a company called Nasco in Guelph."

Andrew soon realized that he wasn't cut out for selling veterinarian and agricultural supplies, and returned to Carleton County to set himself up as manager of Alan Morris's rock group, the Howard Brook Band. Andrew had taken a course in record producing in Florida; and both produced and financed a record for the band. He later opened the Sam the Record Man outlet in Woodstock which he eventually sold.

• • •

The other "poor" McCain family was that of Andrew H. McCain and his wife Marjorie Pearson, whom Barb Carter describes as a "sweet girl from Hartland." Andrew was a director of the New Brunswick Telephone Company and a member of the exclusive Union Club in Saint John. His alcoholism was widely known, but rarely discussed. In 1984, he died of complications resulting from cirrhosis of the liver, four days after collapsing at Margaret McCain's fiftieth birthday party at the Lord Beaverbrook Hotel in Fredericton. Andrew and Marjorie raised six children, two boys and four girls. "The single most resourceful family is Andrew's," says Barb Carter. "You've got Allison, Stephen, you've got Nancy, you've got Linda. They've all got business degrees, and they're all more than capable."

Allison, born in 1949, is the oldest McCain cousin and, until Howard Mann was appointed CEO in 1995, was regarded as the most likely McCain to succeed Harrison in the company's top executive spot. Because he is so much older than the other McCains, and because he spent much of his career working for McCain operations overseas, he is often regarded as the unknown McCain in the bunch. After working for New Brunswick Telephone as an engineer for three years—a job handed him because his father was a director of the company, family friends say—Allison began to work for McCain Foods in 1975. After spending five years at different positions in Florenceville, Allison was appointed production director of McCain Foods Australia in 1980. In 1983 he moved to England, where he works under the tutelage of Mac McCarthy, as McCain Foods (GB) Ltd.'s managing director.

Except for Mrs. A.D.'s short stint as president of McCain Produce Co., the position she assumed after her husband's death in 1953, no female McCain has held a prominent post in the McCain food empire. Of the four brothers' 19 children, 11 are women. No one in Florenceville is holding his breath until one of them is appointed CEO of a McCain company somewhere.

"It's a very patriarchal family," says Barb Carter, who wishes, for the women's sake, that would change. "The girls probably have the most brains. Laura [Harrison's daughter] is the businesswoman. If I was just looking at Harrison's children, the one I would have bet on would have been Laura," she says. "She's got it all: the brains, the ability. Unfortunately, she's a woman."

Although there are seven seats on the family-run Holdco board of directors, none are occupied by women. "The boys have, on average, more business training than the girls," Harrison explains. "Although my daughter, Laura, has more business experience than some of the men on the board."

Indeed, Harrison's daughters are doing very well for themselves. Gillian, his youngest, earned an M.A. in English Literature from New York University, and recently signed her first book contract with a large American publishing house. Harrison is happy about his daughter's early success, but is nonetheless perplexed by the book's subject matter. "It's an oral history of punk rock," he says with a broad grin. "I think it's a little esoteric myself. [She said] 'Look, Dad, you better go to the bookstore and poke around a little bit. It's not so esoteric.'

"She sold to Grove. Got an offer from Random House —not enough money. 'Not enough money,' she's talking. Not enough money? Screw off!"

Harrison is apologetic about the lack of women in management positions at McCain Foods. The reasons for this, he suggests, are twofold: corporate culture and location. "We don't have more women working for McCain Foods in managerial roles and we're very conscious of it," he says. "One, we probably haven't pushed it hard enough. It's probably our fault. Even worse, is getting a highly skilled, trained, educated professional, or a manager, a woman, to live in a place like Florenceville. If she's single, it's not so easy. She wants to be in a place where there's more social activity. Perfectly understandable. And if she's married, well, there's her husband's job—and there's not that many jobs available. It's hard enough recruiting men, so women are even worse."

According to Wallace, McCain women weren't recruited into top executive posts at McCain Foods because of the company's size. There were only a certain number of senior jobs to go around—and the McCain men had already secured

Mr. A.D. as a young man.

Wallace McCain as a teenager.

Mr. A.D. and his four boys. Clockwise from top left: Robert, Andrew, Harrison and Wallace.

Four future directors of McCain Foods Group, Inc. From left to right: Allison, Andrew, Scott and Mark McCain.

From humble beginnings. McCain Foods' Florenceville plant, circa 1959.

A family portrait. From left to right: Wallace, Eleanor, Harrison, Mrs. A.D., Mr. A.D., Marie, Robert and Andrew McCain.

In November 1952, the McCain brothers were inducted as Ancient and Accepted Scottish Rite Masons. From left to right: Wallace, Harrison, Grand Master J.W. Duncan, New Brunswick Lieutenant-Governor D.L. MacLaren, Mr. A.D., Robert and Andrew.

Yousef Karsh

Karsh's portrait of Harrison McCain.

Wallace McCain.

Margaret McCain, Wallace's wife, and Lieutenant-Governor of New Brunswick.

Mrs. A.D. as she approached her 90th year.

Harrison and Wallace in 1984.

The Wallace McCain family at Lieutenant-Governor Margaret McCain's 1994 swearing-in ceremony. Top row, left to right: Eleanor, Scott, Michael and Martha. Seated: Wallace and Margaret.

them. "If you have a large piece of the pie controlled by family members, be careful," says Wallace. "Because you'll have trouble with your other executives who'll say, 'You have to be a family member to get anywhere.' Unless you handle that with great care, you'll have problems. You'll get jealousies. It's a very treacherous road, and obviously we didn't cover it."

CHAPTER EIGHT

Brothers at Arms

BEFORE 1993, FEW PEOPLE COULD SAY HOW THE McCAINS ran their successful company from the tiny village nestled on the banks of the St. John River. Theirs was a privately held company in the K.C. Irving mould: make all the money you can and keep your business affairs to yourself. Why tell the world what you earned—or how—when you had no legal obligation to disclose anything?

Harrison, the more talkative of the McCain brothers, gave few interviews; Wallace spoke hardly at all. When they did open up, it was usually to announce the opening of a new plant or the launching of a new product. All the world knew about McCain Foods Ltd. was that Wallace and Harrison McCain had turned their father's respectable potato business into one of the most profitable food companies around. Their success was a modern-day fairy story set in a fairy-tale village. Harrison and Wallace were its benevolent french-fry kings, the largest processors of frozen french fries in the universe. With 50 production facilities in nine countries, including New Zealand, Holland and Australia, 12,500 McCain employees churned out more than 226,000 kilograms of potato products an hour. In the year ended June 30, 1994, McCain Foods Ltd. sales totalled $3.2 billion, with a net profit of $84.3 million.

Harrison and Wallace accomplished what they did, they liked to say, because they worked together as a team. "We are both heads of the organization," Harrison once said. "We both think alike, we both know what's going on. Whatever answer one of us might give to a certain question, the other agrees to it. He would have given the same answer." They had adjoining offices, connected by an unlocked door. They talked nonstop by intercom or by shouting through the wall.

Harrison and Wallace were descended from a people who were almost wiped out because of a potato famine. In Carleton County, with its 20,234 hectares of potato fields, "blight" is not just a word out of a history book; it is a very real threat that can spell disaster. The McCains shudder to their Irish cores at the word, and worked hard improving fertilizers and chemicals to prevent the disease from killing their profits. But in their quest for success Harrison and Wallace had overlooked the blight that had infected themselves. By the end of the 1980s, Harrison and Wallace no longer worked as a team, and they were no longer best friends.

Harrison said that Wallace was blind with nepotism. Wallace maintained that Harrison was corrupted by the blight of power. In 1990, Wallace appointed his son, Michael, to the CEO's post of McCain Foods Ltd.'s $500-million-a-year U.S. operation, McCain USA. Harrison feared Michael was being groomed by Wallace to take over the company once he and his brother retired. Michael, Harrison argued, was hardly fit to be CEO of the American firm, let alone the entire $3-billion McCain corporate empire. There was no other cure, reasoned Harrison, but to ferret Wallace and his ego-driven disease out of the company.

• • •

The question of succession at McCain Foods first arose in March 1981, when the company was enjoying yet another year of record-breaking profits. A major expansion of their Florenceville plant and cold-storage facility had been completed the previous year. The french-fry plant at Harnes, France, was being completed and plans were being finalized for a third french-fry plant in England. While the future of the company looked bright, the brothers figured they ought to think about their own futures, just in case. In a letter addressed "to whom it may concern," Harrison, then 54, and Wallace, 51, ordered that, in the unlikely event that both of them were killed simultaneously, Charles "Mac" McCarthy, their long-time head of McCain's United Kingdom operations, was to be CEO of McCain Foods. Within 12 months of McCarthy's appointment, a company president was to be appointed, taking over whatever responsibilities the CEO and the McCain board of directors handed him. After an additional 12 months, the board would decide whether to keep McCarthy as CEO, move the president into the CEO's position, or give the job to someone else.

This un-notarized letter of questionable legality suggested who should be put in place if both of them should somehow die together. But they had no succession plan in the event of their retirement, which was, they figured, at least another decade or two away. The question of who should succeed them became more pressing, however, as McCain brothers seemed to be dropping dead at relatively early ages. Robert died in 1977 at age 55; Andrew in 1984 at age 63. "It was certainly spurred by the reality that

Wallace and I were then, or would soon be, in our sixties," said Harrison. "Wallace and I could not be expected to go on forever."

Wallace and Harrison, indeed, turned their gaze to the future and debated how the succession process would work. Gradually the debate became argument and the brothers were at each other's throats, with allegations of bias and favouritism.

By 1989, their fight became so severe that Wallace wanted to hire John Ward, a well-known U.S. family-business consultant, to mediate a solution. "Wallace stood on his head, pleaded, begged, did everything in his power to try and get John Ward in as a guru to guide them through this transition," says Wallace's wife, Margaret. "Wallace did pull Harrison kicking and screaming into a meeting with John Ward," after which, she says, Harrison "quickly pronounced him 'A very nice man, but not very smart.' And that was the end of it . . . That is a tactic Harrison uses to back people off into a corner and get rid of them." If Harrison's assessment of Ward was not very complimentary, neither was Ward's view of Harrison. According to Margaret, "He [Ward] said to Harrison, 'If you don't get your megalomania under control, you're going to destroy the company.'"

On June 18, 1990, after Ward was dismissed, Harrison sat down and, in his take-charge way, composed a draft restructuring proposal that addressed the succession issue head-on, and would "protect the interests" of the other McCain family shareholders. (Harrison and Wallace owned 33.5 per cent each; the remainder was divided among a couple of dozen McCains or their holding companies.) In his document, Harrison pointed out that everything was running smoothly because he and Wallace were co-CEOs. This made sense, he noted, because "the wealth was *created* in the company by Harrison and Wallace." But the company, he stressed, had to look to the future, when he and Wallace would not be around.

McCain Foods Ltd. had been run from its inception until 1984 by a five-director operating board called Opco, headed by Harrison and Wallace. Opco, or McCain Foods Ltd., as it is commonly known, orchestrated the day-to-day operation of all the McCain companies. A holding company, Holdco, known as McCain Foods Group Inc., was formed in 1984 after the death of Andrew McCain solely to own the assets of McCain Foods Ltd. Both boards, however, rarely met, and acted as rubber stamps for the decisions that came from Harrison and Wallace. "[Holdco] was just there for tax reasons," says Harrison. "I don't really know what the tax reasons were, but there . . . was some kind of tax advantage for us."

Harrison now attempted to change that. Harrison's restructuring proposal included the setting up of a two-tier board that would shift power away from Harrison and Wallace to the McCain family shareholders. The top tier, McCain Foods Group, would be composed of—except for one "outsider," McCain Foods vice-president George McClure—family member directors, two from Wallace's family, two from Harrison's, and one each from Andrew's and Robert's families. Holdco would appoint directors for its board and the Opco board, decide who should be chairman and president of McCain Foods, and decide on dividends, sales of securities and acquisitions involving more than $25 million. In other words, a more formal structure would replace the informal decision-making process by which Harrison and Wallace had run the empire.

The families of Andrew and Robert McCain were all for Harrison's changes. Indeed, Robert's son, Andrew K. McCain, joined his mother and sisters in support of Harrison's two-tier board, which would ultimately lead to Andrew's appointment as chairman of the Holdco board. "Many things have changed since 1977 [the year of Robert McCain's death]," they wrote. "And in that time we feel that our ability to contribute to the board has developed. This is the time when we can contribute and we should have direct input to the crucial issues facing the company. Perhaps our viewpoint will assist in devising the most appropriate structure. In any event, our family should have a choice as it is our investment which will be affected while the matter is currently under review by a board which is comprised of a majority of non-shareholders."

As for succession, Harrison proposed the idea that, once a year, he and Wallace would each draw up a list of three contenders for the CEO position. Upon the retirement of either brother, or both, the family-run top-tier board of directors could select from the contenders, although the list was not binding. One of the three nominees he would list at the time, Harrison advised, would be Allison McCain, elder brother Andrew's then 41-year-old son, who was a managing director of McCain Foods in England. "He has the longest and best record," noted Harrison. The new CEO, Harrison stressed, should not be a CEO simply because he is a McCain. Before nominating a McCain to the post, Harrison and Wallace "would both have to be *reasonably* satisfied he is competent to do the job," he wrote. "Desirable, but not essential," was how Harrison characterized the nomination of a McCain to the CEO position after he and Wallace were gone.

Near the end of the document Harrison wrote an aside that seemed to be aimed at Wallace, warning against appointing a McCain CEO who was not well qualified: "He will tend to look after his own family first, tend to be jealous of his cousins, his cousins will tend to be jealous of him, and he will be sorely tempted to use his inside information to increase his strength inside the company. 'Politics' inside the company will grow at an increasing rate, and in my opinion, the Company *will split*."

• • •

In 1986, Wallace's eldest son, Michael, with the blessings of both Harrison and Wallace, was appointed president of McCain Citrus, an American frozen-fruit-juice company the brothers had purchased a year earlier. The new firm had been a money loser, and Michael, a business-administration graduate of the University of Western Ontario, who had held various jobs in McCain companies since 1979, was to turn the company around. According to McCain Citrus executives, Michael did just that, restructuring the company's four plants into one efficient business. By 1990, McCain Citrus was profitable, and when the McCain USA CEO position came open that year, Wallace figured Michael was the ideal candidate for the job.

Wallace appointed Michael CEO of McCain USA on October 4, 1990. "It was not a quantum leap forward from my perspective," recalls Michael, who had spent the previous four years changing the fortunes of McCain Citrus. "It was one step up. . . ." I had been an operating company president for four years, turned the company around, everybody knew that was the case. The job was open, they wanted it filled, the other two candidates were knowingly not candidates—Wallace and Harrison both agreed they weren't candidates—and Harrison wanted to go outside. So Wallace said, 'Why the fuck would you want to do that?'

"All the balls were in motion. Wallace called me and said, 'Look, I'm going to go ahead with this appointment. And congratulations, have fun—I know you're going to do well in it. Give her hell. I'm going to make an immediate announcement."

Harrison, however, saw Michael's promotion as an act of spectacular nepotism. Not only that, Wallace had appointed Michael without Harrison's agreement, which, Harrison argued, broke the brothers' practice of consensus. Wallace maintained, however, that because he was in charge of all McCain operations in North America, he could appoint Michael CEO unilaterally. It was the beginning of the end.

On October 4, 1990, Harrison and Wallace met in Florenceville to discuss Michael's appointment.

"I thought he was taking advantage of the situation in doing that, and I said so at the top of my voice," says Harrison of his meeting with Wallace. "I never claimed that Michael was stupid or that he was lazy . . . I told Wallace that his son's promotion wasn't justified and was far, far too nepotistic." Harrison stormed out of their meeting, jetted off to another, but called Wallace on the airplane's telephone and begged his brother not to go ahead with the promotion. Later, Harrison recorded his conversation with Wallace into a dictaphone:

I just had a telephone conversation from the plane with Wallace: (1) I told Wallace I didn't want him to make the announcement which he threatened to do that Michael was going to become the Chief Executive Officer of McCain USA today.

He said, 'I have already done it.'

I said, 'Just walk out to the fax machine and stop that. You know I don't agree to that.'

(2) He said, 'You have disagreed with that five or eight times in a row and I am going to do it anyway.'

(3) I said, 'It is wrong. Just put it off until we have straightened some other things out. Call the other Directors and tell them you favour it and I don't, and if they take your side, it is perfectly okay with me to proceed.'

He said, 'I don't have to ask the directors who I am going to appoint or what I am going to do. I am going to do whatever I want to do.'

(4) I said, 'Wallace, you are undoing something—it is the first time in our lives that you have split from me. Just keep cool, hang in for awhile.'

He said, 'You've turned that down five or eight times and you will keep on turning it down forever.'

(5) I said, 'Even Michael must be embarrassed.'

He said, 'He is the smartest executive we have in the entire company in the entire world, and why would he be embarrassed?'

(6) He said, 'If I have made a mistake, I will take the responsibility.'

I said, 'You don't have the responsibility or the authority to even make the decision. It is not a question of taking the blame for doing it or not doing it.'

I said, 'You are making a very serious mistake and I would like you to retract it.' (Again) He said, 'I will not do any such thing.'

I said, 'You are going to have to be held accountable for this and you are going to regret it.'

He said, 'Is that a threat?'

I said, 'No, it is not a threat, it is just a statement of fact. You are making a very bad mistake and you can't get off with it.'

I hung up the phone.

I really don't know if he sent the fax or not—I can't believe that he is going to try to extricate Michael from any responsibility for profit. Michael has never made a nickel for us in his life. (Not all his fault either), but he hasn't, and now he will never have to—Any time any company doesn't go well, it will be that president's fault, not Michael's.

He has just escaped accountability except in a very general way.

And the two other top guys in [the] United States, Robinson and Lan, have both been talked to ahead of time, and Lan was promised Michael's job if he was supportive, and Robinson, Wallace said, was 'fully supportive' and nothing had indicated to him as to his future . . . ??

Harrison also believed that Wallace planned to gain for Michael the CEO position of McCain Foods Ltd.

On October 5, 1990, the day after he was informed by Wallace of Michael's promotion to CEO of McCain USA, Harrison completed a sixth draft of his restructuring proposal; he submitted it to the shareholders four days later. This draft included a mention of the possible conflict that could arise when family members were both shareholders and managers. "If they are only shareholders," he wrote, "they would control their board of directors, select good professional managers, and if they didn't suit, fire them. Not nearly so easy when a brother or cousin is a top executive and he has to be fired or demoted." To remedy this, Harrison proposed that shareholder/managers could not be removed unless 75 per cent of the shareholders were in agreement. That way, the two smaller blocks of votes, i.e., Andrew's and Robert's, could not prevail alone against one of the larger blocks. Either Harrison or Wallace would have to vote with them. Moreover, for Harrison and Wallace to prevail against the other, both Andrew's and Robert's votes would have to be won over.

As for succession, Harrison no longer included his nephew Allison on his list of potential candidates. "We do not want our company badly screwed up," he wrote. "I favour a McCain as President/CEO and/or Chairman, but we are risking an enormous amount of money *needlessly* if we say 'it must be a McCain.' The failure of Canada Packers was unnecessary and sickening. An incompetent family CEO protected by his name and relatives was allowed to destroy Canada's largest and oldest food company. There is a lesson to be learned here. We want *excellent* people to run our business. That is the first test, but I am happy to report that I personally see McCains who will be capable of filling the very highest jobs in our organization after they mature and gain more experience."

Harrison's proposal regarding shareholder/managers was a direct threat, not only to Wallace's maneuvering of Michael into the CEO position at McCain Foods, but also to his own position. Wallace believed Harrison was maneuvering his removal from the company should he persist in promoting Michael. If Harrison's votes combined with Andrew's and Robert's, Wallace believed, Harrison would control the ownership board like a puppeteer.

Harrison's rough drafts evolved into a Board Expansion Proposal, which was submitted to the shareholders in January 1991 for approval. In it, much of Harrison's early succession notes had been replaced by broad, general powers that the new, family-run holding company board would wield, including the power to remove either Harrison or Wallace—not with 75 per cent of the vote, but by a simple majority—and the authority to name new CEOs after Harrison and Wallace were gone. The responsibility for selecting such successor was assigned to the newly created Management Resources Committee (MRC), composed of four "outsider" (non-family) directors of McCain Foods Ltd., or Opco. Three directors were soon assigned to the MRC: Imperial Oil CEO Arden Haynes, Noranda Chief Financial Officer Kendall Cork and Aluminum Company of Canada CEO David Morton. Fishery Products International CEO Victor Young would be named to the board in November 1992.

Although he supported the concept of the MRC, Wallace made no bones about his disapproval of the Board Expansion Proposal, and fought hard to change it. In a letter to McCain shareholders on July 18, 1991, Wallace argued against the establishment of a two-tier board, because, he said, a single board that oversaw all aspects of the company's operations would give the minority shareholders "a *better view* of the company, not a *sheltered view*." Wallace saw Harrison lining up the family on Holdco against him, and pointed this out to the shareholders. "The real issue is—when it comes down to a crunch," said Wallace, "who's [sic] interest is it to have a *stacked* board with highly controlled managers on it?"

Among the shareholders, however, Wallace's objections were seen as promoting his family's careers. Wallace denied the charges. "Absolutely not," he wrote. "I have two sons who are active in the business, and both are doing well, I believe. I support their careers, but not to the exclusion of shareholder interests . . . As far as my sons are concerned, all I ask for is an evaluation of their potential without the cancer of family bias involved, in a timetable that fits the needs of our company."

The Board Expansion Proposal provided for one member of Holdco, or McCain Foods Group, the ownership board of McCain's, to sit on the Opco board as a management appointee. Wallace recommended to Harrison that Michael be that member. This suggestion prompted, in August 1991, one of the most vitriolic exchanges of memos between the brothers.

"You mentioned to me a couple of days ago that I should vote to put Michael, now on Holdco, on the Opco Board as a Management appointee," wrote Harrison to Wallace. "You said this would help alleviate 'the bad blood' between him and me. As mentioned to you yesterday—and to which you gave me an evasive answer—'What bad blood?' I'm certainly not angry or 'sore' at him."

The memo continued with a number of stinging rebukes Harrison wanted Wallace to justify:

(1) Is Michael *under*-employed?

(2) Am I knifing Michael in any way?

(3) Was he put in any worse position than any of the other McCains with the Two-board system?

(4) Is *everyone* treated exactly the same with the Two-board system?

(5) We listened patiently to your arguments, for about the 8th day, at the Board Meeting as to what we should change. Did you get a fair vote?

(6) Didn't we compromise and compromise 'The Proposal' to suit you only to find, in the end, that you voted against it?

(7) How do you account for the fact that you led your own family into negative votes that were opposed 100% by all the other Shareholders? Did you ever stop to think that maybe *you* were out of step?

(8) You insinuated that Michael thinks he has been ripped off?

(9) You say that I have been playing politics with the Shareholders for 25 years. Absolutely ridiculous. *A joke*.

Wallace responded to Harrison two weeks later, on September 6, 1991, with an equally passionate response:

1. Q. Is Michael under employed?

A. No.

2. Q. Am I knifing Michael in any way?

A. Blocking him and undermining him is constantly in your mind. It's obvious.

3. Q. Was he put in any worse position than any other McCain with a two board system?

A. No. We are *all* worse off.

4. Q. Is everyone treated exactly the same with a two board system?

A. Yes, badly.

5. Q. We listened patiently to your arguments for about the eighth day at the board meeting as to what we should change. Did you get a fair vote?

A. No!!!! The votes were bought by you!!!

6. Q. Didn't we compromise and compromise 'the proposal' to suit you only to find in the end that you voted against it?

A. No!!! You lost the argument on one clause. You won all the rest with muscle and force, not on the strength of the argument.

7. Q. How do you account for the fact that you led your own family into negative votes that were opposed 100% by all of the shareholders?

A. Easy answer. Your power! Your muscle! Their fear! You lined them all up in a row, and cracked the whip. What I asked for was motherhood and a fair play.

8. Q. Did I ever stop to think maybe I was out of step?

A. Yes. Every day, every hour. My conscience told me I was taking the wise, courageous and honest course. I have preserved my integrity!

9. Q. You insinuated that Michael thinks he's been ripped off!

A. I feel ripped off! We were once equal partners. We were once close friends. We once trusted each other. That is all gone. Yes, I have been ripped off.

10. Q. You say that I have been playing politics with the shareholders for 25 years.

A. Yes, you have been. Not only have you done that,

you brag about your political skills and how you can play politics.

That exchange of memos, Harrison would later say, signalled the end of the brothers' 35-year relationship. They both agreed that it was over, but disagreed on how to effect their divorce. Harrison said simply that Wallace must go; Wallace suggested that, as in any other divorce, there were three possible options: sell the company, split the company in two equal parts, or have one brother buy out the other's shares. Harrison repeatedly refused all three.

There was a temporary truce in March 1992, when Harrison, 65, suffered a heart attack and was flown to Boston for bypass surgery. But his near-death did not soften Harrison's stance; if anything, such acute awareness of his own mortality strengthened Harrison's resolve to keep his brother from positioning his son to take over the company.

● ● ●

The fight remained private until September 3, 1992, when Harrison wrote a letter to his nephew, Andrew McCain, chairman of Holdco, the McCain family-controlled ownership board, and explained, "with regret and guilt," that he and Wallace were at loggerheads over who should succeed them as CEO of McCain Foods. When he got word of Harrison's letter a week later, Wallace fired off one of his own to Andrew, setting out his three options, which he described as a "last resort," and stating that he preferred to let Opco's Management Resources Committee find a solution to the succession problem.

"Since Harrison's illness in March, he appears to have

lost desire to understand the details of the operation of this business which has been a source of frustration (for both of us)," wrote Wallace. "He seems also to have lost interest in the Board Expansion Proposal (BEP) adopted one year ago." Wallace also claimed that Harrison "casually offered to piece me off with 'maybe a plant somewhere' or 'maybe a business in the U.S. somewhere.'" Wallace was insulted. "The success of our company was a PARTNERSHIP between myself and Harrison. I have been, at a minimum, 50% responsible for the overwhelming success in the business. You can well see my lack of enthusiasm for a 'plant somewhere.'" According to Wallace, Harrison wanted to bypass the Management Resources Committee and immediately appoint an executive, who would be trained to take over when the brothers retired.

On September 11 the Holdco board met and ruled that if the brothers' differences were not resolved by October 5, 1992, the board would meet again to consider imposing its own remedy, up to and including firing Harrison, Wallace, or both. They also ruled that the brothers would have the opportunity of addressing the board at an October 5 meeting. Andrew, as chairman of Holdco, informed Harrison and Wallace of the resolution in a September 16 letter. The ultimatum started an avalanche of threats and accusations. Wallace believed that Holdco's letter was really a veiled plot to remove him from the company. Harrison, he believed, not only wanted him out of the way, but was also coercing the Holdco family members board into collaborating.

On September 18, 1992, two days after Andrew's letter, Wallace responded to the Holdco board, saying he was insulted by their proposed solution:

I hasten to remind you that *all* your wealth today is due singularly to the intense effort and *sweat equity* in this business by Harrison and myself over 35 years. As shareholders, your risks have been rewarded many times over. For you to even threaten to discharge either or both Harrison or myself, shows extraordinary ingratitude, for which you should be ashamed. For the sake of the company, I hope and trust your character is infinitely stronger than what you displayed here. In my entire career, I have never responded to threats and have no intention of starting now. I'll support what I think is right for all shareholders, including myself.

Wallace also delivered the following message at the October 5 Holdco board meeting:

This is in response to Harrison's letter to Holdco of September 3rd, [and] Andrew's letter to me of September 16th, 1992.

Harrison and I have had several days of conversation and I wanted to follow through as per your request of September 16th, and have representation of all families present.

I would like to present my position after a lot of careful thought about our operations and the problem as stated by Harrison between us. I would suggest two separate scenes:

1. Operations: In this regard I suggest following an idea that was suggested by George McClure two to three weeks ago! We each have our spheres of operation, we each have specific executives that answer to us. We should

continue this operation and stay out of each other's spheres.

If either Harrison or myself wish to spend capital or do an acquisition over $1 million then we should consult the other party. If no agreement is reached between us then a presentation is made to the Opco board who will make the final binding decision.

Really quite simple and readily workable. Not the least bit restrictive to either of us!!

2. The other obstacle we have, let's face it, is succession. As you know, we had a painful fall in 1991, however, finally a new board structure was passed. A shareholder agreement was voted on and passed. It was your document, I voted against it—you all supported it 100%. Now I ask you to follow it and support what it says. In other words allow the process to work. It is our by-laws and our shareholders agreement.

Finally, it has been suggested by Kendall Cork and the MRC we have a mediator. We have been given a name by Kendall Cork. I am willing and anxious to talk with one now or at any time in the future.

All the above is my first choice!!

Finally, you know I mentioned originally three last resorts:

(I) Split the company. Geographically and financially with two equal companies. Easily done. Harrison would own 2/3 of company A and Wallace would own 2/3 of company B. Each of the other two families would own about 1/6 of company A and 1/6 of company B. Minority rights obviously must be protected. Example, Birds Eye, sometimes parts are worth more than the whole.

(II) A shotgun arrangement. Fair and equitable to Harrison and myself and no disadvantage to the other shareholders! I'll buy or sell with Harrison.

(III) Sell the company in total.

I will comprise [sic] everything except for three issues:

A) I will not be thrown out of this business or demoted after what I've done for all of you (including Harrison). I'll fight that (with every resource) to my grave, and my sons I think will carry on after!

B) I will not allow Harrison to make the management succession decision (including evaluation of my sons). His interest is biased.

C) I will not play second fiddle to Harrison in this organization. This has been a 50/50 partnership and it's going to stay that way or hang on for the ride!!

Everything and anything else is on the table.

I would like to have your suggestions.

I assume Harrison will present his position as well.

Wallace then marched off to his lawyer, John Petch of Osler Hoskin and Harcourt, in Toronto, who informed the board that their proposal constituted "inappropriate interference" in what was essentially a dispute between two shareholders. Petch reminded them that it was the role of Opco, acting on the advice of the Management Resources Committee, to decide whether Harrison's and Wallace's fight justified a review of their positions. Moreover, Petch wrote, Harrison was attempting to bypass the MRC, which, he held, had the authority to resolve the dispute. Holdco, he advised, should stay out of the dispute.

Wallace then offered Harrison a Solomon-like proposal:

split McCain Foods in half. Wallace would take the North American, Australian and South American markets, while Harrison would own the British and European divisions. The plan made sense, Wallace argued, as McCain Foods had been run in these two divisions for years. Wallace would own two-thirds of his company, Harrison two-thirds of his; the rest of the McCain families would own one-third of both companies.

Harrison responded to both Petch's arguments and Wallace's plan in a letter to Andrew McCain, dated October 6, 1992. In it he rejected his brother's proposal as being detrimental to the interests of all the shareholders. He also pointed out that Opco "has a management which is no longer working together [and] the investment of the Holding Company is being adversely affected by this disagreement and could only be worsened if it continued."

Harrison contended that their dispute over succession changed the nature of the Management Resources Committee, which had been formed before he and Wallace began to disagree with each other. "It is now apparent," he wrote, "that Wallace and I differ greatly in our view of the company as Wallace believes that the McCain Companies are effectively a two-person partnership." In fact, the McCain group of companies was a corporation, with boards of directors and specific corporate by-laws; but it was run by Harrison's and Wallace's two-person management team. Both he and Wallace, Harrison wrote, have equal authority to manage the company, which is owned by all the shareholders. "Unfortunately," added Harrison, "we are not working as the team we once were and, in my view, this working relationship could not be renewed."

On October 29, 1992, Opco held a board meeting at the

Toronto law offices of Fasken Campbell Godfrey, where the succession issue and the brothers' feud were brought out into the open. Harrison told the meeting that, because he did not "relish 12 months like the last 12 months," he wanted the succession issue resolved immediately. He also wanted Wallace's son, Michael, removed from his post as CEO of McCain USA. Harrison said he favoured splitting the U.S. business in two, "with a mature, experienced potato executive as the Chief Executive Officer." Wallace erupted, responding that, with $500 million in business each year, McCain USA did not require two CEOs, and that he was "more than satisfied with the work of the current chief executive officer."

Earlier that month, Wallace had written to the three outside directors on the Management Resources Committee and asked them to conduct an objective study of Michael's performance in the United States:

> I am telling you that as far as the USA potato business losses are concerned, *Michael is the solution, not the problem*, and he is now months away from his *second major business turnaround completion* [wrote Wallace]. On the other hand, Harrison is repeatedly telling you and others that Michael is not capable of handling his current position, knows nothing about the potato business, is the *cause* or at least not sufficiently experienced to solve the US problems, and should be promptly removed from his responsibilities. I have not heard a single underlying *fact* that would support this and I'm not sure how he comes to the conclusion, since Harrison hasn't been to a single meeting, sales call, plant visit, or engaged in a single conversation with Michael on the subject in over *four years*!

If the management study should conclude that Michael was capable of handling his position, wrote Wallace, the company was to pay for the study and put the issue to rest. Should the study indicate that Michael was incapable of the McCain USA CEO post, Wallace would pay for the study and ask for Michael's immediate resignation. "I am 1000% confident in my position," he concluded, "and I'm willing to put my money where my mouth is."

Arden Haynes, the Imperial Oil CEO and one of the outside McCain directors named to the Management Resources Committee, told the Opco board meeting that his committee should not be searching for a new McCain Foods Ltd. CEO unless given instructions to do so by both Harrison and Wallace, or by order of McCain Foods' sole shareholder, Holdco. According to the minutes of the board meeting, Wallace objected to this as well, saying that although the ultimate power of authority resides in Holdco, "the six family members or the Holdco Board were never intended to run the business. That was a clear Opco responsibility."

The next day Holdco held their board meeting in the Fasken Campbell Godfrey offices. Noting Arden Haynes' position that the MRC might begin searching for a new CEO for McCain Foods if asked to do so by Holdco, a resolution calling "for an orderly transition of management from the present Chairman and President to the new Chief Executive Officer" was proposed by Allison McCain and seconded by Harrison's son, Mark. The idea was that a new McCain CEO would be sought immediately. Wallace would step down, but Harrison would remain until the new chief executive was confidently in place. Michael and Scott McCain, seeing that their father had been set up, voted against the proposal, but lost the vote five to two. The process of removing Wallace McCain was well on its way.

On January 22, 1993, McCain business took Wallace to Australia. On the day he left, Holdco called a board meeting in Florenceville for January 27. Among the proposed items of business was a resolution instructing Opco that Holdco would not approve, when asked by Opco to do so, the appointment of Harrison or Wallace as chairman or president of McCain Foods, respectively.

Wallace, through Alan Lenczner, one of his Toronto solicitors, objected both to the timing of the meeting and the resolution. But the meeting went ahead anyway, and the resolution enabling Wallace's dismissal was passed.

• • •

The next few months were taken up with negotiations. Wallace's lawyers warned the McCains that if they voted him out he would have no other recourse but to take the battle public. Wallace again suggested splitting the company in two along geographic lines, but was rejected, again, by Harrison. "McCain is a unique global enterprise and splitting it would be unthinkable, and would be at the expense of our family, our Province, and our Country," wrote Harrison. "Half of Canada would be angry if McCain Foods was split. It is like the Biblical solution of 'cutting the baby in two.'"

On May 6, 1993, or "Pearl Harbor Day," Wallace, armed with a $100-million investment commitment from the Ontario Teachers' Pension Plan Board, and a $175 million operating line of credit, attempted to buy 17.5 per cent of Holdco shares from his relatives, to become the majority shareholder of McCain Foods. The Ontario company that

Wallace set up to buy the shares was "Castlefin," after the County Donegal town from which the original McCains emigrated in search of their fortunes.

It was a bold move. Wallace needed 4,886,700 shares to make the deal work, and there was a good chance, given the anti-Wallace climate of the Holdco board, that his attempt would be seen as a hostile takeover bid. Working with RBC Dominion Securities, Wallace offered $55 per share, provided he gained enough shares to control the company. The financing for the takeover would be arranged by Wallace, so that McCain Foods itself would not go into debt. (He had already paid RBC Dominion Securities $1.5 million to put the offer together.)

"I am making this offer because it is the only alternative which I can initiate myself to try and solve the difference of opinion that now exists as to appropriate arrangements for succession to Harrison McCain and me as co-Chief Executive Officers," Wallace wrote in a letter to the shareholders. It was a last resort option, Wallace noted, that could still be withdrawn if the shareholders agreed to let him stay and to split the company, or to maintain the status quo and to allow the Management Resources Committee to find a new CEO while he and Harrison remained in place.

The offer included management changes, one of which might lure Allison into selling his shares. Allison would be named CEO of McCain Foods in Great Britain after Mac McCarthy resigned. Harrison's role in the company, however, would be greatly diminished. "Harrison McCain would be invited to remain as Chairman of McCain Foods and to become Chairman of Group, if he is a director of McCain Foods and Group," read the offer. And then came the change which Harrison would never forgive: "Wallace McCain would remain President and become the *sole* Chief Executive Officer of Group and of McCain Foods." [Author's emphasis]

Although Wallace later admitted that the words "sole CEO" were a mistake and corrected himself, Harrison saw Wallace's takeover bid as a plot to fire him. The attempted purchase of shares was treasonous, fumed Harrison. Later that summer, Wallace received two letters from his brother— one on the management issue and one on his attempt to purchase shares—in the same envelope. The two letters signified to Wallace that Harrison saw the two issues separately, and not as part of the same problem. "The irony is not lost on me that I should receive two separate letters from you on the same date," wrote Wallace.

"I wouldn't get carried away by a couple of letters in a single envelope," shot back Harrison. "Much sadder is to receive a telephone call from Tony Fell at 6:30 in the evening telling me that my brother and long-time and closest associate is making a bid to take control of our company— that night! That was May 5/93. Dazed, I thought it was December 7/41."

Nor did the rest of the family take kindly to Wallace's "Pearl Harbor" offer; within a week, they had signed a shareholders' agreement blocking anyone from selling shares to Wallace without the unanimous consent of all shareholders. On May 20, 1993, Harrison responded to Wallace's takeover bid with "this is not an offer to purchase shares" typed across the top of the page in block letters. "I find the offer of May 6 unacceptable and the manner in which the offer was handled highly distasteful," he wrote. "The bid was made without prior notice to, or consultation with, the Directors and/

or other members of the McCain family—it was a surprise offer, an unwelcome and uninvited offer, therefore hostile." Harrison therefore asked for his brother's immediate resignation. "Your offer has increased the apprehension of our family members that you are not looking out for our interests."

Wallace denied that his offer was either a surprise or hostile. He argued that he had spoken with Harrison, as well as Andrew's and Allison's lawyers, before making the offer to buy shares. He also accused Harrison of sandbagging his attempts to find a peaceful solution to their differences, and of orchestrating the shareholders' agreement that prevented him from buying a majority of shares in the company.

"You want to change the present situation by having me resign," he wrote. "The whole problem began when you initiated steps last fall to try to force me out of my position as CEO. It is you who has initiated the actions which have led to my proposals for other solutions to the succession issue and which led to my offer."

If Harrison continued to press for his resignation, he added, the only option would be to take the whole mess to court and have the McCains' dirty laundry aired publicly. "If litigation ensues because of your actions the McCain family will not be better off and the Company will not be better off. Everyone will lose, irrespective of how the litigation comes out. Litigation will divide our family even further before it is over and make it a public spectacle in the news media."

Wallace's offer to buy McCain Foods' shares expired June 3 without any takers. As the shareholders' agreement effectively blocked Wallace's takeover bid, Harrison suggested that Wallace was left with only one option: to sell his shares to the company. Harrison said that McCain could buy his brother's shares at $40 a share, for a total of $374 million, half in cash, and the rest in 15 equal annual payments, plus interest. Wallace declined Harrison's offer, which was not only too low but would leave the company saddled with debt, as the company, not Harrison, would be buying his shares.

The brothers spent the summer negotiating. By July, Harrison was offering Wallace $150 million, tax-free; plus $81 million in preferred shares, tax-free; plus $55 million, taxable, for Wallace's 9.3 million shares—roughly $30 per share, Wallace figured. If he accepted, Wallace would have to sign a five-year, global non-compete. "We have no intention to fund a rival," wrote Harrison, "who knows all the inner workings of Opco and who has already said that if he leaves 'he will take his two sons and some of the top executives with him'."

By August, Wallace and Harrison had still not agreed on the terms of Wallace's buyout, and negotiations were stalled. On August 5, Andrew McCain, as chairman of the Holdco board, wrote to its members stating that a resolution to end the brothers' dispute would be voted on at the August 13 board of directors' meeting. The resolution, which condemned Wallace's attempt to gain majority ownership of the company, concluded with the statement: "Wallace McCain is removed as President and Co-Chief Executive Officer," to take effect September 30, 1993.

McCain insiders were shocked at the suddenness and finality of Wallace's removal. Victor Young, the CEO of Fishery Products International in Newfoundland and the last outside director named to McCain's Management Resources Committee, wrote to Andrew saying that the resolution was not in keeping with the spirit in which he was asked to join the board. "I . . . am naturally disheartened at the manner in which you are intending to proceed, given its profound effect on Wallace," he wrote. Meanwhile, John Clements, a former Opco board member, scribbled his feelings in pen and faxed them from his home in Australia. "I would like to express my disappointment," he wrote to Andrew, noting that the company's success was due to the efforts of both Wallace and Harrison, "that such a resolution was felt to be necessary."

Two days before the vote, on August 11, Wallace renewed his offer to purchase just over 17 per cent of the shares in McCain Foods, at $55 a share. The offer was open until August 20. Again, Harrison responded angrily to the offer on behalf of the shareholders. "The McCain Group is an asset of the McCain family, is not for sale as far as I'm concerned," he wrote. "You are well aware of this. Accordingly, the offer is, in my view, a device to try to get a high price at which to sell your own shares, if it ever comes to that, and to try to negate any negative impact of the statements in your offer of May 6, where you clearly said you would become the sole CEO and control both Holdco and Opco Boards. In the latest offer you are magnanimous and will keep me on as Co-CEO as well as leaving the other family members with their existing titles. You don't mention your plans re controlling both Boards."

On August 17 the vote was passed with Wallace's sons, Michael and Scott, dissenting. In a joint statement to the board, they blasted their uncle Harrison for "exercising his influence over certain members of this board" and concluded that the resolution was proposed simply to pressure Wallace to agree to sell his shares at a low price "in order to avoid the public embarrassment and humiliation of it becoming known that he has been fired." Given the company's record year in terms of both sales and profits, the two brothers said they were "shocked" that the board would consider firing their father on the basis of a "so-called serious management issue."

The board passed the resolution and, within a week, Wallace and his lawyers were at the Court of Queen's Bench in Fredericton filing for an injunction to stop his proposed dismissal at the end of September. At the same time, Wallace's spin doctors went into overdrive. A few well-placed phone calls from Toronto-based public-relations consultant David McNaughton of Hill and Knowlton had the media all over the story.

About three weeks before the McCains' feud made head-lines, both *Forbes* in the U.S. and *The Financial Post* in Canada printed glowing portraits of Michael McCain, the man in the middle of the fracas. The *Forbes* article painted Wallace's son as a whiz-kid who turned a $10-million loss at McCains' U.S. operations in 1992 into a profit in 1993, by dropping prices by five per cent per kilogram of french fries, while cutting its own profit margins from 10 to six per cent on its "fancy" french fries. This move cut into the American seasoned french-fry market, dominated by bigger processors. With McCain's com-petitors cutting their profit margins to meet the McCain's price-cutting, the price of seasoned french fries dropped, while the price of plain french fries increased. And McCain owns the U.S. plain french-fry market.

Tagged on the end of the article was a paragraph stating

that Wallace wanted Michael to become the next CEO of McCain's, but was running into resistance from Harrison. The gist of the *Financial Post* story was similar— Michael seemed a likely heir apparent, but Harrison was standing in his way. The stories were set up to protect Michael from a purge should Wallace be fired. After all, it wouldn't look good if the company yanked Michael after both *The Financial Post* and *Forbes* had declared the young McCain perfectly fit for the job.

When the story of Harrison and Wallace's feud became public, those who were most stunned by it were the people of Florenceville, where four thousand jobs hinged on the happiness and success of the McCains. Villagers felt betrayed, like children who can do nothing but watch as their parents threaten—Harrison was prepared to move McCain's head office out of the picture-perfect village—and divorce. Equally stunned were residents of Fredericton, where the McCains' battle was to be fought in a courthouse that had not seen intense media attention since the trial and conviction of Alan Légere, the Miramichi axe murderer.

For the McCain family, their public image as the very model of familial harmony faced tarnishing in a highly watched, lengthy court battle. For the McCain business, the effects of a court fight could be equally disastrous. George McClure, a long-time McCain executive, said that the company's competitors were rubbing their hands with glee over the brothers' feud: there are advantages to be won where the competition is unstable.

CHAPTER NINE

A Dynastic Battle

PICTURE THIS: AN AGING KING SHUFFLES BACK AND FORTH across his throne room, stopping now and then before the window. His eyesight is not as strong as it once was, but he stares long and hard, scanning the horizon for a visitor. His ministers had warned him about this day. His doctors, too, had told him it was coming. Even his own bones remind him that it is time to pass on the crown. His two sons, he knows, are not yet ready for the job. His brother's son is full grown, and is ready to accept the crown. Many believe him tried and able. But the king is determined that this man will not be his successor. That is why he keeps staring out the window. He is going to kill his brother's son, as soon as he comes into sight.

There, in a nutshell, is Wallace McCain's theory of why he is fighting with Harrison—and why it is ridiculous to hope the brothers could resolve their differences: they are locked in mortal battle to determine whose genes continue the family's dynasty. It is a fight that Shakespeare would understand well: yes, Macbeth would be king, but Banquo's sons would rule after him.

"It's been happening through time, through history—it's Biblical," says Margaret McCain, Wallace's wife and the first woman appointed Lieutenant-Governor of New Brunswick, a political gift bestowed by Prime Minister Jean Chrétien in 1994, in appreciation of the McCains'—and her own family's—long-time Liberal patronage. Margaret does not like talking about her husband's feud with her brother-in-law. As she says, "I'm Lieutenant-Governor and that wouldn't look right." But in conversation, punctuated with sighs and the welling-up of tears, Margaret did talk. "Every 24 hours," she says candidly, "we live a drama."

It is indeed a drama. According to one of Harrison's closest friends, Margaret is a Lady Macbeth, hounding her husband into a desperate bid for power at the expense of Wallace and Harrison's friendship. Margaret, they say, convinced Wallace that he was just as important as Harrison, and his children were smarter and more talented than those of the other McCain siblings, and deserved to take over the company after Wallace and Harrison were gone.

The history of Canadian family businesses is littered with corpses. Samuel Bronfman, who built Seagram Co. into the largest distiller in the world with his brother Allan, plotted against his brother's sons, Peter and Edward, turfing them out of the company in favour of his own sons, Edgar and Charles. Because Peter and Edward built a successful corporate empire of their own, that family feud ended relatively happily. Most end disastrously. In 1976, Drummie Birk grabbed control of the family jewellery firm from his cousin Robert. Drummie then promoted his three sons to senior positions in the company; they, too, fought for sole ownership. In 1989, eldest son Jonathan bought out the other two, but the company was mortally wounded. In 1993, an Italian firm picked up the pieces, ending 114 years of family ownership. And when Sam Steinberg died in 1978 after building a small grocery store into a \$1.5-billion-a-year retailing giant, his three daughters fought for control. Steinberg's began losing money, and was eventually sold for \$250 million.

There's something quaint and wholesome about a well-run family business, particularly if it has grown from a mom-and-pop operation. Harrison liked to boast that it might take 50 executives to run a massive corporate ship, but he and Wallace alone ran their entire worldwide operation. But family-owned businesses are particularly vulnerable to wars of succession.

"I've seen this situation more often than I can believe," says Wendy Handler, a family-management professor at Babson College in Wellesley, Massachusetts, and a specialist in family-business disasters. "Succession arguments are seen over and over again when a family fails to do timely succession planning. I've seen lots of businesses sold or liquidated because of it." No matter how close a family has been, she says, brotherly love is the first thing to go once the ownership of the family company is at stake.

Ideally, she says, family businesses should run like publicly traded companies, where discussions of who takes over and who steps down must be open and timely; but this rarely happens. "A lot of this is ego, not wanting to deal with retirement, aging or death," says Handler. "'I rule with my brother,' one of them says. 'What does he deserve? What do I deserve? What about his kids? My kids?' And it's very difficult to go back to the days when they were friends, relating amicably. They're at each other's throats, and emotions are running high."

By the end of August 1993, the fight between Harrison

and Wallace McCain was shaping up into a classic family-business battle. With billions of dollars and family pride at stake, the spectacle of Wallace and Harrison barking at each other in open court made their trial date—September 24, 1993, six days before Wallace was set to be fired—as eagerly awaited as a prize fight. That morning, more than two dozen reporters, cameramen, and media technicians circled the Federal Court of Canada offices in downtown Fredericton.

Unlike the Irvings, their sometime-rivals from Saint John, the McCains had built an empire without rubbing too many people the wrong way. The Irvings are generally seen as insatiable robber-barons who would stop at nothing to get their way. But not the McCains. Although they made a lot of money, the Florenceville french-fry barons are regarded as embodying noblesse oblige, meting out benevolence where needed, to friend and foe alike.

The McCain airplanes were always ready to whisk a neighbour or village resident off to a far-away hospital. In 1975, when McCain Foods' cold storage plant in Florenceville burned down, Harrison and Wallace decided to give away the $2-million worth of undamaged food that had been inside rather than dump it. When Harrison learned, in 1985, of a hay shortage in Georgia and the Carolinas, he sent them two hundred truckloads. And when, in 1989, New York City Mayor Ed Koch ordered water fountains shut off because of a severe water shortage, the McCains stepped in. Their tanker trucks hauling orange-juice concentrate from their New Jersey plant to Grand Falls usually returned empty: why not fill them with "pristine New Brunswick water" on the return trips to supply one fountain in New York City's Bowling Green Park?

However self-serving, such acts had contributed to the McCain mystique, and now they were feuding. Not even the Irvings fought in public. In 1992, when K.C. Irving died, he left an iron-clad will designed to keep the company running his way. A year later, Harrison and Wallace McCain were dodging reporters outside the federal courts building in Fredericton, flanked by 18 lawyers armed with documentation.

• • •

Wallace's statement of claim and attached affidavits, from himself and senior McCain officials and the man in the centre of the fire, Michael, were the hors-d'oeuvres: enough to whet the appetite, but leaving a craving for more. Wallace's sworn court documents bore out Margaret's view of Harrison as a paranoid egoist willing to destroy the company to prevent Wallace's son from becoming CEO. Harrison's 37-page affidavit merely hinted that Wallace was a decent manager until somehow he got the idea that Michael should succeed Harrison and Wallace as CEO.

Wallace's statement of claim was a dry, lawyer's document, requesting a court order prohibiting Harrison and his allies on the Holdco board from removing Wallace as co-CEO. It claimed that McCain Foods was in reality a partnership between Harrison and Wallace, although it operated in the guise of a corporation; therefore McCain's family-controlled board had no right to dismiss Wallace. The judge was asked to resolve the brothers' dispute in one of four ways: splitting McCain Foods managerially as well as geographically, with Harrison and Wallace getting equal shares; dividing McCain's into two equal financial groups; implementing a process whereby one brother could buy out the other; or selling the entire company outright.

The statement of claim may have made dull reading, but the three affidavits filed with the claim were fireworks displays. Wallace disagreed with the appointments of Harrison's two sons and those of nephews Andrew and Allison to senior posts in McCain Foods and on the Holdco board of directors. "Andrew McCain is not in any position to speak on this issue," wrote Wallace in one affidavit. "He has the title of Chairman of Holdco, has attended three or four board meetings . . . and has very little knowledge of the day-to-day business operations of McCain's." Harrison's son Mark received even shorter shrift. "Mark has never occupied, to my knowledge, any meaningful position in a McCain Company. He is located in Toronto, has the title of Analyst and a few times a week sends me clippings from business magazines and newspapers. His knowledge of the daily business operations and strategic decisions of the McCain Companies is virtually nil." Wallace saw nepotism in the appointment of Harrison's son Peter, who was then Vice-President of Export Sales of McCain Foods Canada. Wallace pointed out that Peter reported directly to his father, rather than to Archie MacLean, the chief of Canadian operations. "The appointments of Mark, Peter and Allison were not, in my opinion, based on merit. However, I supported them in the past and I continue to support my nephews as I believe in family harmony and believe that family members should be extended every opportunity in our company."

Wallace's first affidavit, sworn in February to scare the company out of dismissing him, drove home his point that McCain's was a brotherly partnership and not a corporation.

Variations of the phrase "Harrison and myself" appear 50 times in the 52-page document. "Opco was incorporated by me and my brother Harrison McCain in 1956 . . ." The affidavit was filled with so many references to the jobs Wallace and Harrison did together, one might be forgiven the impression that the brothers picked potatoes together, strapped aprons on, and worked the giant french fryers too. About the only aspect of the business that was not shared was the sizzle. "Harrison assumed responsibility for public relations and promotion of the company and its products. As a result, while I shunned publicity, he was identified in the public eye as being in charge, although internally, our executives and bankers knew that we were co-equal Chief Executive Officers."

In his affidavit, Wallace stated that their troubles began in 1988, when the two brothers first discussed restructuring the board of Opco and the succession process. "Harrison McCain wished to control the process," said Wallace. "At the same time, he feared that he might be the first to leave and that if I were left in charge I might designate my son Michael as the heir apparent. This troubled him greatly." Wallace held that their dispute grew when Michael was later appointed CEO of McCain USA and Harrison began to subvert the succession process agreed to in the company's Board Expansion Proposal. In the spring of 1992, when Harrison underwent heart bypass surgery, Wallace acted as sole McCain's CEO for three months. On Harrison's return, Wallace found him a changed man. "After his return from his illness, Harrison became impatient with the [succession] process . . . He wanted to control the succession and the process of succession and feared that, if he had another heart attack, he might lose control over both. Thus, in the summer of 1992, he began a campaign of attempting to circumvent the process or, alternatively, to accelerate the process."

In September and October that year, Wallace continued, Harrison planted the idea in the minds of the Holdco board of directors that the friction between him and Wallace was a management problem that might adversely affect the running of the company. Although Wallace admitted the two were fighting, it was certainly not having an impact on business. On the contrary, Wallace pointed out, McCain Foods sales were up 12 per cent in the first six months of fiscal 1993, over the same period in 1992; profits were up 16 per cent overall, and the McCain Foods divisions for which Wallace was responsible increased profitability by 52 per cent over the previous year.

"There are no serious disagreements between Harrison McCain and myself regarding the operations of the businesses," claimed Wallace. "As we have responsibilities for different geographical areas of the business, there is not much room or opportunity for conflict. I hold Harrison responsible for stirring up trouble where really none exists." As recently as August 1993, Wallace went on, he and Harrison held more than half a dozen meetings that were "cordial, friendly and without rancour."

Moreover, it was incorrect to suggest that the appointment of Michael to the top American spot had destroyed the trust and confidence between the brothers. After all, they disagreed on many things, including the appointment of Harrison's two sons to two key McCain positions and the appointment of Andrew's son Allison to a senior post in McCain's United Kingdom operations. "When Allison McCain was appointed to his position in 1983 in the U.K.,

I was not in agreement. Harrison, however, said he wanted to make the appointment and since the U.K. was in his sphere of responsibility, I did not make an issue of it." The dispute between himself and his brother was solely a succession issue, and did not impact on the orderly management of the company.

Because the McCain group of companies was in reality a partnership between himself and Harrison, Wallace argued, the rest of the McCain family had no place in this fight. The two older brothers had simply invested $20,000 each to get McCain Foods off the ground in 1956, and remained passive investors. Why should his brothers' heirs, he asked, play such significant roles in the company now?

Harrison objected to many of Wallace's assertions, but took particular offence at Wallace's suggestion that their company was a partnership, not a corporation created by the family. When the company was founded in 1956, said Harrison:

The plan was that Wallace and I would work in the McCain "downstream" business while Robert and Andrew H. would continue to direct and control the established "upstream" potato and seed potato supply business . . . Andrew H. and Robert took less active roles than Wallace and I did in the management of the downstream frozen potato business. However, this has nothing to do with their, and now their families' ownership interests. Their investments in the business have always been and continue to be substantial. From the start, the business was conducted as a corporation with four co-venturers. The evolution of ownership has occurred quite naturally as the new McCain generation, the grandchildren of Andrew D. McCain, has matured. Indeed, I believe that it was the expectation of my brothers and me that the family business would evolve in this way.

McCain Foods, Harrison asserted, always was and always would be a family business, run soundly for the benefit of the McCain families. "I do not agree with the statements made in Wallace McCain's affidavits that there was any understanding between us or of the other brothers that he or I were to continue in the management of the business as long as we wished. To the best of my recollection the point was never discussed. I do think it is fair to say that I expected that, as long as we were able to function as a team, we would remain active in managing the business if we so wished."

The brothers functioned happily together as co-CEOs, said Harrison, until the day Wallace appointed Michael CEO of McCain USA. Since then, "an atmosphere of distrust, intrigue and maneuvering has existed." When Holdco voted Wallace out of his senior executive post, their action was spurred by the directors' common interest in the company, not subversion, said Harrison. The problem, he continued, was that Wallace was too interested in himself and his family and not in the company. This attitude, he said, is evident in Wallace's petitioning the court to maintain the "status quo," i.e., allow him to stay on as co-CEO, although the majority of the shareholders wanted him out. "Wallace assumes that the 'status quo' means that he and I remain as 'co-CEOs.' The real 'status quo' is that the majority of the Holdco board have passed a resolution, as they are entitled to do, in order to obtain a new CEO of Opco in whom they have confidence."

Indeed, some of the most damning testimony against Wallace came from his four nephews sitting on the Holdco board. All saw Wallace and Michael as divisive, promoting their side of the family even if it meant destroying the company.

"Prior to Michael McCain being made President of McCain's U.S. operations, his father, Wallace, had been pressing for Michael to become President of that operation," states Peter's affidavit. "The juice business which had been run by Michael in the U.S. had been losing money and Harrison was concerned about Wallace promoting his son to be President of the U.S. operations. Harrison . . . was opposed to promoting Michael until he showed an ability to profitably manage the U.S. juice business, as it would send a wrong signal to the other executives."

Peter's older brother Mark agreed that Michael's performance in the U.S. was anything but successful. "From 1986 to 1990," said Mark in his affidavit, "during Michael's tenure as the head of that business, the McCain U.S. juice business lost over $11.2 million (U.S.), before taxes." Mark also suggested that Michael's quick rise through the McCain ranks was due only to the fact that his father was co-CEO. "Michael had joined McCain while in his early 20s. To my knowledge, he has never worked for any company other than McCain, and he has never worked for any ultimate superior other than his father."

In his affidavit, Michael contradicted his cousins, contending that in fact he had made McCain Citrus profitable:

In 1986, I was promoted to the position of President of McCain Citrus, Inc. in the U.S.A. and took up residence in Hinsdale, Illinois. This promotion was supported by both my father, Wallace, and my uncle, Harrison, who wished me well in my endeavours in the U.S.A. Harrison also advised me that the Company had some serious difficulties and that it would take some time to turn the Company around.

Contrary to what is asserted by Mark McCain, until 1986 I never reported to my father, but reported to other senior management within the McCain Group of Companies. As president of McCain Citrus, Inc., I did report to my father as he was responsible for the McCain interests in the U.S.A. I completed the turnaround of McCain Citrus, Inc. by 1990 and was then promoted to the presidency of McCain U.S.A. Inc. When I left McCain Citrus, Inc. it was profitable and continues to be so to this date.

Michael's assessment of McCain's citrus-juice business was supported by the affidavit of Richard Lan, current president and CEO of McCain Citrus Inc.:

According to corporate records, in 1986 McCain Citrus Inc. was losing money. By the time Michael McCain was promoted to the position of President and CEO of McCain U.S.A. Inc. in October 1990, McCain Citrus Inc. was making money and has been profitable ever since. During the four-year period that Michael McCain was the President and CEO of McCain Citrus Inc. he was ultimately responsible for restructuring the company and putting into place a completely new management team and organization, which continues in place today. As President of McCain Citrus Inc., Michael McCain led a team which: 1) consolidated four acquisitions into one efficient company and in the process turned McCain Citrus Inc. into a low cost producer; 2) re-strategized the business; and 3) refocused the purchasing programs. Michael McCain's leadership led to innovation, ideas, ingenuity, and dedication that turned McCain Citrus Inc. from a money losing operation into a profitable company with a sound structure so as to ensure profitability for many years to come.

Nevertheless, Wallace's nephews blamed the breakup of Harrison and Wallace's close business relationship on Wallace's efforts to promote his son. Peter's affidavit sets out their version of events:

When Wallace appointed Michael President of the U.S. operation over Harrison's specific objections, I believe that the relationship of trust and cooperation, to the extent it then existed between Harrison and Wallace, was destroyed. Events since that time have made it clear to me that that relationship is not capable of being restored.

Over the past several years, I have become aware of a number of incidents where Wallace has sought to run the operations under his control without, as had traditionally been the case, reviewing and coordinating with Harrison major decisions . . . It appears also that information has actively been concealed by Wallace and his son Michael from Harrison. I have been advised by Harrison and believe that McCain U.S. undertook a significant legal risk when it embarked upon a price reduction strategy in the face of a U.S. patent infringement action. I have been advised by Harrison that he was not made aware of the existence of this risk until December of 1992 though Wallace had been advised of the risk in June, 1992. This and other incidents have contributed greatly to the lack of trust between Harrison and Wallace and has led me to the conclusion that they can no longer function effectively as a team.

Prior to Wallace's promotion of Michael in the U.S. and the resulting breakdown in the relationship between Harrison and Wallace, each of Harrison and Wallace had concentrated on parts of the business. However, each historically had significant input into major decisions in the other's area. To suggest, as Wallace does . . . that Harrison and Wallace had historically operated their business independently is not what I have understood to be the case. Rather, I believe that Wallace has attempted in the past several years to insulate those parts of the business which are his responsibility from Harrison's influence. I believe that this has and, if continued, will foster negative internal competition with McCain which will significantly harm the company's ability to compete.

As an example of the breakdown of Harrison and Wallace's business relationship, Peter submitted the following memo, written in February 1993, from Wallace to Harrison regarding crossed signals the two brothers were sending to

McDonald's, the huge international fast-food chain and one of McCain's most important customers:

> All in all Harrison, to give it to you straight, you are screwing me up. I don't know why you are doing it. I know what you are doing is wrong, and I have asked you two or three times to please not interfere with what we are trying to do with sales to McDonald's in Canada and USA, and South America to a lesser extent. You continue to stick your nose in it. I've asked you. Now I'm telling you, please, please get out of this and stay out of it. You can talk to McDonald's all you want—just don't make an initiative to them on the areas that you are not looking after, because it is screwing me up unmercifully and you are going to screw up the company unmercifully. I guarantee you are going to have repercussions in other areas. If you aren't satisfied with this, then obviously this will have to go to higher locations to give you some direction, and I hope that is not the case. Please Harrison, get off it.

The memo, said Peter, "demonstrates the state of deterioration of their relationship" and exemplifies why he chose to vote Wallace out of the co-CEO position. "I could not support the company being managed for another several years with joint CEOs who did not trust each other and could not work together." More important for Peter, however, was his personal distrust of Wallace:

> As a result of my dealings with and during my time at McCain, as well as actions he has taken recently, I can

simply say I do not trust him. In all of my direct dealings with Wallace in the McCain business, I have not found him to be a person whom I could deal with on an open and honest basis . . . He sought to interfere with or undermine my area of responsibilities (notwithstanding that I report to Harrison), my dealings with customers and issues relating to customers, and in some cases inserted the authority of his sons, Michael or Scott.

The following exchange of memos, in November of 1992, in which Wallace strips Peter, then McCain's vice-president of export sales, of his responsibility for selling McCain's dehydrated potato flakes, and Peter's indignant response, shows the strained relationship between uncle and nephew. First, Wallace's memo, addressed to Peter and his colleague David Morgan, with copies to Archie McLean, Bill Mabee and Harrison McCain:

For the last year or two, David Morgan has had the responsibility of looking after inventory of potato flakes, but there have been some problems with the sale of same for different reasons.

To clear things up and hopefully make it better for the company, effective immediately, dehydrates will all come under McCain Foods Limited, and no longer under Export Sales. Peter, I'm sure, will continue to get any leads he can on flakes whether it be in the Philippines or Taiwan, but will channel them back through Dave Morgan who will look after the final sale of such.

This, I think, will hopefully keep everybody satisfied and be better for the company in total.

Bill, would you please see that if Peter has a plus or minus on his budgets from flakes, that it is changed and moved to the parent budget from Export Sales. We'll just handle it then as another sale through our regular McCain Foods Limited sales.

I appreciate everybody's cooperation in this matter. If there are any questions, please give me a call.

Peter's response to Wallace came a week later:

Let's just slow down a minute here. On November 12, you and I agreed to meet with Dave Morgan sometime after December 2nd to resolve this matter. One day later, I receive a memo stating I am to be relieved of all my duties regarding flakes.

I haven't discussed flakes with you in over a year. I've received second-hand copies of memos sent to other people indicating you felt the whole flake problem was Export Sales fault. I sent a memo to you describing the problem and what we were trying to do. No response. I suggested a meeting with other interested parties. No response. Clearly, you have a strong opinion on this matter, but unfortunately, it seems to have been formed before listening to all sides of the story.

We produced too much flake last year. Period. Everybody's scrambling to sell off the excess. As for the alleged poor performance by Export Sales, let's look at the numbers. Sales by all departments are summarized below.

Are sales by Export too low? Could be. On the other hand, with a 71 per cent increase—the highest in the company—I have some trouble swallowing the charge that poor sales by Export have put us where we are. It just doesn't wash.

We sold flakes last year and we're still selling flakes. I confirmed four loads to the Far East just two days ago.

I want a meeting. I'm not interested in giving up any of my responsibilities. I'll be back in the office the week of December 7th.

P.S. In future, if a change in my status is contemplated, I'd appreciate it if I was notified in *person* and in *private*. Getting the 'news' via a memo circulated to my colleagues is a bit much.

Peter submitted another memo to Wallace with his affidavit, written in May 1993, complaining that Wallace bounced him from the McCain's account with McDonald's in Latin America—and replaced him with his son, Scott:

Scott McCain phoned me late last week to tell me that Dick Widman, a Regional Manager for McDonald's Latin America, had contacted him for clarification on a price quote sent out of my office.

I know Widman well and telephoned him. Towards the end of our conversation, I asked him why he'd called Scott, the Vice President of Production, on a sales issue.

Widman replied that Larry Jackson—your chief contact for the Region—had told all his people that Scott was the new McDonald's contact at McCain and that *all* issues and concerns were to be addressed to him. I very diplomatically told Widman that there was a misunderstanding, that Scott's role in the company was confined to production, and that I'd get the matter cleared up.

The Purchasing Agent for Costa Rica told Paul Berger the same thing. At a recent Convention in Sao Paolo, it was announced *to the floor* that Scott was now the man in charge.

Today, as I was writing this letter, I received a call from Paul Berger. Paul had called the Guatemalan Purchasing Agent to discuss general business matters, and in the course of the conversation, the Agent stated she'd received a letter from Scott today concerning some quality problems she'd experienced. She said Scott had been dealing with the matter for about a week. Was Paul, the Manager in charge of the account, made aware of the problems? No! Was I? Of course not!

I'd like an explanation and then perhaps we can discuss *how* we go about clearing up this 'misunderstanding.' I *earned* the right to look after that account. Any recent problems we had with McDonald's were caused by producing poor quality french fries. I'm not trying to hang Scott for that. He's an excellent employee and an excellent guy and these things happen. But to expand his role under the circumstances, and curtail those of the people who built up the business, and continue to build it up, is just another depressingly familiar example of the nepotism and political maneuvering [I] have come to expect from you. You set me up.

It was incidents such as these, not merely the promotion of Michael to CEO of McCain USA, that caused the nephews of Wallace McCain on the Holdco board to propose their resolution to drop Wallace from the company. Harrison's 1992 heart attack added to their concern. Should Harrison die, they thought, there would be nothing to stop Wallace from promoting everyone in his family ahead of themselves.

"A further event which had an impact on the management issue was the heart attack that Harrison suffered in the spring of 1992," said Harrison's son Mark in his affidavit:

Harrison's health condition further influenced him in seeking to have the successor issue dealt with, but I believe that it also had a significant impact on the other McCains who had relied upon Harrison over many years as the guiding spirit of the corporation and family, and became anxious to see a satisfactory resolution of the successorship to the CEO position of McCain as soon as possible. Other than the members of Wallace's immediate family, I do not believe that the other shareholders of Holdco are satisfied to have Wallace hold the position of sole CEO of McCain, today or in the future.

I was not, in the fall of 1992, nor am I now, willing to have Wallace as the sole or co-CEO of Opco. Furthermore, I do not believe that Wallace enjoys the trust and confidence of any members of the McCain family other than his own immediate family. Furthermore, and particularly judging from my observations of Wallace's conduct in relation to his son Michael, and his handling of other inter-family relationships, I do not believe Wallace will put the interests of the larger McCain family and the overall interests of the McCain companies ahead of the interests of his own family.

According to executives who have worked with Michael, however, Wallace had good reason to promote his son to the

CEO post of McCain USA—and probably was right to put him forward as the next CEO of McCain Foods. Richard Lan, the McCain Citrus president who worked with Michael to improve the juice company from 1986 to 1990, said in his affidavit:

> Since October 1990, Michael McCain has used the same talents, skills and commitment to turning around the potato business in the U.S.A. with the result that this business is now making a profit and is poised, with its new management team and structure, to become a significant contributor to the overall profitability of the McCain Group of Companies for years to come. Michael McCain's management talents and leadership in the potato business are highly regarded throughout this organization in the U.S.A.

William Voss, the president of McCain USA, and former president of an $800-million-a-year poultry company, said that Michael McCain has made the company's U.S. potato business profitable. "Prior to Michael McCain's assuming the role of President of McCain Foods, Inc., the potato business was undergoing a difficult time owing to the cut-rate competition that existed in the United States," states Voss's affidavit. "Michael McCain took the situation in hand and over the past 16 months has engineered a turnaround of McCain Foods, Inc. He has revitalized management and staff, refocused the direction of the company, and made it cost efficient and profitable."

The affidavit of Tim Driscoll, the president of McCain Ellio's Foods, Inc., the McCains' American pizza operation, and former vice-president of operations for Lipton's Foods in Canada, described Michael as an intelligent leader:

I was hired as the vice-president of manufacturing of McCain Citrus in 1989 and was given the task of improving the manufacturing operations. I was hired by Michael McCain and over the next four years worked closely with him. Together, we closed some manufacturing plants, built a factory and generally improved the entire manufacturing line. My efforts and those of Michael McCain contributed to the turnaround that the citrus operation is now enjoying.

Approximately two years ago, Michael McCain asked me to take over as senior vice-president of operations of McCain Foods, Inc., the McCain U.S.A. potato business. It too was suffering stiff competition and cut-rate prices. Together with Michael McCain we worked hard at refocusing the business, revitalizing management and improving the organizational structure and the working methods. As a result, that business is beginning to enjoy the fruits of our labours and will be a very profitable business in the years to come.

Over the last four years, drawing on my 25 years of experience with Lipton's, I have been most impressed with the integrity, candor, commitment and intelligence of Michael McCain. He sets out to improve the businesses for which he is responsible, is unafraid to put in teams that can achieve his goals and promotes a willingness amongst staff and management to follow his lead. The result of his leadership is that the three businesses in the United States have all been re-positioned to make substantial profits.

Allison McCain, who worked most of his career at McCain Foods in England, and Andrew McCain, who never worked for McCain Foods in any significant capacity, had little to say about day-to-day problems involving Wallace or Michael. But Allison's affidavit did say that Wallace not only voted against the Board Expansion Proposal Harrison submitted to the family in 1990, but moved many amendments to it—"Some of which in my opinion, were motivated by his wish to position himself to significantly influence the succession process," said Allison. "I had been aware for some time that there was a growing rift between Harrison and Wallace McCain, dating back to October 1990, when Wallace appointed his son Michael as CEO of McCain Foods Inc., the U.S. operating company. At that time Harrison told me that he had opposed the appointment, but that Wallace had made it anyway. This was the first time that I had known either of them to implement an important decision with which the other clearly disagreed."

The most extraordinary information to come out of the nephews' affidavits was contained in nephew Andrew's 39-page statement. In it, he gave a detailed account of how the sons of Andrew H. and Robert McCain, Harrison's and Wallace's deceased brothers, became involved in the Holdco board. Andrew, who became Holdco's chairman, engaged in what Margaret McCain calls "a re-writing of history," inflating the roles of both Andrew H. and Robert in the growth of the frozen-food company, to counter Wallace's claim that McCain Foods Ltd. was a partnership between himself and Harrison, not a corporation under which Wallace could be fired by the shareholders: "In 1956, my father, while working with Andrew H. McCain, developed the idea of starting a frozen-food business and convinced Harrison to join Robert and him in starting such a business," stated Andrew. "They then convinced Wallace to leave his employment and join them. It was agreed that each of the four brothers would invest a share of his inheritance in the frozen-foods business which was incorporated in 1956 as McCain Foods Limited. From the outset, each of the four brothers was a director of the Operating Company.

"Harrison and Wallace played key roles in the development of the business. However, my father and his brother Andrew were also very much involved in it, being consulted regularly and on an informal basis."

Although it was true that Andrew and Robert each invested $20,000 in McCain Foods and were directors of the Operating Company until they died, there is no indication in any company history, or in any interview with Harrison or Wallace, that Andrew and Robert were more than silent partners in Harrison's and Wallace's venture. In fact, Andrew and Robert ran McCain Produce Co., the seed-potato business they inherited from their father.

Attached to his affidavit, Andrew submitted a three-page history of the McCain group of companies, which was full of the kind of factual errors contained in his sworn statement. "In 1956, three years after their father's death," he wrote, "Harrison and Wallace McCain were young men of twenty-five and twenty-three years of age respectively." In fact, Harrison was then 29 years old, and Wallace 26.

"They were both employed in the Irving group of companies." Wrong again. Harrison had left Irving Oil in the fall of 1955, to sell Christmas trees in Florida and look for a business in which he and Wallace could invest their inheritance.

Wallace stayed on at Thornes Hardware in Saint John, but only for the first few months of 1956: he resigned that spring to start up McCain Foods with Harrison.

"Robert and Andrew H. McCain recognized their talents and convinced them to join the family business." Harrison and Wallace did not join the "family business." Moreover, the family business was the buying and selling of seed potatoes. McCain Foods sold frozen food.

Andrew McCain emphasized the importance of Robert and Andrew H. McCain's involvement in McCain Foods: "Particularly in the early years, consultation among the four brothers was regular and informal as they worked together and were neighbours in Florenceville, New Brunswick . . . McCain Produce acted as a major supplier to the Operating Company. McCain Produce and some of its subsidiaries and affiliates also continued the commercial links within the family business, which was, for many years, operated by the four brothers as an integrated whole. For example, McCain Produce supplied the Operating Company with seed potatoes; McCain Produce's equipment division provided equipment to the Operating Company for its field production and occasionally and when necessary shared harvesting duties with the Operating Company.

"During the formative years of the Operating Company, the Robert McCain family lived next door to Wallace McCain and his family in Florenceville. Robert and Wallace spoke regularly about business matters. A two-way radio was set up in the backyard of Robert McCain to help run the farms worked by the Operating Company and by McCain Produce. Robert McCain was often on the radio offering his assistance and advice." That Robert had a two-way radio in his back yard only confirms that he was only involved in McCain Produce, the seed-potato business the brothers inherited from their father. Robert and Andrew H. worked, at best, as suppliers to the frozen-food business.

These were the accusations the brothers hurled at each other, as sterilized by their lawyers for public consumption. But in Wallace and Margaret's home, away from the cameras and reporters' notebooks, the rift between the McCains became an all-consuming issue.

• • •

Margaret McCain was sworn in as Lieutenant-Governor of New Brunswick in June 1994. Ironically, the theme she chose to espouse during her term of office was "family violence." Except for her own immediate family, no McCains attended her swearing-in ceremony. Harrison says they were not invited. Margaret says they weren't asked to come because they didn't show any interest in attending.

The war of words had extended beyond their depositions. When I interviewed Margaret, and later, a friend of Harrison's, the air reeked of a seventeenth-century revenge play: in the heat of the moment, both sides were hurling hyperbole.

Margaret believes the root cause of the feud is not only Harrison's envy of Wallace's children, particularly Michael, or that Harrison is willing to short-circuit the company to prevent Michael from becoming CEO. The fight, she says, is caused by Harrison's inability to relinquish power. Harrison, she says, needs to control the company, even from the grave. Wallace and Harrison may be loath to discuss their feud, but Margaret is exasperated by the spin the family has put on the story. "We were drowning," she says, "in a cesspool of lies and dishonesty. And half-truths, especially."

Harrison's problem, says Margaret, is that he believes he is a king, despite the democratic structure of the McCain corporation. "He has that personality," she says. "Monarchs equate retirement with death. Monarchs equate succession with death, and the successor as the assassin. Succession, assassination. Successor, assassin. Their personalities become so entwined with their creations, the objects of their creations are inseparable. Anyone perceived to be a real threat is an assassin and must be eliminated. It's not succession, it's power. Because succession means taking away power, successor means taking away power."

The McCain story, Margaret admits, would make a wonderful Hollywood movie. "What was it about Michael that the rest of the family hates? Why did Harrison hate him so much?" In answer to her own questions, Margaret considers Henry Ford and his family: "Ford destroyed his own son. He raised him, he nurtured him, he taught him, he had a close relationship with him—until he realized he had created a force. Then he realized he had to get rid of him . . . The seeds of destruction are there. When power takes over, it eventually will destroy."

It all began, she says, with the way Harrison and Billie raised their children: "Harrison's wife very much followed the traditional line. She did what he expected of her, which was to entertain and keep a perfect house and raise perfect kids." The only problem, according to Margaret, was that Billie was not allowed to raise children talented enough to succeed their father. In fact, she says, Harrison's two sons, Mark and Peter, were deliberately stunted by their father. "Harrison had two sons who could have been good, too. They could have been. Their oldest son [Mark] had spirit—and he killed it. I adored that little boy. He was spirited, he was screaming for attention."

Not that Wallace, at first, was anyone's champion dad, she concedes. "When we were first married, I knew that the company was first, I was second, and the kids were third," she says, laughing. After 15 years she decided that it was time the family moved up in the Wallace McCain pecking order. When their sons were pushing ages 10 and 13, Wallace had scheduled a long business trip to Europe. Margaret insisted that he take the children with him—it would be an ideal opportunity for father and children to become close. "The bonding, it happened, and he's the first one to admit it and give me credit," she says. "I sound like I'm bragging, but I carried a healthy parenting model into our relationship and I was prepared to give 100 per cent to our kids, and I expected him to give too, and he gave it."

By way of illustrating Wallace's progress, Margaret recalls an altercation between Wallace and their daughter Eleanor, then in grade 12. The upshot was that Eleanor picked up a book and fired it across the room at her father saying, "That's the worst fucking thing you could say to me." Margaret, who was Chancellor of Mount Allison University at the time, got an earful over the phone from Wallace about Eleanor's behaviour:

> They were having dinner together, and she was telling him about her day, events at school. She was directing a play, and she had to chew out one of the male performers for not cutting the mustard. And he said, "You were too aggressive . . . I just don't think a woman should

speak that way." She said, "You wouldn't have told Scott and Michael not to speak like that," and he said, "That's different, they're men." And pow, he got the book. She was right. He deserved it.

Margaret later persuaded Wallace to apologize to Eleanor for his remark, and told him that both Eleanor's behaviour and his ability to apologize were marks of strength.

Over the years, Margaret pulled Wallace out of meetings at McCain Foods to attend his sons' hockey or basketball games, or parent–teacher nights at school. She made him babysit so he would learn how to put his kids to bed, how to bathe them, how to read to them. "It got so, gosh, he wouldn't miss a hockey game for anything. We went to five a week, I think," she says. But the Wallace McCain family solidarity, in the end, turned the other McCain families against them.

It became a wonderful weapon to use, which Harrison used to implant in the rest of the family an attitude that because Wallace was such a strong family man, he was biased to everybody else . . . and would promote only his own sons. And that was implanted before we realized what was happening. And you know what? We couldn't get past it. You know what's sad, what is really sad? He [Michael] wasn't the most talented, his talents were just allowed to grow. And the rest of them were stunted. And weak people never judge strong people well. As long as one guy over here is performing well, it makes the rest of us look pretty sick, doesn't it? Let's get rid of him.

Even before Harrison and Wallace began fighting, Michael's positioning as heir apparent polarized the McCain families; it was everyone against Wallace and Margaret. "We didn't play by the family rules," says Margaret. "The rules were set down . . . in fact, it was articulated to us: submit or you're out. It was a gang-up, let's face it. And it's absolutely fascinating to think that people as intelligent and as well-educated as members of this family could march in lock-step and speak with a single tongue. I don't know how they do it. My four kids don't speak with a single tongue. Gee whiz, our family dinners can be wild and woolly, because they're all individuals and they express their opinions. But I think that's a mark of strength. To see people march in lock-step, that's a mark of weakness."

And so, with the McCains "in lock-step" behind him, Harrison created the two-tier board, filled with the sons of Andrew and Robert McCain.

The family has tried to deny, or minimize, Wallace's role in the company, to suit their own purposes. [Wallace is] far more responsible for the company than anybody else. He'd be the single biggest factor in the success of the company, but he's the unsung hero. And now, the families of the other two sons want to believe that their fathers had as much to do as Wallace did. All they did was put $20,000 apiece in the company. They had nothing to say. They didn't draw a salary, they weren't even invited to the Christmas office parties. Isn't that significant? No, the governing structure in place now is only there as a vehicle for Harrison to continue to pull strings. To perpetuate his control, his power.

Margaret is confident that Harrison's lust for power will eventually destroy him and the company:

> I think he's got to make a choice, between power and public relations. I think he believes that he'll take the power and deal with the public relations later. But I don't think he understands that by doing this, he's created almost a psychosis that he might never break out of, which will cause the company to implode. People aren't going to work today in that kind of environment. I think that's going to be a killer more than anything else.
>
> There are two rules in the family: his and everybody else's. He can't read other people. The self-absorption is so total . . . he's got four out of five kids on the company payroll. There's another one, we just found out about— one of his daughters. I got into trouble when I confronted him and told him. Accused him of hypocrisy. And it was the first time any woman has ever challenged him: don't you find it ironic that the rationale for this whole feud and breakup was Wallace's nepotism? Blind nepotism?

The holding company board is a disgrace, she says, because it was filled by Harrison with relatives who know nothing about the business. "We built a house in this community, my husband is a senior executive, my children were born here, they go to school here, our future is dependent on this company, and you have these shareholders up here, most of them haven't done anything but carry empty briefcases, sit in offices and clip coupons, buy expensive toys."

If Margaret seems like a woman obsessed with how Harrison ruined her family's relationship with the rest of the McCains, it's because she *is* obsessed—and it is this single-minded placing of her family's welfare above everyone else's that is more responsible for the feud than anything else, says one of Harrison's closest friends, a former New Brunswick politician who often vacationed with Harrison and Billie. "God, she's an obsessive woman," he says. "All of the things she says about Harrison can be directly applied to herself. Look, she's terribly ambitious, very focused, and plenty egocentric too. She calls Harrison a megalomaniac, but you know, the shoe's on the other foot. I tell you, Harrison's got a very powerful woman on his hands. The other thing too, is that she manipulates Wallace like nobody's business."

The story making the rounds in Harrison's circle is that Wallace was moulded by Margaret into the strong man she wanted him to be. "Wallace is really not a bad fellow, you know. I always liked Wallace—it's just that he's the weak sister in the thing," says Harrison's friend.

Margie really controls him. Family nourishment means nourishing Wallace in the direction she wants him to go. She just manipulates Wallace like a toy doll. My God, she drove a stake into Wally's scrotum. She is so full of shit. Wallace for years deferred to Harrison. Wallace recognized that he was the leader, but then Margie started to work him over, I know damned well.

You know, I just can't get over how nasty she can get. And you know that goddamned Margie, she has no sense of humour at all. She's devoid of it. She gets pretty snide about how she can only talk with Billie about recipes for so long, and she makes Billie out as some kind of idiot.

Well, I tell you, Billie was no twit. She was a very supportive spouse and she did a lot to further Harrison's interests, but you know that was fair ball. You have to ask yourself, why did she hate Billie so goddamned badly? This has become a passion with her. Harrison has become a monster in her eyes. She's political right up to her goddamned tits. All this stuff about Harrison playing politics is just such a crock of bullshit.

"My God, she's no one to have as an enemy. And you know, all this talk about Mark, you know Mark wasn't even with the damned company. And Peter, he soldiered away. He's a good, capable fellow. But Harrison never kidded himself that either of them could take over the company. Harrison certainly had ambition for his kids, but Harrison is a realist. He certainly didn't see them as that kind of material. No way. Harrison is very hard headed, and there's no way Harrison would move somebody in unless he had absolute confidence in their ability to handle the job.

As for Michael, the view from Harrison's side of the fence is that he's not as competent as either Margaret or Wallace make him out to be. "I met Michael a little while ago, at their house, and he was just a fresh young upstart at that point," says the same friend. "But I tell you who is a really nice fellow, and that's Scott. I always liked him. Michael seems to turn them all off. He's not a public relations guy. He's arrogant and gets carried away with himself. But Harrison won't talk about them, won't say negative things about them at all. I've yet to hear Harrison bad-mouth members of his family."

• • •

Certainly, no one got to hear Harrison publicly bad-mouth members of his family from the witness box. Both Harrison and the Holdco board desperately tried to avoid a public airing of the family's dirty laundry. Indeed, Holdco attempted to convince Wallace to keep the family feud private. In a letter dated the day Wallace was to bring his action to court, Andrew McCain, as chairman of Holdco, suggested that Wallace's decision to go public was selfish:

> I understand that you are on the verge of deciding to "go public" about your disagreement with the Group board resolution of August 17. I am extremely upset and worried about that possibility. I believe you have been advised that such a move would advance your business interests, but in my opinion, it would cause irreparable harm to the company and the shareholders as a whole. Furthermore, I am personally very concerned that such public exposure would also make all of us and our children vulnerable to the dangers that go with a heightened public profile.
>
> Wallace, while I am not in agreement with your position, I respect your right to adopt that position and defend it but I implore you to consider the consequences for all the McCains of defending your position in the public spotlight.
>
> I fear this is a reckless course of action which will have long-term effects on all of us. I ask you to please reconsider before taking this irrevocable step. The concerns of all parties can be addressed fully and fairly by a private court without a public airing.

Moreover, bringing the dispute to court, said Harrison, was evidence that Wallace was not acting in the best interests of the company, and deserved to be fired:

> I agreed with Wallace that the publicity would be harmful and suggested a form of private alternate dispute resolution. I have raised this point repeatedly with Wallace but received no satisfactory response. Some Opco directors, as well, have urged Wallace to use some form of private dispute resolution . . . The suggestion was not accepted. This further cements my view that Wallace's family is acting in its own self-interest and not in the interest of the other McCain families or the McCain business.

At least 18 lawyers showed up to argue the brothers' case in court on September 24 before Judge Ronald Stevenson of the Court of Queen's Bench of New Brunswick. "This is the annual holiday for the Bar Association of Ontario," laughed Harrison outside the courthouse. Asked what he thought would happen, Wallace answered: "Buy more french fries." His flippant remark held a great deal of truth. After all, neither Harrison's nor Wallace's world would come crashing down, whatever the outcome. Indeed, the dispute may have been a publicity gift: who can buy advertising on the front page of *The Globe and Mail*? Should the judge decide that the family could kick Wallace out, he would still own one-third of the company and more than nine million McCain shares.

On the eve of the court date, Harrison issued a brief press release, re-stating his position that Wallace's removal was in the best interest of the McCain families and the company:

The fact remains that Wallace and I are two business-men in our sixties sitting atop a $3-billion enterprise that is in great shape. To make sure that it stays that way in the future, we need to find a new CEO to take over. It's time for transition. There are lots of reasons. Three families that include most of the shareholders think so. Wallace's family has a different opinion. I have reconciled myself to changing my role in the company. I think it's time Wallace did, too. The issues will get settled through negotiation or a legal process, or both, and we will start looking for a new CEO. We want the best person for the job from inside or outside the company, it doesn't matter. We just want the best.

The spectator sport was over before it started. Lawyers and McCains scurried from room to room in the federal courthouse in a last-ditch attempt to keep the battle from going public. Harrison and Wallace agreed to drop the court case in favour of binding, private arbitration and settlement by April 30, 1994. Judge Stevenson, who would have heard the case, agreed to arbitrate. It was scheduled to begin in January at the University of New Brunswick's Wu Conference Centre, which the McCains would rent for the hearing. The arbitration would not include deciding who would succeed Harrison and Wallace as co-CEO, but only whether the Holdco board's resolution to fire Wallace was proper or whether Wallace had been "oppressed" by the other family members.

Harrison's friend scoffs at Wallace's suggestion that he is being "oppressed." It is Harrison, he says, who is suffering most. The worst tragedy, he says, is that Harrison lost his two closest confidants in the same year: Wallace, his brother and friend, and Billie, his wife. On March 30, 1994, nine months after the brothers were scheduled to begin their court case, Billie died after a lengthy battle with cancer. Wallace attended the funeral service in Florenceville and paid a sympathy call to Harrison in his home; but the rest of Wallace's family stayed away. They weren't at the graveside ceremony, even though Harrison had asked them to come.

"It hasn't been a good year for the McCains," says Harrison's friend. "Especially Harrison. And you can imagine the terrible effect it's had on him, to have lost his best friend in Wallace. And they were so close over the years, he was so fond of Wallace. And there's very few people a fellow like that can talk to, you know. And now his wife's gone, which makes it pretty worse."

CHAPTER TEN

Divide
and Conquer

WALLACE'S AND HARRISON'S BATTLE FADED FROM THE PUBLIC
view when the arbitration hearing settled in at the University
of New Brunswick's 10-room Wu Conference Centre. The
brothers agreed that a New Brunswicker rather than a
retired "Upper Canadian" judge should settle their feud.
Justice Ronald Stevenson, a devout Anglican who had been
chancellor of the Diocese of Fredericton and chancellor of
the Ecclesiastical Province of Canada, was appointed arbitrator of the McCain dispute by the McKenna cabinet, under
the province's Judge's Act. The McCains picked up the tab
for the arbitration hearings, including the rental fees for the
conference centre, salaries for court reporters, and travel
expenses, as well as their lawyers' fees. Judge Stevenson,
however, would continue to draw his salary from the federal
government.

Why would Wallace, whose ace-in-the-hole against the
McCain family had been his threat to air in public the family's business and personal lives, withdraw his civil suit and
agree to private arbitration? Family insiders say that Wallace
acted to avoid embarrassing the family. A more realistic
motive, however, is that it was quite possible that, had the
suit gone ahead in court, Wallace would lose his request for
an injunction against the Holdco board's resolution removing

him from the co-CEO post. Had that happened, Wallace might have languished on the sidelines for months, if not years, while his lawsuit dragged through the courts. Whatever the reason, Wallace and the family agreed on private arbitration, which would take weeks rather than months, signing an agreement that Judge Stevenson's ruling, which would come no later than April 1994, would be binding on all parties.

In mid-January, the brothers and their entourage set up camp in Fredericton for the six-week hearing. On days when he appeared in the makeshift courtroom, Harrison stayed in the apartment he keeps in Fredericton; his lawyers were put up at the Lord Beaverbrook Hotel near the city's legislative buildings.

Wallace and Margaret rented Room 717, the $450-a-night Royal Suite at Fredericton's Sheraton Inn. It is perhaps the fanciest hotel suite in New Brunswick; its balcony overlooks the St. John River and the rooms are fitted out with dark-stained hardwood floors, antique furniture, king-size bed, fireplace, dining room for twelve, bar, CD-stereo, whirlpool and a telephone in the bathroom. Wallace also provided rooms at the Sheraton for their lawyers.

"They kept the rooms on the weekends, even when they weren't there," says a former Sheraton bellhop. ". . . They'd still have the same rooms when they got back. We held the rooms for them."

Hotel staff were in charge of keeping Margaret's car running; its engine was not meant for cold New Brunswick winters. "She had a BMW that didn't have a block heater in it, and we had to go out and start it for her at night and let it run for about 20 minutes. Otherwise it wouldn't start in the morning," remembers the bellhop. "A lot of times we had to boost it. The thing wouldn't start. After a while, it became a pattern and she'd leave the keys with us to start it. I was quite excited, it was the first time I ever drove a luxury car. I drove it around the parking lot—it was great."

The hotel bill, which ran into the hundreds of thousands of dollars, was the largest in the hotel's history.

The number of Ontario lawyers attending the arbitration became a running joke for Harrison. Walking into a strategy meeting at the Lord Beaverbrook one day, Harrison pulled one of his lawyers aside and said, "Tell me, how many lawyers would you say there would be in all of Toronto?" The lawyer, who could see he was being set up, said, "I don't know, maybe three thousand?" Harrison said, "Well, I bet that if you look into it, you'll find maybe five or six that aren't working for one of the McCain families in this dispute. And I'd like you to find them and hire them. Put them on the payroll. There's no reason why they should suffer."

When the lawyers' accounts were submitted, there was little laughter heard around McCain Foods. The lawyers' bill for the four McCains on the Holdco board sued by Wallace came to $7 million. Harrison's legal fees came to $6 million. Wallace's legal bills amounted to $6 million. Add in travel, time and expenses, and the feud cost the McCains over $20 million.

The private arbitration began in mid-January and continued for 10 weeks, rather than the expected six. McCains from all over the world flew into Fredericton to testify as to why Wallace should be removed as co-CEO of their family food empire. Although the hearings were private and both families vowed not to discuss the arbitration, snippets of testimony sometimes leaked out. At one point, Wallace was being questioned by a lawyer representing his nephews; the lawyer was attempting to get Wallace to admit that he didn't have much confidence in his nephews' business skills. After much poking and prodding, Wallace finally blurted out that his dog Zack had more business smarts than all of his nephews combined.

Another piece of the McCain dispute became public when a 149-page transcript of an examination for discovery, containing statements by Allison, Peter and McCain Foods' vice-president George McClure, given at the discovery the previous fall, was mysteriously "leaked" to Eric Reguly of *The Financial Post*. In the document, Allison admitted that, "If I can do the job in a positive manner, I would like to be CEO some day." He also explained why he didn't think Wallace's son Michael would make a good CEO: "Because I believe that he has been a disruptive, divisive influence in this whole affair. And I have some serious concerns that Michael has no interest in what the other shareholders want to do, or what the other family members want to do, or the continuance of this company as an extended McCain family-owned company. Michael has a very great interest in Michael McCain."

Harrison's son Peter said that the only reason Michael was not fired was to dampen the feud between Harrison and Wallace. "I believed that Michael deserved to be fired," said Peter, "but I also believed that it would create further friction between Harrison and Wallace."

Although their battle changed venues, the scope of the hearing remained the same; and family members, as they had done in their affidavits, flung mud at one another. Lawyers for Wallace argued that he had been unjustly removed as co-CEO of McCain Foods, and that this action constituted "oppression" by family members on the Holdco board. They asked Judge Stevenson to order one of the several remedy scenarios proposed by Wallace, such as dividing the company or selling his shares. Lawyers for Harrison and his nephews argued that Wallace's dismissal was within the corporation's bylaws, and that the judge could not undo their decision.

The hearing was over by the end of March, and Judge Stevenson delivered his ruling in April. The judge found that Holdco's resolution removing Wallace from the co-CEO position was invalid because it was not done in the proper manner: the Holdco board alone could not remove Wallace from office, only the shareholders of Opco had that power. Once the Holdco board received that power from Opco, he wrote, the Holdco board might start the process again and might "withhold its approval of Wallace McCain for reappointment." He also found that Wallace had not been oppressed by other family members, so there was no need to rule on possible remedies to the succession dispute. "The removal of Wallace McCain would not be oppressive and would not unfairly prejudice him or disregard his interests as an officer." Stevenson then stretched his judicial responsibilities a bit and wrote a personal letter to Harrison and Wallace, outlining his concern for their relationship and the future of the company. He suggested, as Wallace had all along, that the Holdco and Opco boards be combined into one expanded board, and that the McCains sell 20 per cent of the company to the public:

> While the arbitration hearings were going on a number of people suggested to me that I should meet with

Harrison and Wallace and attempt to bring about a reconciliation or resolution of their differences. In each instance I responded that I was an arbitrator, not a mediator, and that I could not do anything that would compromise my adjudicative role.

Barring some matter being remitted to me by the appeal tribunal or by a court, I have completed my duties. I have decided to convey to you some of my thoughts of the past four months. They are the views of one who is detached from the family and the companies but who now has a wide knowledge of their affairs and some insight into their problems. There is little here that is new. It may seem to be a mosaic of suggestions that others have made. I have arrived at some of the same conclusions that people like Mr. McCarthy and Mr. Haynes had come to.

The CEO's authority should be clearly defined and respected.

I am no expert in corporate governance and do not have a crystal ball, but I am concerned about the future of the McCain business and think that with some concessions and forbearance it can remain a successful business for a long time.

Reduced to fundamentals there are two problem areas —management succession and corporate governance.

Management succession is by far the more important. If the companies fail to provide efficient and effective management the business will suffer and will not survive as we know it. To ensure effective management in the immediate future most family members are going to have to swallow some pride. I do not see any hope of

Harrison and Wallace working together again as they did in the past. It seems Harrison is prepared to retire from his present role but Wallace is not.

While it was not mentioned during the hearings I have been aware of the side agreement of September 23 last authorizing the MRC [Management Resources Committee] to identify suitable candidates for the position of CEO. I assume that process has continued and that candidates have been or are about to be identified.

Harrison and Wallace should continue to be directors and should have prominent consulting roles. I do not suggest any particular titles for them. It's their advice, not their titles, that will be important and invaluable to a new CEO who should be free to call on either or both of them at any time.

All of the members of the second generation who are employed with the company should continue their employment. Those who aspire to higher positions must be patient. One or more of the second generation may eventually serve in the position of CEO. But a normal selection process should be allowed to operate—the cream will rise to the top. All of the cousins must put aside their jealousies and animosities and develop a respect for each other. (The public perceive the McCain family as a tight-knit unit. They do not realize that because of age differences and other factors few close relationships developed among the members of the second generation, other than among siblings in each of the four families.) The cousins must recognize that each of them has his or her own strengths. They must refrain from looking for and stressing petty failures or shortcomings either in individual personalities or in the company operations for which some of them are responsible.

When it comes to shareholders meetings all shareholders must put the interests of the group above personal feelings and personality conflicts.

Corporate governance is another matter. It is fine to look at textbook models of various kinds but every company has its own peculiarities, not least the McCain company. A company must either develop its own model or adapt someone else's model to its circumstances. In my opinion the two-board system has not worked, and will not work, for McCain's.

Unquestionably family representation was essential and overdue. One of the avowed purposes of the Holdco Board was to allow shareholders to become familiar with the company. But five of the six family directors are company employees who obviously have that familiarity in varying degrees. Andrew is the only non-employee McCain who has been placed in the director role. Other non-employees should be considered.

In the family ownership situation that now exists the Holdco board as presently established will, because it is structurally removed from management, attempt to interfere with or exert an influence on management when it should not do so. In his memo of May 1993 Mr. Haynes suggested giving the Opco board final authority for all executive and officer appointments. The corollary to that was the giving up by Holdco of its rights to approve such appointments.

While Mr. Haynes' suggestion had merit, in the long run it will be better if the same people serve on both boards. Both boards should consist, in the immediate future, of

1. Harrison
2. One of Harrison's children
3. Wallace
4. One of Wallace's children
5. A member of the Robert McCain family
6. A member of the Andrew McCain family
7. The CEO
8, 9, 10 & 11. Four outsiders

I deliberately use the words "children" and "member" as the women in the family should be considered as well as the men. Eleven of the 18 members of the second generation are women.

I understand the articles of Opco may have to be amended to allow for a larger board but that is not a serious obstacle.

When a McCain is CEO, the representation of his family group on the board would be reduced by one.

The presence of four or five non-family members (the CEO being the fifth) on the board would have a leavening influence and should deter inter- and intra-family disputes.

A consensus should be sought as to whether family members in the employ of the company (other than Harrison and Wallace) should serve on the board. Some of them may withdraw voluntarily. In the present climate it might be better if most or all of them did not take seats on the board for a year or two. If the configuration I suggest were adopted one of Scott or Michael and one of

Peter or Mark would be eliminated in any event.

Once things have settled down and a strong public image of McCain's has been restored, the company should seriously consider a public equity issue. It would not be appropriate for Holdco to make such an issue. It could create a temptation for a family member or members to buy enough shares on the market to give them majority control. A share issue by Opco would not affect control. Holdco would continue to hold a majority of Opco shares. Again, the presence and influence of non-family shareholders, like the non-family directors, would act as a restraint on inter- and intra-family disputes.

I make these comments with some reluctance. It may be inappropriate for a sitting judge to do so. But the importance of the McCain business to New Brunswick, and my personal acquaintance with Harrison and Wallace, justify what may be a departure from the normal rules of judicial conduct.

I address this memo only to Harrison and Wallace and their counsel for two reasons. First, I knew Harrison and Wallace before the arbitration. Second, unless some of my suggestions find favour with both of them there is little point in conveying my thoughts to the other parties. You are free to pass my comments on to the other directors and shareholders if you see any value in doing so.

• • •

While Wallace celebrated his victory at the Sheraton in Fredericton, the rest of the family went back to the drawing board to ensure that, when they fired him again, he would stay fired. In August Wallace wrote to Harrison, asking that he accept Judge Stevenson's recommendations. Harrison refused, saying the company's shareholders would decide the fate of McCain Foods. Rather than wait for the company to dismiss him again, Wallace launched a pre-emptive strike against Harrison and the rest of the McCain family. In September 1994, he filed another lawsuit, in Moncton, asking the court to accept Judge Stevenson's proposals to restructure the company and sell some of its shares to the public.

His relationship with Harrison, wrote Wallace, was at a "complete, absolute and irrevocable end." Wallace argued that because McCain Foods was a partnership between himself and Harrison—and not a family business as Harrison and the rest of the family claimed—the judge had the power to dissolve the partnership and force Harrison's side to buy out Wallace's shares at a fair price. During the impending court action the brothers once again fired angry letters at each other.

"I would have thought that despite our differences, my older brother and partner would not have so consistently tried to distort the facts," wrote Wallace. "To accuse me of trying to manipulate people is akin to the pot calling the kettle black in the extreme." Wallace said he was sorry that he was forced once again to go public with his fight with his brother. He was, he wrote, "sorry for our family, our company, and our province that you have not seen fit to support these recommendations."

Harrison, noting that he began to get telephone calls from the media shortly after he received Wallace's letter, accused Wallace of writing the letter for purely "cosmetic reasons." Wrote Harrison: "You are trying to mislead the judiciary, our employees and the public in general. You put your own self-interest before our family, our company and our province."

On September 12 Wallace went to court; on the same day, McCain Foods' shareholders were carefully studying Judge Stevenson's ruling, which outlined how they had wrongfully demoted Wallace, to make sure they got it right this time. Holdco first transferred to itself from Opco the power to demote Wallace, and then voted to demote Wallace to corporate vice-chairman, a hands-off title Wallace would not accept. But the vote by the Holdco board, which would make Wallace's ouster official, would not come until after Justice Paul Creaghan, the New Brunswick judge hearing Wallace's latest suit, ruled.

Alan Lenczner, the Toronto lawyer representing Michael and Scott, who had moved to suppress Holdco's dismissal of their father, opened the proceedings with a question: "I ask rhetorically—What is the rush?" Wallace's team argued that there was nothing in McCain Foods' balance books to indicate that Wallace needed to be fired immediately; indeed, McCain Foods' profits had increased 40 per cent in the year ending June 30, 1994. Lenczner accused Harrison and the Holdco board of withholding information on their search for a new CEO from Wallace, and that Wallace had a right to participate in that search. "He has an enormous investment of money in this company," he said, "and he has given his life to this company. He is most interested in having a say in who is the CEO who will govern his investment." Lenczner also said that the McCain business in England and Europe, which had been controlled by Harrison for years, was in trouble—and needed Harrison's complete attention. "Harrison

McCain can't fulfill the sole job of CEO. The company is too big," he said.

But Charles Whelly, the lawyer representing Harrison and the Holdco board, said that increased profits didn't mean that a protracted battle between the brothers wouldn't hurt profits later. "There is a management problem that is being addressed by the board," he said. " . . . The shareholders have the right to decide what they want their company to do."

Inside the courtroom, the battle lines drawn by the brothers were evident even in the seating arrangements: Wallace and his supporters sat on one side of the courtroom; Harrison and his faction on the other. The brothers rarely looked at each other. Outside, relations seemed a little warmer. During a break, Wallace hustled to a nearby Tim Hortons donut shop and returned with a tray of cups of coffee, which he brought into a meeting room with his lawyers and children Eleanor, Michael and Scott.

A few minutes later, Harrison was walking down the hallway just as Eleanor swung the meeting-room door open. Wallace passed Eleanor one of the cups of coffee. "There's your coffee right there, Harrison," Wallace called out to his brother. Eleanor gave Harrison the cup and Wallace returned to his meeting.

At another break, June Hayes, a former restaurateur from Petitcodiac, slipped Harrison a note. Harrison laughed and said, "This isn't a subpoena, is it?" Hayes, who had met Harrison in 1958 when both were starting out in business, was volunteering to arbitrate the family feud. All she needed was "15 minutes of your time," she said.

But her offer came too late. By the time Wallace and Harrison went to court the next day, 65 per cent of McCain

Foods' shares had voted in favour of removing Wallace; the Holdco board merely waited for Judge Creaghan's ruling to make it official. John Campion, the lawyer representing the McCain food empire, told the judge that, as they had fired Wallace according to Judge Stevenson's recommendations, he was simply trying to forestall the inevitable. As for Wallace, Michael and Scott's claim that they should be allowed to participate in the succession process, Campion argued, Wallace rejected that right by not agreeing that Herbert Stone, a consultant hired to find the new CEO, should begin his search. "They are the authors of their own misfortune on that information and the lack of delivery of it to them," he said.

In their closing arguments at the three-day hearing, lawyers for McCain Foods said the judge should dismiss Wallace's suit for two reasons: first, it was based on a set of facts already ruled upon by Judge Stevenson; second, that part of Wallace's lawsuit asking for remedies to the feud was based on a provincial law that governs the liquidation and dissolution of companies—and therefore, McCain Foods' lawyer Charles Whelly argued, did not apply in this case.

Lawyers for Wallace and his family argued that the judge should block Wallace's removal from the company. Lenczner argued that Wallace, because of his large stake in McCain Foods, should be allowed to stay with the company at least until a new CEO was chosen, suggesting that the company desperately needed Wallace's business smarts, and that profits might suffer if he was fired.

"Wallace McCain," he said, "is absolutely interested that that not occur. He says, 'I'm running my side of the business perfectly well but there are problems on the other side that require attention.'" Harrison's half of the McCain pie,

Lenczner said, had lost $7 million in one month that year. "[Harrison] is not capable on an interim basis of operating the whole company anyway, but particularly when the U.K. and Europe companies require attention."

Lawyers for Wallace asked the judge to consider three possible remedies to the feud: replacing both Holdco and Opco boards with one expanded board; ordering that Holdco allow 20 per cent of McCain Foods' shares to be sold to the public, thereby allowing some shareholders to bow out; or, in the last resort, ordering a buyout of Wallace's shares at a fair market price.

Judge Creaghan's ruling, which was reserved until the end of September, came down squarely on the side of McCain Foods. He dismissed Wallace's and his sons' applications for an injunction halting Wallace's dismissal as co-CEO. Such an injunction would cause the company irreparable harm, the judge ruled. Wallace, he said, had made "a significant contribution to the success of the company in the past." But that, he added, "is not to say the company cannot successfully operate in the present without guidance" from him. Creaghan said the Holdco board was well within its rights to fire a CEO, and that the courts should not interfere with corporate decision-making. The judge also ruled, however, that Wallace could come back to court to seek an order that would force McCain Foods to restructure its boards, sell some of its shares to the public, or buy out the Wallace McCain family shares.

Wallace's dismissal—more precisely, his demotion to corporate vice-president, which he refused to accept—was effective almost immediately following Judge Creaghan's ruling. Although Wallace was fired for promoting his family's interests above those of the company, Harrison promoted his son Peter to President of McCain Foods International, Inc., a couple of weeks later. Wallace's family seethed.

"Don't you find it ironic that the rationale for this whole feud and breakup was Wallace's nepotism? Blind nepotism?" asked Wallace's wife, Margaret. "And did you see what happened, ten days later? Don't you find that ironic or slightly hypocritical? The real irony is that this son who was appointed was the one who articulated why Wallace had to be fired. He was at the meeting. It's in the minutes. He was the one who said, 'Yes, he has to be fired for appointing Michael to that job in the United States against Harrison's wishes.' That's the reason, right? And ten days later, look what happens. Where are these people? I mean, where are their minds?"

In January 1995, Wallace and his lawyers went before Judge Creaghan again, to order McCain Foods to buy out his shares in the company, as suggested by Judge Stevenson in his "side-letter" to the brothers. (Wallace and Harrison had been negotiating the price of Wallace's shares for months. Wallace demanded between $700 million and $800 million for his 34-per-cent stake in McCain Foods, while Harrison refused to budge beyond $400 million.) Lawyers for McCain Foods argued that Wallace could not start another legal proceeding because he had forfeited that right when he signed the contract giving Judge Stevenson the final say in the dispute. Under section 13 of the contract, the parties were not allowed to initiate "injunction or other proceedings" on the same matter. "If he has misfortune," said McCain Foods' lawyer Lorne Morphy, speaking of Wallace, "he is the author of it."

It took Judge Creaghan less than two weeks to rule on

the matter. He decided that because Holdco acted legally in removing Wallace as co-CEO, it could not be forced to compensate him. He also ruled that the partnership between the brothers had been dead for a number of years, replaced by a corporate-board structure. Because Wallace was asking for relief under a provincial law governing the winding down of partnerships, he could not sue. McCain Foods, he concluded, "was not operated as though it was a partnership but was subject to the norm of majority rule [which] is binding on the parties to the present action."

Three strikes, and Wallace was out, outplayed, as he saw it, by his older brother in a long power struggle that involved the winning of the support of their nephews. Wallace was simply unable to read people: he just didn't see all the McCain shareholders, except those in his own immediate family, lining up against him—until it was too late.

"It never crossed my mind," Wallace says, looking back at the events that led to his dismissal. "We always ran as a partnership, we operated as a partnership. I never thought it could possibly happen. At the time, my wife said, 'You know, you're going to get fired.' She told me that in 1990. She said, 'You're going to get fired by your brother.' It almost caused a divorce right then. I was so mad that she could think such a thing. But it was true. She said, 'I can see it coming. You're going to get it.'

"Yeah, she saw it happening. I didn't. And I knew I didn't. I trusted. I trusted my brother 100 per cent, and unfortunately, Harrison has a thousand good attributes, but he doesn't trust people. He doesn't trust anybody. Nobody, including me. And I trusted him, and I generally trust people. And that was my downfall, actually. But if I had not trusted him, I wouldn't have founded the company initially. If I had not trusted him personally, I couldn't have worked so closely with him."

Although he will generally smile and tell reporters that he has put it all behind him—the public humiliation of being fired by his own family, the feud with his brother—his emotions come to the surface easily. At one point when he discussed how painful it was to move from Florenceville to Toronto, Wallace wiped tears from his eyes.

He is reluctant to call his battle with Harrison a power struggle—"There wasn't power as far as I was concerned, because I agreed that I was leaving and someone else was coming in," he says. Rather, he recounts the events leading up to his dismissal and leaves it to others to figure out what was going on.

His first mistake, said Wallace, was not wooing the sons and daughters of Andrew and Robert McCain, as Harrison had done, after their fathers died. "We should have recognized—and you can blame me as much as Harrison, at least as much—we did not bring the other two families into the company. We ran it for so long by ourselves. Andrew and Bob were passive investors who really had received very little dividends that made a lot of money out of the deal. So they had received the dividends, but they never gave us a hard time.

"And when they died, we should have recognized and we should have got involved. I think Harrison did some, without my knowledge actually, some of that personally, because I saw that in some of the files of the court case where he was sending some information to members of the family. He didn't tell me. Not that it was wrong. It was right, but we should have done it together."

Wallace admits he was high on Michael becoming CEO one day, but only because he believed he was qualified to do the job. "Michael had said, since the time he was four or five or six years old, that he wanted to work in the business. Scott never said for sure he wanted to go into the business until he finished university. [I] wanted them to join the business, but I didn't pressure them at all. His mother, to the contrary, would have been happy if he [Michael] didn't join the business.

"I think [Michael] is a good executive. He's stubborn, but he's got a good reputation. I've worked with him long enough to know that he's a good executive, he has good rapport with his employees, but he's hard enough too that he's got some backbone. He's hard to handle, but I think that makes a good executive. Michael is not a yes-man. I don't mean that he likes to argue, but if he doesn't agree with you, he'll certainly tell you. And he doesn't care if it's you or the pope. . . . That has not endeared him to some of his relatives. We brought up all our children to be independent, and they are."

The fact that Wallace trumpeted Michael as future CEO of McCain Foods after he and Harrison retired had nothing to do with the fight. "That was an excuse. I'm perfectly satisfied in my own mind that . . . the scenario with Michael was a red herring.

"The problem used to be classified as all Michael. Then the problem was classified as all my wife. In between there was me. It was all Michael, it was all Wallace, it was all Margaret. But to say it's one of those three things as the leading cause, there's no facts to support that. None. Zero."

In the late 1980s, when Wallace met and hired John Ward, a family-business consultant from Chicago, one of

Ward's first pieces of advice was to stop promoting Michael. "He's a great guy," said Wallace of Ward.

I met him once or twice, and then Harrison and I had two meetings with him. And I changed all my positions, all my thoughts about what I should do after I talked with him. I learned a lot about what I should do and what not to do with family businesses from him.

He said, "The best thing you should do is, a: get your family involved." Good advice. Put them on the board. "Have one board, not two, if you want them involved." Number two, he said, "Get the outsiders on the board on a committee and let them do the succession." And he said, "Wallace, shut up about who you think should run the company. Shut up about Michael." He was right. I did shut up about it then, but I had talked about it too much. He said, "Drop it, Wallace," and I did drop it. He said, "Put in one board, put in the outsiders, and have them choose it."

I got the outside committee, and I got part of what I wanted—I had the outside committee, and they were going to choose a successor. And then Harrison got the two-tiered board—which he had in the back of his mind for a long time, I found out afterwards—and he controlled that board . . . but I didn't catch on, I didn't.

The MRC [Management Resources Committee] had a mandate. There was supposed to be four on the MRC. One [Arden Haynes] resigned over this thing here. The other three stayed, and what they were supposed to do was when Harrison or I retired or resigned or dropped dead, whatever, they—not me, not Harrison, they—were supposed to pick the successor. They just followed the deal. I clearly told them whoever they picked, I would support. I told them that, written, verbally, 20 times. . . . My brother decided that they might not pick someone who [suited] him, and he changed the rules . . .

Harrison always has been a good businessman. He just changed his personality after he had that heart attack. That's when he changed his personality . . . He was a good salesman. First-class salesman. And he was always conservative in our financing, which helped us. And he's aggressive, a hard-working man, always worked very hard, so he has natural instincts in that regard. He's a natural entrepreneur.

Some of his power things and his ego got out of control. That started before, power and ego, and unfortunately, after he had the heart attack, that affected his judgment. I could be wrong, but I think it did. Today he's not the same man I worked with for 35 years. Back in the eighties, I think he took some decisions about what he was going to do. Harrison is the type who would think ahead, and I think he made himself up a plan then. But when he had his heart attack, I think he jumped the pattern. He just made some personal decisions that were very erratic.

The manipulation that Wallace suspected of his brother by the late 1980s, however, was evident to Michael much earlier. At a sales meeting in Quebec City in the early 1980s, Michael and Harrison locked horns over what Michael saw as Harrison's control of the family. "I was raised on a strict diet of direct communications," says Michael. "Jesus, the rhubarbs we get into in our family would just make your feet rattle. That's Wallace's style—he's a very direct, open, blunt, honest communicator. And I was raised on that style. And I was taught that being a blunt straightshooter is important. I don't remember how we arrived at this topic, but we were talking about being political. I said, 'You know, Harrison, I always thought that you were like that, too. Everyone always said that you were a direct, straightforward shooter.'

"You know what he said to me? He said, 'Michael, I am. And that's right—except when it comes to family. The family can't handle the truth.'"

According to Michael, Harrison confessed to being a "student" of Machiavelli. "Harrison was under the weather at a cocktail party one night," says Michael, "and I used the adjective, 'so-and-so was Machiavellian.' And it struck a chord. He pulled me over to the corner and said, 'Have you ever read *The Prince*?' And I said, 'Well, no, I've never read it, but I'm familiar with the doctrine.' And basically he went on a long diatribe about how he was a student of the doctrines and principles and the techniques that were articulated in this book. I didn't pay a goddamn bit of attention to it until the last several years. I went back and researched it a little bit, because it stuck with me. And Jesus, he's true to form."

Harrison, however, says that his thinking about succession, and his concern later about Wallace's "nepotism," was anything but extraordinary—or manipulative. Moreover, he says, Wallace was in favour of the Board Expansion Proposal until it came time to vote. "He contributed substantially to all the things that make up the two-tier board system that I had signed," says Harrison. "In fact, we changed those structures repeatedly, to see him satisfied. And then when it came back to the board, he voted against it. Which did surprise me."

Harrison calls it ridiculous to suggest that he courted the shareholders and aligned them against Wallace. "These people, they all have university degrees, one or two degrees apiece," he says. "They're not 15 years old. There's only a few of them in their twenties. Most of them are in their thirties or forties. Well, are you going to line up 15 or 20 of your nephews and nieces with a whip or something like that? They're all well educated, they all have money . . . I definitely didn't go to talk to them at all. Wallace went and talked to them all."

According to Harrison, the rest of the McCain shareholders didn't need convincing that Wallace had to go. They had all seen him advance his two sons over the interests of the company. "I wasn't satisfied, nor any other individual shareholder—save Wallace's family—to have Wallace as CEO. Not because he wasn't a good business executive, but because they couldn't trust him in his judgment about family matters. Like appointing Michael . . .

"And neither I nor the rest of the family want to lose our fortune in order to satisfy Michael's ambition. Because we didn't think he was capable of doing it, we were risking our fortune. And we didn't choose to do that, and that was an opinion shared by everyone. Each and every one, individually, except Wallace's family. Another reason I was against it [Michael's appointment as CEO of McCain USA] was it would have been nepotism. That was transparent. It was a bad business decision. And it was not the way we ran the company for all those years. That's why I was so shocked by it."

Wallace's appointment of Michael against Harrison's veto

upset Harrison most of all. It was a time-honoured tradition between the brothers that they would not act on anything against the other's disapproval. "[Wallace] de facto did it," says Harrison. "What could I do, shoot him? Unplug the fax machine? What would you want me to do? We had a mutual veto for a long while. That day he didn't acknowledge the veto. That's what was earth-shaking to me."

There was no other remedy, says Harrison, except to remove Wallace from his position—and the majority of shareholders didn't need much convincing. "If [Wallace] had been CEO by himself, well, he would have been happy—and everybody else would have been sore. The others that were sore were 65 per cent of the votes. So you know what would have happened to McCain Foods? Bye-bye."

• • •

An old friend of both Harrison and Wallace, Bev O'Keefe is a big, intimidating man who tends to shout rather than speak to his visitors. He worked with them for K.C. Irving in the 1950s, after Harrison hired him as a junior salesman in the oil business, and again in the 1960s and 1970s, serving first as McCain's sales manager for Eastern Canada, and later, as the head of Thomas Equipment, the McCain farm machinery subsidiary. In 1977 he became the majority shareholder in Juniper Lumber, the old sawmill that had become a financial disaster for former premier Hugh John Flemming. After Harrison helped bail the company out, O'Keefe put $75,000 of his own money into the lumber company and worked it night and day until it made a profit. He has great respect for people like the Irvings and the McCains, who devoted all their time to business. One of the highest compliments in O'Keefe's sometimes earthy parlance is, "You know, that fella has a fucking smell for the dollar."

O'Keefe has lived in Florenceville for more than 30 years now, and has worked with or befriended just about every member of the McCain family. In the past few years, however, O'Keefe says his respect for his old friend Harrison McCain has disappeared. He saw the feud brewing long before Michael McCain and the whole succession question was made an issue.

"I worked with Harrison one day and Wallace the next day," he says. "Or I'd have to go to someone for a decision, it didn't make any difference which one you went to, there was harmony among the ranks. They displayed love and respect, call it what you may, for one another. That went on for a long, long, long while. And I could see that changing."

Harrison began "hobnobbing," as O'Keefe puts it, with movers and shakers such as Jim Pattison in Vancouver, who owns 100 per cent of the Jim Pattison Group, his $3-billion-a-year company. "Harrison wanted . . . to have virtual control of McCain Foods," says O'Keefe.

He had made up his mind that he was going to have the controlling interest in McCain Foods. And the first move he could make was when Bob died in 1977. Sixteen per cent of the shares there.

And then Andrew died in September of 1984. So that was another 16 per cent. Up until that time, young Allison wasn't going anywhere with McCain Foods. He had been an engineer with the telephone company, because his father was on the board of directors. So then Harrison started courting that family. So you see, he was jockeying in for 16 and 16. He had 34 and Wallace had 34.

Then he decided what he should do was have two boards, an operating board and a holding board. And Wallace relied a lot on Harrison's judgment, because Harrison was always the up-front man, saying, "I'm the fellow who does all the financing and this is how it should be done." As far as I'm concerned, that's where the whole problem started. Michael's situation was only a front, but a real front, because Michael had the up-and-coming brains to be, someday, the CEO. Because Wallace's family, both Michael and Scott, were making contributions to the company when Harrison's two sons were not making any contributions to the company.

O'Keefe saw all the moves, but being a friend to both brothers, decided to remain neutral. But when word leaked out, in the fall of 1992, that Harrison was attempting to remove Wallace and was blaming the move on Wallace's promotion of Michael, O'Keefe marched over to Harrison's office in Florenceville and gave him an earful. He remembers the conversation like it was yesterday, and in true New Brunswick fashion, tells the story in loving detail:

Harrison often said to me, he said, "You know, O'Keefe, you and I are good friends. Anytime you ever see me getting greedy or too goddamned big for my britches, come tell me, will ya?"

I said, "Sure, I'll do that."

So I would say about three years ago, I called Harrison one day, and I said, "Harrison, I'd like to come have a chat with you."

He said, "Sure, when would you like to do it?"

I said, "Well, I'm in Juniper, and maybe I'll leave a bit early and I'll come in and have a chat with you."

So we chatted for a few minutes, but then I said, "Harrison, I'm here for a purpose. More than on one occasion, you often said to me, 'If I ever get too big for my britches, and greed stands in my way, for Christ's sake, come and talk to me.'" I said, "Do you recall that?"

He said, "Yes, I do."

I said, "Well, I'm here to accept that invitation, because that's what I want to talk to you about right now."

He said, "Jesus, what the hell are you talking about?"

So I told him. I said, "Jesus, what I'm hearing on the goddamned streets and around the telephone poles here at night, under the lamplights, when I travel around Montreal, Toronto and New York, in business circles, Jesus, for two brothers that went and built a business with love and respect for one another, what I'm hearing on the street, Jesus Christ, Harrison, it's ludicrous."

He said, "You understand what this is all about?"

"Well," I said, "based on what I hear on the street, it's succession."

"Well," he said, "that's right. I owe it to the shareholders to make sure they get a good deal."

I said, "Harrison, Jesus, you're only 65 years of age. You and Wallace got a deal that you're going to continue until you're 75. And at age 75, you're going to do something about it. So what stirred this thing up so fast?"

"Well," he said, "I don't think that Michael is ready to take this over."

I said, "Did Michael ever say that he was going to

take this thing over?"

"No," he said, "but I didn't agree with my brother when he appointed him."

I said, "Did your brother ever say anything to you, when you appointed Allison managing director in England?"

"No, but he opposed it because he didn't think Allison was a good decision-maker."

"Well," I said, "he allowed it to happen because you were running that company, and you're on your own, and hip-hip."

So one thing led to another, and he said, "You know O'Keefe, you got your goddamned nerve coming here and talking to me about this."

"Well," I said, "do you want me to leave? I came here because you invited me to come here a few years back. And I'll tell you something, I'm not picking sides."

"Tell me," he said, "how is it you know so much about this?"

I said, "It's pretty goddamned simple. You got your nephew down there, Andrew in Woodstock . . . he runs big speedboats, all kinds of goddamned ski-doos, all kinds of cars, does whatever the hell he wants, collects a goddamned big dividend off his father's stock in this company, and you got him as chairman of the board of the holding company. Christ, Harrison, he doesn't have the goddamned brains to keep his fucking mouth shut. And he's telling everybody, so it's becoming common knowledge on the street."

"Oh," he said, "he's a smart young fella."

I said, "Lookit, Harrison, don't give me that fucking

bullshit. Smart young fella? Jesus Christ, I remember coming here and he was in diapers. What the hell does he know about the fucking food business?"

"Well, you know," he said, "his mother's smart."

I said, "What the fuck does she know about the goddamned french-fry business? Anyway, that's beside the point. You fellas got a deal for another 10 years."

He said, "How do you know that?"

"I know it. It's a fact. And you know it's a fact, too. You can't dispute it."

"Well," he said, "it is a fact. I don't know how the hell you learned it, but it is a fact. At any rate, I appreciate you coming in and having a chat with me, but I've got things to fix in my mind now. But I'll tell you what I'm going to do. I'm going to call Wallace and let him know that you were in to see me."

"I hope you do," I said. "Because you know where my next call is? It's to Wallace McCain. Because I'm going to have the same goddamned conversation I'm having with you. And I may not even stop there. I may even call some of your CEOs that I know quite well. Because if this keeps on going, you're going to create some major problems in your business."

He said, "Lookit, O'Keefe, you don't know what the Christ you're talking about. Furthermore, about 17 or 18 years ago you got the opportunity to go into the lumber business. Just don't ever forget it. I helped you, I put you there."

I said, "Lookit here, McCain. Eighteen years ago, in order for me to get into the lumber business, it cost me 75,000 bucks. I had to raise a new mortgage on my home,

I raised a second mortgage on my home, and I borrowed some money on my own, and I raised 75,000 bucks, and I put it in that fucking business. I've gone through two fucking recessions, I've worked like a son of a whore. Don't you ever, ever tell me that you passed me on a golden platter the lumber business, because it ain't fucking true. And I don't wish to, want to talk about that anymore."

So Wallace wasn't at home, but I got him in Toronto, and I talked to him along the same lines. The next one I called was Archie McLean. I said, "Archie, what the hell is going on here?"

Then I called Mac McCarthy in England, who I know very well. That conversation didn't last too long, because he had taken his side already. He was with Harrison. I talked with Tim Bliss, and I talked with John Clements. I tried to treat it in a neutral way, because of the love and respect I had for both those fellas. Because you know, we were just kids when we started growing up in business. And for the life of me, I couldn't understand why two brothers would do what they were doing.

But the more O'Keefe thought about it, the more he understood why Harrison was making his power play. With his eye perpetually on publicity and on having friends in the right places, Harrison maneuvered his way into the limelight, orchestrated so that he, rather than Wallace, would get the glory and make the cover of *The Financial Post Magazine*. "Harrison started to make it known that Wallace was making some bad deals, and that Harrison was carrying Wallace on his back," says O'Keefe, when the opposite was true:

When they built their first french-fry plant in England, it was a fucking disaster. Mac McCarthy started as the manager of Caterpac, and became the manager of McCain International. His brother, James, who I got to know and became a good friend, was hired by Harrison. But to be a production manager, it wasn't his forte, and the business was going to hell in a handbasket. And the fellow that stepped in to salvage that business wasn't Harrison, it was Wallace. Wallace said, "I've had enough. I'm going to England and I'm going to clean up this goddamned mess, and you can do whatever the hell you want with James McCarthy. If you want to set him up in some other kind of business, between you and Mac, you do whatever the hell you want to do with him. Put him in the ice business, selling ice to the fishermen down at the goddamned wharf, but he's coming the hell out of here. Because I'm going to fix this deal up."

Wallace McCain fixed that deal up in England . . . Otherwise, they would have been in real fucking trouble. It affected their businesses elsewhere, where they were making money, and the bankers were saying, "Hey, Christ, maybe you fellows have gone far enough, and you don't have the ability or the capacity to go any further."

And it was Harrison, says O'Keefe, who made the decision in 1985 to buy Bodine's, a Chicago-based juice company, from Edward M. Boden and his son Edward Jr. The Bodens were fined, and Edward Sr. sentenced to a two-year jail term, after being convicted of illegally diluting their orange-juice concentrates with artificial ingredients and sugar. Because McCain Foods bought the company prior to charges being laid, the company was never directly linked to any wrong-doing. But the acquisition came with a large bill for legal fees.

"Harrison and [George] McClure bought this business," says O'Keefe. "But because the United States was Wallace's business, his responsibility, he had to try and pull the goddamned thing out of the fire."

Recently, the European and British pieces of McCain Foods, which are controlled by Harrison, have been losing money—$7 million, according to court documents. O'Keefe notes:

> They made some very serious errors in Europe and Great Britain, in contracting potatoes at high prices. There was a surplus of potatoes last year and potato prices were low. Their competition didn't contract potatoes, and now they're buying them at low prices, while McCain's has to buy them high.
>
> I was with them long enough to see certain acquisitions and deals going through, that if they had of been left with Harrison, they would have been a goddamned flop. And the fella who pulled him out of the goddamned fire was Wallace. Wallace worked the trenches, and he carried the water, and his brother was a promoter and went for the glory.
>
> Harrison—as was Wallace—they both were excellent salesmen. They both were on equal footing. When it came to be promotional, or somebody up front, to take the lead, make the announcements and all of that, that was Harrison. Wallace stayed back in the background, he made sure that there was lots of funds when they were tight for cash. He signed every goddamned

cheque that ever went out of that goddamned place, not Harrison. And I've seen him night after night with bundles of cheques on his desk, signing cheques, approving purchase orders, salary increases, bonuses, and all of that stuff. And he had a tremendous capacity for that. He had a capacity to look at a situation and say, "That is not going right, it's not going in the right direction. You may have to change an individual, or you may have to change the methodology."

Harrison never had that capacity. He just had to be on the move. Harrison had the capacity to sell stuff, work up a profit. Wallace was just the opposite. He could make deals as good as Harrison, but he managed the cash. Wallace would never allow anybody subordinate to him to spend a capital dollar. And that's no different than the success of the Irvings today. There's not one person, in all of the Irving organization, who can step out and buy a car, or a half-ton truck, unless it's approved by an Irving. And that's what Mr. Irving recognized in Wallace McCain that he couldn't recognize in Harrison McCain.

Irving likened Harrison and Wallace to a sailboat, says O'Keefe: Harrison was the sail, catching the wind and driving the ship onward; Wallace was the rudder, keeping the speeding sailboat on course. Without Wallace, Irving noted, the McCain ship would go nowhere fast.

CHAPTER ELEVEN

To the Victor

IF YOU TURN RIGHT AFTER LEAVING HARRISON'S OR Wallace's driveway on River View Drive and continue up McCain Hill, on your left you'll see the H.H. McCain family graveyard overlooking the St. John River. The tiny plot of land, maybe 23 metres square, is surrounded by a short, white picket fence. H.H., the family patriarch, is in the middle of the graveyard, his 1.5-metre-high tombstone towering over all the other monuments. In front of H.H. is a single row of gravesites for his only son, A.D. McCain and A.D.'s sons. Almost directly in front of H.H. stands A.D. and Laura McCain's tombstone. To A.D.'s right lies Andrew's grave, pressed right up against the picket fence, and to his left, Robert. Harrison's grave and the remains of his wife Billie, who died in 1994, are crammed up against the opposite fence. There is no room for Wallace's grave in the A.D. McCain line.

Whether an oversight by the family when the gravesites were plotted or maneuvered after Harrison and Wallace began to fall out, Wallace's banishment from the final resting place of his brothers and parents is perhaps a poignant symbol of his ejection from the McCain family.

Wallace McCain knew that sooner or later his brother would succeed in separating him from McCain Foods as well. "They tried to fire me twice before," he says. "I was fired twice and I snuck in the back door again. But I knew it was coming . . . it was only a matter of time before they nailed me." When he was finally demoted from co-CEO to vice-chairman in October 1994, Wallace was 64 years old, one year before the legal retirement age, when many people decide that it's high time for a little rest and relaxation. But Wallace was a man with a fortune in the bank and little else. He had been fired by his own brother from the family-owned firm he helped build, and was shunned by the other McCain families as well.

Wallace was now merely the owner of one-third of McCain Foods' shares, and a single, small voice on its board of directors. It was only a matter of time, Wallace knew, before Harrison would fire both Michael and Scott. (Harrison had placed Michael on probation the previous December for unspecified acts of insubordination.) "I knew I'd have to get into something else," says Wallace. So in March 1995, Wallace announced that, through Castlefin, his family-owned holding company named for the small Irish town of his ancestors, he had plunked down $150 million toward a $1.06-billion takeover of Maple Leaf Foods Inc., Canada's largest food-processing company.

Wallace was also taking one of McCain Foods' key executives with him, McCain's senior vice-president Archie McLean, the 55-year-old head of McCain's Canadian operations. McLean, who admits he spent more time being loyal to Harrison than to Wallace ("I spent the first 20 years with Harrison and the last three with Wallace," he says), stuck his neck out for Wallace in the brothers' court dispute. In an affidavit filed with Wallace's statement of claim, McLean stated: "Wallace McCain has an enormous reputation in the food business in Canada and is widely respected by our suppliers and customers. He has always been active in making sales calls upon our customers and his removal as co-CEO would, in my opinion, have a negative impact on our Canadian food business." In December 1994, McLean had given Harrison six months' notice, but on the day Wallace announced his Maple Leaf takeover attempt, he moved his resignation date up to March 31. McLean, Wallace announced, would become CEO and President of Maple Leaf once the deal was cemented.

To help fund the takeover bid, Wallace enlisted the help of an old financial ally, the Ontario Teachers Pension Fund, which had backed Wallace on his two unsuccessful attempts to take over majority control of McCain Foods in 1993. The $30-billion pension fund put up $150 million in cash to match Wallace's private investment. The Toronto Dominion Bank lent Wallace the balance of $760 million. "We got it quickly, painlessly," says Wallace of the bank loan, which the family sees as a vote of confidence in Wallace's business skills, which had been called into question by his dismissal from McCain Foods. "It feels like we're making it on our own now," says Margaret.

Publicly, Wallace was saying that he was looking ahead and felt no bitterness about the feud with his brother that cost him his job. In the privacy of his Forest Hill apartment, however, Wallace sulked about his dismissal, and the family politics that were responsible for his banishment from the family. "Does it ever tick me off?" he asks sarcastically. "Absolutely it ticks me off. I should say so. It's very painful, very painful. If you said, 'Would you rather have this company [Maple

Leaf Foods], or would you rather still be involved in the family business, and let things happen naturally?' I'd take the latter, naturally. Oh, it's painful. Painful. My father lived there, my grandfather, great-grandfather. Five generations . . . I'd just as soon be home. I feel homesick for home."

Yet Wallace must have felt some familiarity with Maple Leaf Foods. After all, it was not the first time a McCain had attempted a takeover of the company. During the 1970s, Harrison and Wallace bought about 12 per cent of the shares in Canada Packers, which would become Maple Leaf Foods after Maple Leaf took it over in 1990. At the time, Canada Packers was owned by the McLean family, who refused the McCains a seat on its board of directors. Years later, Wallace looks back at the irony of it all: "We thought we'd buy a piece of it, get on the board, take a good look at it, and if we liked it, we'd buy control of it," says Wallace. "And then the financial people we talked to in those days didn't think we could get control of it. Because of the McLean family that owned it with the pension fund, they owned too big a piece of the pie, and we couldn't get control of it. We couldn't get on the board to find out a bit more, so we dropped it."

In 1985 Maple Leaf Foods was four times the size of McCain Foods, but by 1995 both companies had recorded just over $3 billion in sales for 1994; however, Maple Leaf had shied away from costly expansion projects and was virtually debt-free. McCain Foods, riding a 30-year expansion bonanza, was saddled, according to company insiders, with some $700 million in debt. The bulk of McCain Foods' sales came from overseas and from frozen foods, whereas Maple Leaf was largely into domestic processed meat and bread. Some of its brand names include: Maple Leaf,

WiseChoice, Hygrade, Shopsy's, Country Kitchens, York, Monarch, Tenderflake, Nutriwhip, Dempster's, Olivieri, Homestead, Fearman's and Shur-Gain. Maple Leaf also owns Country Style Donuts, with 190 stores from Quebec to the Prairies. As for direct competition, Maple Leaf has one potato farm in P.E.I. and a french-fry plant in Lethbridge, Alberta. McCain Foods and Maple Leaf compete principally in Quebec, where Maple Leaf's processed meats go head to head with McCain-owned Bilopage. "I'm into hot dogs now," Wallace told reporters at the press conference announcing his takeover bid.

Wallace has big plans for Maple Leaf. He suggested that Hillsdown Holdings, the company's major shareholder, had been too conservative with regard to expansion: only 24 per cent of Maple Leaf's products are sold outside Canada. Wallace, with an international business sense inherited from his father and grandfather, felt that it would be natural for Maple Leaf to expand worldwide. Having grown up with one brand name—McCain—Wallace was confused by all the brand names Maple Leaf produced. It might be best, he said in his offering to Maple Leaf shareholders, that the company adopt the Maple Leaf brand name for all its products. "There's room," he said, "for a sharper brand focus and a sharper marketing focus."

Yet there was more to Wallace's new venture than changing corporate logos: in fact, his whole life was about to change.

● ● ●

Not only was Wallace leaving the french-fry business, he was moving into the business big leagues. McCain Foods is a private company, with all 28 million shares held by the McCain family. Wallace, who owns more than nine million shares of McCain Foods, didn't have to worry about whether the company's shareholders would approve of his decisions —until 1992, when the family began his ouster. Maple Leaf Foods, on the other hand, is a publicly traded company, with thousands of stockholders to keep happy. Wallace could shun the media attention at McCain Foods, but at Maple Leaf he would have to be front and centre.

With private companies, Wallace said, "you always make decisions on what's best long-term, but with public companies sometimes you have to look at the long-term, medium-term and short-term. How it's going to look in the newspaper and all that stuff. That's what I'm told. I don't know enough about it."

Wallace began taking a good look at Maple Leaf Foods in the summer of 1994, while still the co-CEO at McCain Foods Ltd. The following December Wallace made an offer, but it was rejected by Maple Leaf's parent company, Hillsdown Holdings. Although he considered making his bid more attractive to Hillsdown, Wallace decided, on Michael's advice, to walk away from the deal. Michael had argued that Wallace would have had to borrow more money, which would leave Wallace's family fortune highly leveraged: risking all was not worth it. It was advice that Wallace did not want to hear. "He really wanted the company," says Margaret, "yet he knew that Michael was right." Indeed, Michael's advice paid off. "It was like walking away from a car dealer's first offer," she says, "because they came back later and said, okay, we'll take your offer."

Meanwhile back in Florenceville, McCain Foods' 15-

month search for a new CEO came to an end. On February 28, the company announced that British-born Howard Mann, a 48-year-old former executive with the Heinz and Mars companies, was taking the helm. As he had vowed since the fight with his brother began, Harrison announced he would step aside and become chairman of the board—"If elected, because I can't appoint myself," he says, adding that he had no plans to fully retire. "I expect I'll have something to say about the operation of the company, strategy, and so forth and so on. But all the day-to-day business, he'll be running it."

Mann, who worked as a labourer to put himself through night school, is proud of the fact that he was able to move from East-End London to Britain's corporate ranks, most recently as managing director of food products at Ranks Hovis McDougall, a large British food company with annual sales of $2.3 billion.

"He [Mann] is running a group of companies that's organized not unlike McCain Foods," says Harrison. "I think he has about 13 companies reporting to him. And he has strong experience in sales and marketing. He fits our culture also. This is not some posh Englishman. This is some guy who came out of the East End of London, and got a university training after high school in night school. He's got his feet on the ground, he's smart, good humoured. First-class guy."

Mann might have impressed Harrison, but in the tiny village that has been dominated by the McCain name for more than three generations, the news that a non-McCain was going to occupy the top spot of McCain was greeted with disbelief. Harrison or some other McCain must still be going to run the company, because a non-McCain, let alone an unknown from England, as company CEO, was unfathomable.

"Oh shit, nobody believes that this guy is going to run McCain Foods," said one Florenceville resident. "Oh yes, sure. And how many strings are on his back? Yeah, sure, he's going to run it. Nobody would believe that in a million years. If you're not going to pass it on to your nephews, you're certainly not going to pass it on to some stranger . . . Look, these guys are really hands-on. They might have some big contract somewhere, but they'd be down there walking the floors, checking the potatoes."

Along with the announcement of Mann's appointment came the long-feared news that he would be working out of Toronto. For Florenceville, one of the most frightening revelations to come out of Harrison's and Wallace's public feud was that Harrison had long considered moving the company's head office to one of the world's financial capitals. That scenario shook Carleton County, which relies so heavily on McCain for jobs. Mann attempted to allay those fears, saying that while he would work out of Toronto, the company's head-office operation would remain in Florenceville.

"I don't intend to be sitting on my backside in an office anyway," he said. "This is a global company, after all . . . The McCain business is part of Florenceville and the McCain business will remain part of Florenceville. I look forward to meeting people who are there where the company started. The impact I will have on them geographically will be minimal. It will probably be non-existent."

Harrison also stated his commitment to keep the company in Florenceville. Only Mann and a handful of office staff, he said, would move to Toronto. "We have all these people who worked here all their lives," he says. "They have a loyalty to us, and we have a loyalty to them. They owe the company, and the company owes them. We can't say we're going to close this office up and rent space in Toronto. It's not fair. We're not going to do it. The global business will be in Toronto."

Wallace wished Mann well, which is not surprising given that Wallace and his family still own 34 per cent of McCain Foods. In fact, Wallace's move to Maple Leaf created a conundrum. He hired Archie McLean and Michael McCain, but Wallace risked a talent drain from McCain Foods if he hired a good number of loyalists. "If I hired 10 per cent of the people who called me who would like to join me," he said, "there would be a disaster." If McCain Foods began losing money, so would Wallace. The key to keeping executives from fleeing McCain's, he said, was Mann's winning the confidence of his employees.

"I'd say it all depends on how good or bad the CEO is, and I can't speak to that because I don't know him . . . This is by far and wide the biggest job he's ever done in his life. Whether he'll sell all the troops to get behind him, time will tell . . . Harrison is going to run the company as long as he's living . . . But I sure wish him well and hope he can do it. Because it's to my advantage. It's not to my advantage to knock McCain Foods."

The two companies, with their assets in widely diverse areas of food production, might even collaborate, suggested Wallace's new President and CEO, Archie McLean, setting out various possibilities: Maple Leaf might consider selling its french-fry plant to McCain's; it may package hot dogs and other meat products for McCain's; and it may use the McCain-owned trucking firm, Day and Ross, to haul its products. "One could make a case that two of the largest food businesses in Canada might be able to co-operate a great deal more than compete," said McLean. "Maybe there's an opportunity there."

While Wallace and McLean said they were loath to do anything that might hurt McCain Foods, Harrison wasn't so sure. On March 7, the day after Wallace announced he was trying to buy Maple Leaf Foods, Harrison fired Michael, who was informed of his dismissal by letter. "Since Wallace McCain was removed as president and co-CEO of McCain Foods Ltd., you have engaged in acts of insubordination which caused the board to place you on probation," wrote Harrison. "As of the date of this letter, your employment with McCain group, and specifically McCain Foods USA, is hereby terminated."

Michael turned his dismissal into an opportunity to attack his uncle. "Harrison McCain is a man who prefers to be surrounded by people who perpetually agree with him. If being a man of my own mind makes me insubordinate, then I plead guilty," said Michael. "I've always been like that: blunt, direct, and it sure as fuck didn't curry me any favors. And at the end of the day, I don't give a shit. I really don't care. I have five children whom I love more than anything in this whole world —who are everything to me—and that's all that matters to me, and that's all that I care about. And we'll have fun, whatever we're going to do. Maple Leaf Foods today looks very appealing. So there.

"You want to know what's truly on my mind? And this is the gospel truth. I harbor no disrespect for any of them. Any of them. Because I can understand the circumstances that they were in, what caused them to do it. I really don't think it's their fault—it's not. They were led by one very domineering individual."

Michael also vowed to stay on the Holdco board, even after he begins working for Maple Leaf Foods. "He [Harrison] can't remove us from the board—absolutely not," said Michael. "My family still owns one-third of the stock in the company and we will be safeguarding that as an investment."

The day before he fired Michael, Harrison changed the locks on Wallace's, Michael's and Archie McLean's doors. The following signed memo from Harrison was sent to senior McCain executives, explaining Harrison's actions:

I am sure some of you will be concerned and saddened about Michael's departure and I think I should spell out the situation in which I found myself.

1.) For some months, Michael has declined to take my specific direction on various things I wanted done. I pressed and pressed but he declined to follow my direction, saying sometimes 'My only responsibility is to the shareholders, nobody else.'

2.) Because I had trouble with him last year and worse trouble this year regarding authority, our board of directors only agreed to his appointment on a provisional basis, i.e. he had to do better about supporting the team.

3.) Wallace made an offer to buy Maple Leaf Foods. If successful, as I believe they will be, they will have a French fry factory in Lethbridge, Alberta (10 tons/hour, I am told), and of course, will be a competitor to us in our Bilopage meat business in Quebec. Although I telephoned and congratulated Wallace, I took the French fry acquisition very seriously and ordered that Wallace, Michael and Scott's offices have the locks changed.

At about the same time, Archie McLean resigned to

become CEO of Maple Leaf Foods. I had his office locks changed also.

4.) After sending a message to him, Michael telephoned me and I asked him if he was part of the offer to buy Maple Leaf Foods and he said 'Yes, he was.'

5.) The next morning having thought the whole matter over carefully, I came to the conclusion that I should wait no longer so I wrote Michael saying I was discharging him.

6.) I have not talked to Scott McCain but he is due to see me when he returns from his holidays in mid-March, as he was so advised by letter.

I believe Michael was treated exactly the same as if an executive of McDonald's decided he was going to invest, and probably help run a KFC franchise ... It just won't fly and I could not stand for it any longer.

Michael was told that he had been fired, by a *Telegraph Journal* reporter who received Harrison's letter before Michael did. "It was pretty comical, actually," says Michael. "Harrison said, 'I treated him just like I would have treated any other employee.' You tell me how many 16-year employees get fired, locked out of their office—by fax to the media—without a nickel in severence pay."

Harrison later characterized Michael's executive performance as "fair, not brilliant." He added, however, that Michael was thrust into a difficult position as CEO of McCain USA. "He had quite a hard row to hoe," said Harrison. "But I didn't think his performance was brilliant ... He's not too bad an executive. I don't know, it's too early to say. He's too young. He's too young to decide that and write it in stone."

Harrison also fired Wallace's and Michael's secretaries, escalating the level of paranoia between the families. Wallace and his family became loath to telephone people at the McCain head office, fearful that Harrison had bugged the telephone lines. Yet Wallace vowed to retake his Florenceville office, with or without Harrison's approval. "When the time comes," Wallace says, choosing his words slowly and carefully, "I'll get in one way or another."

On the day that Harrison fired Michael and called in the locksmith, Andrew McCain, Wallace's nephew and erstwhile small-time rock music impresario and chairman of McCain Foods' family-owned holding company, said that Wallace's bid to take over Maple Leaf Foods might put him in a conflict-of-interest position. "As a shareholder, it's not a difficulty," said Andrew, "but if he wants to be a director, that would be different." By the end of the week, Andrew was suggesting that Wallace sell his shares—even to the public. "We're not holding Wallace or keeping him captive," he said. "The shares are his to do with what he likes and he can sell them tomorrow if he wishes. He can sell them to Joe Blow or ten Joe Blows. It has nothing to do with us. We might prefer that he doesn't sell them to one of our competitors, but we can't stop him from disposing of his shares in whatever way he wishes."

During the two years prior to his buying Maple Leaf, Wallace had tried a number of times to get Harrison and the McCain family to buy out his shares at fair market value. He had even gone to court, but failed to force the family into buying him out, or selling shares to the public. But now Wallace rejected Andrew's suggestion that he sell them. "They're not for sale today," he said.

Scott McCain, Wallace's oldest son and McCain Foods' vice-president in charge of production, returned to Florenceville from holiday at his family's compound in Jamaica on March 15, the day before he was scheduled to meet his uncle Harrison to discuss his future with McCain Foods. Scott was not, however, worried that he would be fired. Scott is not only the most popular McCain in all Florenceville, but the father of four is also the most popular man in the village. Even those who refuse to be in the same room with Wallace, Margaret or Michael hold no grudge against Scott: if the village held a referendum to decide the CEO of McCain Foods, Scott would win hands down.

"Nah, he's not going to fire me," said Scott the night before his meeting with Harrison. "I do what I'm told and Harrison can't argue about that. My uncle likes it when he can line everybody up like a coat-rack on the wall, all the pegs lined up in a row." And he was right—Harrison did not fire him. Scott put in his resignation, effective March 31.

Wallace said that Harrison's decision not to fire Scott was the only decision he could make. "Scott is, without question, the most popular guy in Florenceville," said Wallace. "I think they would have had a hanging if Harrison would have fired him."

● ● ●

Life on the home front being no less tumultuous, the McCain family was simultaneously swept by a different sort of tragedy. Harrison's and Wallace's older sister, Eleanor, whom Margaret called "the glue that held the brothers together," died after a two-year battle with brain cancer. Of all the brothers and sisters, Eleanor, only a year older than Harrison, had been closest to both Harrison and Wallace. Like Harrison and Wallace, Eleanor made something of herself by herself, graduating with an arts degree from Acadia University, a commerce degree from McGill University, and teaching at a private school in Palm Beach, Florida. Like her two younger brothers, she also "married up," to an Oxford-educated teacher named Patrick Johnson, who later became principal of Upper Canada College in Toronto. She also served on the boards of the Lester B. Pearson College on Vancouver Island and of the Toronto-based Street Kids International.

Like her mother, Eleanor was a bundle of energy, forever trying to manage the lives of everyone around her. Part Florenceville hick, part Forest Hill socialite, she was a small packet of rural New Brunswick amicability mixed with upper-crust Toronto gentility. She spoke her mind whenever—and to whomever—she chose. "Eleanor always walked in," said a friend, "where angels feared to tread."

Eleanor, however, may have been too close to her younger brothers. She did not attend either Wallace's or Harrison's wedding, because, as she admitted to Margaret years later, the thought of giving up her brothers made her uncomfortable. Years later, McCain Foods rented a house for Eleanor and her husband on Dunvegan Road in Toronto's exclusive Forest Hill from Ted Rogers (the Toronto cable television tycoon). He and his wife, Loretta, lived next door, and the two houses shared a tennis court. "That tennis court was the centre of social activities for years," said Linda Camp, one of Eleanor's oldest friends. "Eleanor made many friends through that court."

Eleanor, through her husband's connections at Upper Canada College and her growing circle of friends in Toronto, served as Harrison's conduit to Toronto's old money. "The more money the McCains made, the more legitimate she became," said Camp. Margaret said that Wallace refused Eleanor's introductions because he couldn't see the point of rubbing shoulders with the country's movers and shakers. During Harrison's frequent jaunts to Toronto, Eleanor would cook his meals, arrange to have his laundry done, and drive him around town. And was glad to do it.

Eleanor became caught in the middle of her brothers' feud, and it tore her in two. She loved Wallace but was apt to bow to Harrison, and struggle as she might, Eleanor was forced, in the end, to choose sides. By 1990, three years before Harrison and Wallace's fight went public, Eleanor had clearly picked Harrison. She flew in from Toronto that July and spent two weeks at Harrison's house, but never telephoned Wallace to say that she was just next door. Eleanor and Wallace met finally, by accident, at the annual McCain picnic. "Christ, El," said Wallace when he spotted her, "what are you doing here?" Eleanor and Wallace had just begun chatting when one of Harrison's daughters pulled her away by the arm. Later, Eleanor greeted Scott, who towered a good foot over his aunt. She wrapped her arms around his waist and said, "You know I'll always love you, Scott." But before they could talk, Eleanor was again hurried away by Harrison's daughter.

And when Harrison and the Holdco board were trying to fire Wallace, Eleanor would telephone Wallace. "Don't worry," she'd say, "it's just that they need a new CEO. You're going to get another job in the company. It's nothing against you." Wallace became so frustrated with his sister's phone calls that he hung up on her one day. "It wasn't in anger," recalls Margaret. "She was just in another world over the fight. Wallace felt that he just couldn't say anything to her."

Harrison's and Wallace's feud took its toll on Eleanor. By the summer of 1993 she was exhibiting symptoms of agoraphobia. She was afraid to leave her house. Margaret suggested to Eleanor that she see a therapist. "You've got to talk about this," said Margaret, "or it'll drive you crazy." Margaret also told her that keeping her feelings locked up inside might damage her physically as well as emotionally.

Shortly after Wallace filed his lawsuit against his brother and nephews, Eleanor, on the verge of mental collapse, phoned him. "Wallace," she said, "I'm sick." The irony was not lost on Wallace: in her moment of need, Eleanor reached out to the brother she had turned away from.

Wallace spoke with Harrison about how they could help their sister. Wallace was in favour of sending Eleanor to the Lahey Clinic in Burlington, Massachusetts, where Harrison had had his open-heart surgery. There, Wallace argued, their sister could get a complete, head-to-toe physical in just three days. It would take weeks, he said, for Eleanor to receive comparable medical care in Canada. Harrison said that she could be better cared for by a specialist in Toronto.

Harrison won the argument, and Eleanor was admitted to a Toronto hospital days later: she had a brain tumour. By the time of her admission, Eleanor, a math whiz and stock market aficionado, could barely count to 10. As Eleanor was terrified of being alone, her husband Patrick, Margaret and Wallace took shifts staying with her. "She was in a panic all the time," says Margaret, who more than once crawled into the hospital bed to hold Eleanor.

Although she was later released from hospital and underwent radiation therapy, Eleanor's cancer was incurable. In the fall of 1994, her husband died in his sleep of a heart attack. Eleanor attended the funeral service, but according to family friends, was never really aware that it was Patrick's funeral. Later, she recovered enough, Margaret said, to be aware of things, although she couldn't speak: "Wallace was in there one time and he said, 'You remember so-and-so, she ran a brothel right next door to brother Andrew, don't you remember her?' And Eleanor rolled her eyes—she couldn't speak, she just rolled her eyes—as if to say, 'Boy do I remember her.'"

Eleanor died at her home in Toronto March 20, 1995, just weeks after one of her beloved brothers locked the other out of his office and the second brother announced his move to a new company far from Florenceville and the McCains. Wallace and Margaret were there to watch over her when she died. Eleanor's son Derek Johnson and his fiancée had been taking care of her since her release from hospital in November, but couldn't bear to watch the moment of her death. "They were with her every minute, but in the end, it's pretty hard to sit and watch your mother die, so Wallace and I were with her."

The brothers' feud was not interrupted even by their sister's funeral. At the Humphrey Funeral Home, where Eleanor lay until her funeral on March 24, Eleanor's two sons were receiving visitors. When Harrison arrived, 48 hours after Eleanor's death, he positioned himself at the head of the receiving line, so that he was the first person every caller would meet. Soon, Andrew, chairman of Holdco, the McCain "kiddie board," stood beside him sporting his trademark Quick-Draw-McGraw mustache. Andrew had rolled up to the funeral parlor in a white stretch limousine of the kind typically rented for high-school prom nights or by visiting entertainers. The chauffeur couldn't maneuver the limo into the parking lot: it was longer than the hearse.

When Wallace arrived with Margaret, Harrison stood at one end of the room, greeting visitors; Wallace and Margaret stood together at the other end of the room to thank them for coming. Yet both Harrison and Wallace took the death of their sister hard. "They looked terrible," recalls a friend who visited at the funeral home. Linda Camp, Eleanor's long-time friend, recalls Harrison's saying, "It's been a hard year." Camp recalls that they both were "pretty badly shaken up."

Eleanor's funeral service, at St. Michael and All Angels Church, was attended by more than seven hundred people, including such financial movers and shakers as the Rogers family and Lord Thomson. Derek Johnson delivered a eulogy that captured the essence of his mother's character. "It's very rare when you go and hear a eulogy that has everyone in stitches," said Margaret. "He translated her character to perfection . . . she was one-of-a-kind. She was a character. She was the quintessential matchmaker. She was trying to get young people paired off all the time. She was a frustrated entrepreneur. And everyone would get involved in peddling all this stuff she got involved in, because she'd get herself into hock and it would kill her to lose a penny. I remember we were in Florida with her one time, and she fell in love with these thongs. And she ordered something like 15,000 pairs. She had to sell seven thousand pairs before she could break even. There are still some size tens left in the basement."

Although it was an Anglican service, reminders of Eleanor's Baptist New Brunswick roots thundered through the church in "The Battle Hymn of the Republic." It was the sort of strange mix that Eleanor McCain Johnson might have enjoyed. The McCain children, all Anglican like their mother, had nonetheless been raised on the Baptist hymns their father taught them. "Eleanor Johnson, who couldn't sing a note at all, sang lustily every chance she had," said Margaret. "You have no idea how bad her voice was. My daughter and I would go to church with her and she would sing at the top of her lungs, and she couldn't sing, but she thought, 'Who cares, that didn't matter.' She wanted to sing."

Harrison and Wallace did not speak to each other at the funeral, and greeted guests at the funeral reception at Upper Canada College as they had done at the funeral home—from opposite ends of the room. Yet there was family solidarity of sorts: Eleanor's pallbearers included her two sons; Wallace's son, Scott; Harrison's son, Mark; Robert's son, Andrew; Marie's son, Andy Sutherland; and Andrew's son, Stephen.

Eleanor was buried, next to her husband, on March 27 at a private family ceremony at the McCain family cemetery.

● ● ●

Although Harrison and Wallace avoided each other at their sister's funeral, they nonetheless showed occasional flashes of brotherly love. Days after Eleanor's burial, they sat together at a Canadian Business Hall of Fame dinner in Toronto. Harrison had even brought Wallace's tuxedo; Wallace had left it at home in Florenceville. On April 9, Wallace's birthday, Harrison telephoned his brother to wish him the best in his sixty-sixth year.

It is difficult to understand how Harrison could put the fight with his brother aside, particularly since Wallace's son,

Michael, had just launched a wrongful dismissal lawsuit against him. "Michael is now suing me and three companies for wrongful dismissal, mental anguish, and hurt to his reputation . . . that kind of jazz," said Harrison. "And Wallace is appealing the last decision. So it's not over yet."

Perhaps Wallace could forget about the feud now that he was wrapped up in his attempt to take over Maple Leaf Foods. After all, until a majority of Maple Leaf shareholders approved the buyout on April 20, Wallace's bid remained up in the air. Financial analysts agreed, however, that unless another buyer came along with a better price, Wallace's offer would be accepted.

On April 11, Iowa Beef, the billion-dollar American meat-processing firm, privately announced to Maple Leaf's board of directors that they were interested in purchasing the company and began negotiating a deal. It was a scenario that Wallace and Margaret hoped would not happen: they were eager to put the bitter memories of McCain Foods behind them. Besides, they had a peaceful Easter holiday planned for their family at their Toronto apartment that weekend, and now it was ruined. Wallace and Michael would be trying to head off Iowa Beef's bid in last-minute meetings with Maple Leaf.

Their fretting, however, was all for nothing. A week after Iowa Beef began negotiating with Maple Leaf, they backed away from the deal. Iowa Beef's chairman, Bob Peterson, sent Margaret a bouquet of flowers, with his apologies for ruining her weekend. On April 20, precisely one year after Judge Stevenson ruled that Holdco was legally entitled to oust Wallace from his position at McCain Foods, Maple Leaf shareholders voted 99 per cent in favour of Wallace's takeover.

Wallace phoned Margaret at 4:00 a.m., to tell her the news. "It was the first time I had woken up happy in months," said Margaret.

Even Harrison said he was happy for his brother. "I'm just glad he got it, sure. He got it at the right price, and he can run it," he said. "I wrote him, to congratulate him." Harrison acknowledged, however, that Wallace's new title as chairman of Maple Leaf Foods might conflict with his role as a director of McCain Foods. "They have a french-fry factory in Lethbridge, Alberta; and we're in the meat business in a smallish way compared to them—but we do compete with them—in Quebec, principally; and the potato business in P.E.I. So we share a few areas of competition.

"I don't know how it can be resolved. They [Maple Leaf] are many times a supplier of ours, you know. We buy petroleum products from Irving, cooking oil from [Maple Leaf]. If it's the best deal on the supply side, they can have the business. I don't care where they come from. They can become suppliers, warts and all."

Wallace's cooking-oil business might be welcome in Florenceville, but it was Toronto that accepted him as a corporate citizen. Wallace, firmly planted in his Toronto apartment, had not been home for months; Margaret, when she wasn't with Wallace in Toronto, lived at the Lieutenant-Governor's residence in Fredericton.

Scott has put his house up for sale, and is moving to Toronto to work for his father at Maple Leaf Foods. Michael is moving to Toronto as well, and is selling H.H. McCain's house. But Michael is taking the McCain patriarch's relics with him. Michael's most precious mementoes, which he kept in his den at home in Chicago, are H.H.'s spectacles, roll-top desk framed picture and business ledger from 1892.

Only memories live in Wallace and Margaret's plantation-style home: indeed, the four walls of one upstairs room are covered with family photographs; on a table next to a freezer in the basement two dozen boxes, containing every transcript of testimony in the brothers' private arbitration hearing, slowly gather dust. Just as his dismissal from McCain Foods—and his takeover of Maple Leaf—was final, so too was the departure of Wallace and his family from the village his ancestors settled in, in the 1800s.

The Wallace McCain family are packing to spend their lives in the glare of a public company. From now on, everything they do will be out in the open.

Chapter Notes

CHAPTER ONE: In the Beginning

The remark by Alden Nowlan, Eric Swanick, "[Review of] Jean M. Moore, compiler . . . The Alden Nowland Papers . . . " *The American Review of Canadian Studies*, vol. 23, no. 4 (Winter 1993): 645.

Description of settlers' life in New Brunswick, William S. MacNutt, *New Brunswick—A History: 1784-1867* (Toronto: Macmillan of Canada, 1963).

Information on Irish emigration to Canada, Winston S. Churchill, *A History of the English-Speaking Peoples, Volume Four: The Great Democracies* (New York: Dodd, Mead and Company, 1958).

The early history of the McCain family and life in Buttermilk Creek, Hugh J. Gordon, *The McCain Family of Florenceville, New Brunswick, Canada* (privately printed, 1983).

H.H. McCain's steam-powered press was given an inch of column space in *The Hartland Advertiser*, 26 February 1902.

Heber Hatfield's potato expeditions to Florida, Michel Cormier and Achille Michaud, *Richard Hatfield: Power and Disobedience* (Fredericton: Goose Lane Editions, 1992).

Information on the Combines Investigation of 1924, "Investigation into the alleged combine limiting competition in the marketing of New Brunswick Potatoes," *Interim Report of the Registrar* (Department of Labour, 1925).

Quotes from Harrison McCain are from the author's interview with him.

CHAPTER TWO: Boys Will Be Boys

The chronicle of the growth of A.D. McCain's family and business fortunes is based on the author's interviews with Mary Walters, Helen Depow, David Watson, Ernie Stickney, Nancy McNair Moody, George Urquhart, Gus Higgins, Bev O'Keefe, Fred McCain, Harrison McCain, Wallace McCain and Margaret McCain. All quotes are from these interviews unless otherwise indicated.

Details of the dwindling fortunes of Carleton County potato farmers are based on *Potato Brief,* written by the New Brunswick Department of Agriculture and a group of potato shippers (including A.D. McCain), and submitted to the federal government in 1938.

The description of the potato dehydration process was noted in two magazine articles: C.R. Allen, "Dehydration Plant in Hartland, New Brunswick, is now in Operation," *The Maritime Advocate and Busy East,* vol. 33, no. 6 (January, 1943): 7-13; and Aida McAnn, "New Brunswick's Potato Drying Plants," *The Maritime Advocate and Busy East,* vol. 35, no. 4 (November, 1944):5-8.

Andrew McCain's quote about his mother administering the discipline in the McCain household, Harry Bruce, "Meet the McCains of New Brunswick," *Macleans* (November 1973): 25-26, 90-102.

CHAPTER THREE: The Fries That Bind

The information on Clarence Birdseye and how he single-handedly invented the frozen-food industry, Alex Groner et al., *The American Heritage History of American Business and Industry* (New York: American Heritage Publishing, 1972); Nicholas von Hoffman, *Capitalist Fools: Tales of American Business, from Carnegie to Forbes to the Milken Gang* (New York: Doubleday, 1992).

The involvement of the New Brunswick government in the McCains' decision to go into the frozen-food business is based on the author's interviews with Cy Sherwood and Fred McCain, and on the *Synoptic Report of the Proceedings of the Legislative Assembly of New Brunswick*, March 30, 1954. Quotes from Hugh John Flemming are from this report.

Harrison and Wallace's actions in Saint John, John DeMont, *Citizens Irving: K.C. Irving and His Legacy* (Toronto: Doubleday Canada, 1991).

Description of the entrepreneurial spirit of the 1950s, including McDonald's slogans, David Halberstam, *The Fifties* (New York: Fawcett Columbine, 1993).

The story of how McCain Foods Inc. was founded is based on the following newspaper and magazine articles:

"Tax Concessions Requested For New Food Processing Plant," *Telegraph Journal*, 21 June 1956.

"Carleton County Council Asked For Tax Concession, Building Plans Under Way," *The Daily Gleaner*, 21 June 1956.

"Federal Government Aids East Florenceville Storage Plant," *Telegraph Journal*, 31 August 1956.

"New Food Plant Formally Opened," *Telegraph Journal*, 25 February 1957.

"The McCains and the Murphies," *Family Herald*, 24 September 1959.

Family friend's quotes: "It is a rare thing . . ." ("Third Generation Building Family Business in Produce," *Telegraph Journal*, 2 March 1957.)

Harrison's quotes: "We pinched the idea . . ." and "He made it . . . we sold it" (John Braddock, "The Very Remarkable Brothers McCain," *The Atlantic Advocate*, vol. 59, no. 4 (December 1968): 16-23.)

McCain Foods' near-disaster with peas, "The McCain Story," *Quick Frozen Foods Magazine* (January 1969): 3-41, International Edition.

Further information on the early history of McCain Foods taken from the author's interviews with Harrison McCain, Wallace McCain, Margaret McCain and Franklin Hickling. All quotes are from these interviews unless otherwise indicated.

CHAPTER FOUR: All Work and No Play

Quotes from Harry Ebbett, Darrell McLaughlin, Joe Palmer, Margaret McCain, and all but seven from Wallace McCain, are from the author's interviews with them.

Government loans to McCain Foods, "A report on the situation of New Brunswick potato farmers for the National Farmers Union," Senopi Consultants Ltd., May 1980.

Wallace McCain, "We said the hell with it" ("No Small Potatoes," *The Financial Post*, 14 August 1993.)

All quotes from Harrison McCain are from the author's interview with him, except for the following:

Harrison's memo, outlining his bold prediction, Merle

MacIsaac, "Picking up the Pieces," *Canadian Business* (March 1995): 29-44.

"Those guys who think . . . ," (John Godfrey, "Canada's CEO of the Year," *The Financial Post Magazine* (December 1990): 8-15.)

"Both Wallace and I . . ." (John Braddock, "The Very Remarkable Brothers McCain," *The Atlantic Advocate*, vol. 59, no. 4 (December 1968):16-23.)

"As with any small business . . . ," (Dean Walker, "McCain Foods: Branching Out on a Spud-Spangled Strategy," *Executive: The Magazine for Presidents* (December 1983).)

"It's a lot of satisfaction . . ." (Ibid.)

"Harrison spent most of his working hours . . ." (Ibid.)

"We put money into areas . . ." (Ibid.)

"It's well-known in Rotterdam . . ." (Ibid.)

"Our strategy . . ." (Ibid.)

"I can only recall two . . ." (Ibid.)

"I feel sorry . . ." (Ibid.)

"It is a necessary step . . . ," ("N.B. Firm Confirms Plans for U.K. Plant," *Telegraph Journal*, 30 January 1968.)

"If they said tomorrow . . . ," (Robert Neilson, "McCain's equals spud power," *Atlantic Insight* (December 1979).)

"Peeling potatoes is such a mean job . . . ," ("Common touch, global outlook keys to McCain Foods' growth," *The Globe and Mail*, 11 September 1989.)

"By God, we aren't . . . ," ("McCain . . . chip wagon to the world," *The Financial Post*, 15 January 1990.)

Wallace McCain: "But we had a tremendous . . . ," ("The McCain Saga," *Quick Frozen Foods International* (January 1982): 17-33.)

"We didn't expect . . ." (Ibid.)

"We were reaching . . ." (Ibid.)

"Despite suggestions that the brand name . . ." (Ibid.)

"Maine's location . . . ," ("The International Favorite Enters the United States," *Quick Frozen Foods* (August 1978):147-166.)

"One might say . . . ," ("McCain Returns French Fried Potatoes to France," *Quick Frozen Foods International* (January 1982): 3-16.)

George McClure: "If you can sell something . . . ," ("McCain . . . chip wagon to the world," *The Financial Post*, 15 January 1990.)

CHAPTER FIVE: Politics as Usual

The section on Harrison and Wallace's early support of Pierre Trudeau is based on the author's interviews with Gordon Gibson, Harrison McCain, Fred McCain and Senator Louis Robichaud. All quotes are from these interviews.

A.D. McCain's political misfortunes, Arthur T. Doyle, *Front Benches and Back Rooms*, (Toronto: Green Tree Publishing Company Ltd., 1976).

Information on early provincial government loans to the McCains, *Minutes of the New Brunswick Industrial Development Board, 1956–1960*, Provincial Archives of New Brunswick, Fredericton.

The $3.2 million the McCains received from the Robichaud government, and the $5.2 million from the Hatfield government, "A report on the situation of New Brunswick potato farmers for the National Farmers Union," Senopi Consultants Ltd., May 1980.

The McCains' first DREE grant, Walter Stewart, *Hard To Swallow: Why food prices keep rising—and what can be done about it* (Toronto: Macmillan of Canada, 1974).

The summary of how the McCains' Portage La Prairie plant was built largely with government money, "A report on the situation of New Brunswick potato farmers for the National Farmers Union," Senopi Consultants Ltd., May 1980.

Harrison McCain's comments on government loans, Dean Walker, "McCain Foods: Branching Out on a Spud-Spangled Strategy," *Executive: The Magazine for Presidents* (December 1983).

"That was a very good investment . . ." from the author's interview with Harrison McCain.

"[The grants] are not sufficient . . ." (Dean Walker, "McCain Foods: Branching Out on a Spud-Spangled Strategy," *Executive: The Magazine for Presidents* (December 1983).)

Information on some Carleton County farmers indebtedness to the McCains, Wendy Lill, "Working for the (Corporate) Man," *Harrowsmith* (October 1979): 56-7, 67-8, 97.

"We have become virtual serfs," (Ibid.)

Wilhelmine Thomas, "The View from Hartland, N.B.," *Maclean's* (December 1971): 4.

The section on cursing and Liberalism is based on the author's interviews with Don Marmen, Margaret McCain, David Cameron and Wallace McCain. All quotes are from these interviews.

CHAPTER SIX: The Great Potato War

Reference to K.C. Irving's wealth, John DeMont, *Citizens Irving: K.C. Irving and His Legacy* (Toronto: Doubleday Canada, 1991).

"There's no feud . . . ," from the author's interview with Harrison McCain.

The section on the growth of Day and Ross is based on the author's interviews with Elbert Day and Joe Palmer. All quotes are from these interviews, except Palmer's: "We were as welcome . . . ," ("Day and Ross Relocation," *Telegraph Journal*, 16 September 1980.)

The description of James Kidd Flemming, Arthur T. Doyle, *Front Benches and Back Rooms* (Toronto: Green Tree Publishing Company Ltd., 1976).

Quotes from Dalton Camp, Jackie Webster and Bev O'Keefe are from the author's interviews with them.

Information on C.M. McLean Ltd. is based on the author's interview with Mitch McLean.

"The government urged us . . . ," from the author's interview with Wallace McCain.

J.K. Irving's quote: "We're in the business . . . ," ("Irving Group Planning Food Processing in N.B.?," *Telegraph Journal*, 11 October 1979.)

McCain and McLean lawsuit over packaging, "Battle of the Brands," *The Financial Times of Canada*, 7 July 1980.

The McCain-Cavendish Farms' "water knife" lawsuit, "Cavendish Farms Upheld in Potato-Slicer Case," *Telegraph Journal*, 18 February 1984.

The Irvings' land purchases and ensuing protests from P.E.I farmers:

"P.E.I. Farmers Worried As Irvings Eye Island Property . . . Legislation Restricts Purchases Over 10 acres," *Telegraph Journal*, 7 December 1979;

"Irving To Move P.E.I. Firm Unless Land OKed?," *Telegraph Journal*, 5 September 1981;

"Irving Land Purchase Bid Receives Setback," *Telegraph Journal*, 10 September 1981;

"Farmland Controls Proposed," *Telegraph Journal*, 1 February 1982;

"Irving Company Request Denied," *Telegraph Journal*, 2 August 1985;

"Irving land purchase sparks ruckus in P.E.I.," *Telegraph Journal*, 26 April 1990.

Information on the $80 million Cavendish Farms' plant is from the author's interviews with Harrison and Wallace McCain. All quotes are from these interviews unless otherwise indicated.

Simon Reisman: "Such a scheme is insane . . . ," (*Evening Times Globe*, 19 January 1990.)

McCain counter-moves to the proposed Cavendish Farms' plant, and quote from Archie McLean, "McCain offers P.E.I. deal," *Telegraph Journal*, 24 January 1990.

The McCain-Irving battle over the Grand Falls' plant, "Spud feud: Irving versus McCain," *The Financial Times of Canada*, 3 December 1990.

Quotes from Gordon Ritchie, Senator George Mitchell, Premier Frank McKenna and Robert Bonnell, "Chips and Gravy," *The Globe and Mail*, 8 December 1990.

Robert Irving: "We do over 50 per cent . . ." ("Spud feud: Irving versus McCain," *The Financial Times of Canada*, 3 December 1990.)

Robert Irving: "The slowdown in the economy . . ." ("Spud spat sputters," *The Globe and Mail*, 23 November 1991.)

Quotes from Harry Fraser and Harrison McCain are from the author's interviews with them.

CHAPTER SEVEN: All in the Family

This chapter is based entirely on the author's interviews with Margaret McCain, Wallace McCain, Michael McCain, Harrison McCain, Stephen Morris, Alan Morris and Barb Carter.

CHAPTER EIGHT: Brothers at Arms

Along with their statements of claim, the McCains filed over 1,000 pages of affidavits and memos in their court battle. All quotations are from these court documents except where otherwise indicated.

Harrison McCain: "We are both heads . . . ," (John Braddock, "The Very Remarkable Brothers McCain," *The Atlantic Advocate*, vol. 59, no. 4 (December 1968): 16-23).

Harrison McCain: "I thought he was taking advantage of the situation . . . ," (Peter C. Newman, "Feud of the Century," *Maclean's* (September 26, 1995): 29.)

Quotes from Michael McCain and Margaret McCain are from the author's interviews with them.

Reference to *Forbes* and *The Financial Post* are from Toddi Gutner, "What's yours is mine," *Forbes* (August 2, 1993): 68-9, and "No Small Potatoes," *The Financial Post*, 14 August 1993.

CHAPTER NINE: A Dynastic Battle

All information and quotes are from the McCains' court documents, unless otherwise indicated.

Quotes from Margaret McCain are from the author's interviews with her.

Quotes from Wendy Handler are from an interview with Charles Enman.

CHAPTER TEN: Divide and Conquer

The amounts of the McCains' legal fees are based on the author's interviews with McCain family members.

Allison's and Peter's statements in their examination for discovery, "Inside the McCain feud," *The Financial Post*, 2 April 1994.

Judge Stevenson's reasons for judgement and side-letter to Harrison and Wallace were filed as exhibits in Wallace McCain's Moncton court action.

The September 1994 exchange of letters between Harrison and Wallace, "Breakup of empire possible," *Telegraph Journal*, 9 September 1994.

Quotes from lawyers Alan Lenczner and Charles Whelly, Wallace and Harrison McCain and June Hayes, "McCains expected to dump Wallace," *Telegraph Journal*, 13 September 1994, and "Breakup of empire possible," *Telegraph Journal*, 9 September 1994.

Quotes from John Campion, Charles Whelly and Alan Lenczner, "We can fire him," *Telegraph Journal*, 14 September 1994.

Judge Creaghan's ruling, "Court says board free to fire Wallace," *Telegraph Journal*, 27 September 1994.

Quotes from Margaret McCain are from the author's interviews with her.

Information on Wallace's second appearance before Judge Creaghan, "McCain lawyers argue in battle already lost," *Telegraph Journal*, 31 January 1995, "McCain lawsuit remains on hold," 1 February 1995, and "Wallace McCain: no deal," 10 February 1995.

Quotes from Wallace McCain, Harrison McCain, Michael

McCain and Bev O'Keefe are from the author's interviews with them.

CHAPTER ELEVEN: To the Victor

The information on Wallace McCain and his family and his purchase of Maple Leaf Foods is based on the author's interviews with Wallace McCain, Michael McCain, Scott McCain, Margaret McCain, Harrison McCain, Archie McLean and Linda Camp. All quotes are from these interviews unless otherwise indicated.

Quotes from Howard Mann, "McCain's new Mann at the top," *Telegraph Journal*, 3 March 1995.

Archie McLean's statements about cooperation between Maple Leaf and McCain, "Will the profit motive bring McCains together?" *Report on Business*, 11 March 1995.

Reports of Michael's firing and Harrison's memo concerning the locking of doors, "Michael McCain fired," *Telegraph Journal*, 8 March 1995.

Michael's quotes: "Harrison McCain is a man . . ." and "He [Harrison] can't remove . . ." (Ibid.)

Quotes from Andrew McCain on the selling of Wallace's McCain shares, "Wallace can sell McCain stock," *Telegraph Journal*, 10 March 1995.

Index

ABOUT THE AUTHOR

MICHAEL WOLOSCHUK is a seasoned reporter and has worked for CBC Radio, the Saint John *Telegraph Journal* and the Kingston *Whig-Standard*. In 1992 he won a Southam President Award for Investigative Journalism. In 1994 he was nominated for The National Magazine Award. He divides his time between his two homes in Maine and New Brunswick.